SAINTS OR SINNERS?

General Editors

✠ Maurice Couve de Murville, Archbishop of Birmingham
Fr David McLoughlin
Fr David Evans

Oscott College was founded near Birmingham in 1794 at a time when students and staff from the English Catholic colleges abroad were being driven home by the French Revolution. In 1838 it occupied new buildings at Sutton Coldfield, built in the Gothic style, in a move which inaugurated an ambitious phase of the Catholic Revival in England. Oscott is the seminary of the Archdiocese of Birmingham which also has students from many other dioceses.

The Oscott series aims at continuing the role of Oscott as an intellectual and spiritual centre of English Catholicism for close on two hundred years.

Other titles in the series are:

J. D. Crichton

SAINTS OR SINNERS?

Jansenists and Jansenisers in Seventeenth-Century France

Oscott Series 9

VERITAS

First published 1996 by
Veritas Publications
7-8 Lower Abbey Street
Dublin 1

Copyright © J. D. Crichton 1996

ISBN 1 85390 330 2

British Library Cataloguing
in Publication Data.
A catalogue record for
this book is available
from the British Library.

Cover design by Bill Bolger
Cover illustration © Roger-Viollet
Illustrations supplied and copyright by the Roger-Viollet agency,
Paris, France
Printed in the Republic of Ireland by Criterion Press Ltd, Dublin

CONTENTS

PREFACE

This book is not about Jansenism. It is about people. It is about the people who in various ways were involved in the Jansenist controversy of the seventeenth century. Some were not Jansenists, for example Mère Angélique Arnauld, the reformer of the monastery of Port-Royal. Another was Jean Duvergier de Hauranne, usually known as the Abbé de Saint-Cyran, who, though the friend of Jansen, did not absorb his teaching. He was, like many others in seventeenth-century France, an Augustinian who took a dark view of human nature. There was Antoine Arnauld, theologian and polemicist, who first defended Jansen's *Augustinus* and then, over the years, almost imperceptibly abandoned his teaching. In the monastery there was the brilliant young nun, Angélique de Saint-Jean, niece of the older Angélique, who seems to have known a good deal about Jansenism and who had a great and an unfortunate influence on Port-Royal.

There are others, the curious and often idiosyncratic 'solitaries' who gathered round Port-Royal-des-Champs: old soldiers who had turned away from their sometimes dubious past; the 'beloved physician', Dr Hamon, who looked after the bodies of the nuns and who had to become their spiritual physician when they were excommunicated and cut off from the world; the Englishman, Mr Jenkins, self-appointed gardener to the monastery, who worked without pay for more than forty years. All these are eminently worth writing about but their portraits can be found in the pages of Sainte-Beuve's *Port-Royal*. These and many others were not in any sense Jansenists.

7

However, although this book is not about Jansenism as such it was necessary to give a brief account of it and to situate it in the religious and ecclesiastical history of seventeenth-century France. This will be found in the first two chapters. However, in my ruminations on the Jansenist affair over many years I have come to the conclusion that it is necessary to distinguish theological Jansenism from what I call moral Jansenism. Very few seem to have adhered to the former and Jansenism as it was known in France was almost exclusively a matter of ecclesiastical (papal and episcopal) authority, rather than a controversy about grace and predestination, though that is how it started. By moral Jansenism I mean that austere way of life that became characteristic of Port-Royal and those who attached themselves to it. It was associated with rigorism in morals and in the exercise of the sacrament of penance, infrequent communion, personal austerity (strict observance of the Church's fasts, at least), and a general sobriety in daily living. It is not surprising that it appealed to converted French Huguenots. It is this moral Jansenism which was identified by so many generations as Jansenism *tout court*, a Jansenism which took two centuries to exorcise from the life of the Church. Much that was attributed to this kind of Jansenism derived from the prevalent Augustinianism of the seventeenth century. Original sin and its alleged consequences weighed heavily on the minds and consciences of many for a very long time and it could be said that it is only in the twentieth century that a more balanced view of that doctrine has become general.

Because this book is concerned with the Jansenist controversy as it occurred in France I have felt inclined to refer to *French* Jansenism. As the controversy waxed and waned the Jansenism of Jansen had less and less to do with it.

As I state in the bibliography (p.278ff), the literature by Jansenists or about Jansenism is very extensive – even for so unpretentious a book as this I have had to read a great deal though, since work on the subject still continues, I may not have been aware of

8

all that has been published in the last few years. Some references to works of one kind or another will be found in the notes (p.265ff) but I have tried to keep these to a minimum. My rule generally is that I provide a reference only when quoting directly from contemporary accounts. The nature of the subject-matter of the book has often necessitated quotations from the French which I have translated. To have given the original in every case would have lengthened it unduly.

In a book like this which has involved the reading of a great number of books, not always easily available, I have contracted a number of debts and I wish to make grateful acknowledgement to the following:

Fr Dermot Fenlon, Cong. Or., who read an earlier draft of chapter 1, Fr David McLaughlin who read the whole script, Fr David Evans and George Every, Librarians of Oscott College, Fr Michael Sharratt of Ushaw College and the Librarian of Downside Abbey, all of whom made books available to me.

I wish to thank especially Mrs Elfriede Dubois who, out of her great knowledge of seventeenth-century France, has helped in many ways with advice and proof-reading. Opinions and errors are, however, my own.

Finally, I wish to thank Fiona Biggs for all her help in seeing this book through the press.

J. D. Crichton

1

THE CONDITION OF
THE FRENCH CHURCH

It is an understandable illusion to suppose that once a General Council of the Church has promulgated its decrees they will be put into effect speedily and in an orderly fashion. In 1600 it was more than thirty-five years since the closing of the Council of Trent which had gradually produced a certain reform of the Church in various places and in different aspects of ecclesiastical life. The new active religious orders and the congregations of men and women who largely derived their spirit from the Council of Trent set up new currents of the spiritual life which gradually changed the face of the Church. But the weight of reform fell on the bishops. It has been reckoned that they were required to introduce no less than two hundred and fifty reforms and changes as well as giving 'an example in dress, behaviour, charity, modesty – and no doubt by implication good temper'.[1] But the bishops had to be reformed first. Some were still acting like Renaissance princes, most were royal nominees and few were marked by a strong pastoral sense. In France, by the Concordat of 1516 between the papacy and the monarchy, bishops became royal nominees, though the pope appointed them and could reject those nominated, as he sometimes did. The new arrangement was some improvement on the chaotic situation in the fifteenth century when nobles and others jockeyed for bishoprics for their candidates. Even so, the French bishops remained beholden to the monarch. Even after the Concordat royal patronage did not prevent certain sees becoming almost the appanages of certain families. Thus, Richelieu had to be ordained a priest so that the see of Luçon could be kept in his impecunious family. The see of Paris was occupied for just over a hundred years by the Gondis, nephew following uncle without a break. On the other hand, Bossuet, who received his bishopric for his preaching, was without family support and had to be content with the remote and obscure see of Condom. Meaux, which he later exchanged for it because it was nearer the court, was not one of the greater sees of France.

At the beginning of the seventeenth century, then, most bishops were of noble or near noble families and neither for them nor for priests was there any pastoral or spiritual preparation. It was not until Vincent de Paul began his pre-ordination retreats that some preparation was provided. It is not surprising then that in the first decades of the century it is difficult to find bishops of outstanding merit. Cardinal du Perron, renowned as a great controversialist, was not particularly edifying in his private life. There were some good bishops – Orcibal lists nineteen[2] – and of these Cardinal de la Rochefoucauld, Bishop of Clermont, was outstanding. He saw that 'the real end of authority was the service of the people' and that this service was frustrated by the system of the times. He was also clearly aware that the remedy lay with the clergy who needed to be 'imbued with a sense of vocation and mission, rooted in sound doctrine, in discipline of life and prayer'.[3] But it would not be until the middle of the century that the situation improved. There was also, of course, Francis de Sales who, though not a French national, was much liked by Henri IV for his candour and charm, and who exercised a considerable influence then and for long after by his *Introduction to the Devout Life* and by his own pastoral example.

The reform of the religious orders, by now very necessary, was made peculiarly difficult by the prevalent evil of royal provision, the *in commendam* system, to abbacies of both men and women. These benefices were under the control of the king (though endorsement from Rome was usually required) and he did not hesitate to use his power. Clerics, whether priests or not (tonsure was the minimum requirement) were regularly appointed to monasteries and their lawful inmates were not only deprived of income but were also prevented from reforming their way of living. The monasteries of women were treated in the same cavalier fashion, abbesses being made and unmade at the whim of the king. These houses in any case had become the repositories of the surplus daughters of the nobility and gentry. They were without vocation and felt no obligation to live a life to which they had no call. There was often a complete lack of religious discipline and sometimes there were scandals. Community life had become a thing of the past, the nuns aped the world as far as their meagre pensions allowed, and some from time to time received personable young men at their parties. Reform progressed slowly in the first decades of the century: it was only in 1618 that the Benedictine Congregation of St Maur was inaugurated. Its establishment marked a return to strict observance and to the tradition of monastic learning for which it was to become so famous in the next hundred years. The Cistercians underwent a change even later; the order's most spectacular reform was that of the Abbé de Rancé who set up his idiosyncratic rule at La Trappe. Both these congregations managed to evade the *in commendam* system.

Yet the tide of religious life was flowing strongly and found expression in new orders both from within and from without the country. There was the new and rapidly spreading order of the Visitation, the joint work of Francis de Sales and Jeanne Françoise de Chantal. Intended at first as an active order for work among the poor, under episcopal pressure it became an enclosed order. The foundation of active congregations of women only began with Vincent de Paul who recruited young country women of strong physique, able to stand the strain of looking after the sick in their homes and caring for abandoned children. He evaded the Roman regulations by making sure these women were not 'nuns' in the strict sense of the word; they took only simple, temporary vows. There were others also, like the Canonesses of St Pierre Fourrier, who were engaged in the education of girls, and the Calvairiennes of Père Joseph, Richelieu's *eminence grise*.

But the great feature of the religious life of the time was the emergence of corporate bodies of secular priests who lived in community. Of these the Oratorians of Cardinal de Bérulle achieved considerable renown – and ran into opposition from the Jesuits over their founding of schools. Hiving off from these were the priests of St Jean Eudes who gave himself entirely to the training of priests for missionary work among the dechristianised. There was also the Company of St Sulpice, founded by Jean-Jacques Olier, much under the influence of Bérulle's teaching, which undertook the founding of seminaries throughout the kingdom and eventually in North America. Vincent de Paul founded his Congregation of the Mission whose priests were to work at home, especially in rural areas, and eventually abroad. Because they were new, and perhaps because they had no wealth, all these foundations and others like them remained outside the grasp of the monarch.

Among women's religious orders brought in from outside France, thanks to Madame Acarie and the energy of Bérulle, the Carmelites were notable. They rapidly attracted vocations and it was to them that Louise de la Vallière fled to escape the amorous embraces of Louis XIV. There she was professed and became a wholly admirable religious. Convents multiplied and the affective Christocentric spirituality of the Teresian Carmelites stood in sharp contrast to the 'abstract' mysticism that had come to France from the Netherlands and the Rhineland. The Ursulines, founded in Italy by St Angela Merici, set up schools for girls in their convents, doing a very necessary work, and the notoriety they gained from the 'Devils of Loudon' affair was not at all typical of what they were.

The Capuchins had been resident in France since the sixteenth century. They lived austerely, were popular preachers and worked among the poor. Among other things, they provided the only sort of fire brigade that France knew at the time. This austere and humble order attracted men noble by birth and in spirit. There was Anne de Joyeuse who, from a soldier became a friar, from a friar a general and commander in the French army and then, finally, friar and provincial for the last nine years of his life. There was Père Archange, called 'of Pembroke', who was a spiritual director of repute, although he never completely mastered the French language. With him we must associate William Fitch, like Archange a convert, who was clapped into prison with a Scot named Campbell when they imprudently returned to England. Fitch, better known as Benet of Canfield, became famous with his deeply mystical Rule of Perfection, which influenced the spiritual life of many, including so unlikely a man as Père Joseph le Clerc du Tremblay, the very active agent of Richelieu.[4]

The Jesuits could be said to have their origin in France in 1534 when Ignatius of Loyola and a handful of companions made their first commitment at Montmartre to serve the Church, especially as missionaries to the heathen. Their rule was authenticated by the papacy in 1540, but although the Jesuits made a spectacular contribution to the missionary work of the Church in Asia and the Americas, they were largely absorbed by Rome in the reclamation of the Church in Europe from Protestantism. Their vow of special obedience to the pope made them unwelcome in Gallican eyes and their beginnings in France were uneasy. It is ironical that though they came to be regarded as pillars of the monarchy later, in the last years of the sixteenth century they were banned from the country because it was thought that they were not monarchist enough. The attempted assassination of Henri IV in 1594 was made by a former student of theirs. In the campaign to get rid of them it is interesting that a decisive role was played by Antoine Arnauld, lawyer and father of the numerous tribe that became the spearhead of French Jansenism. His highly rhetorical plea for the expulsion of the Jesuits, made in the name of the University of Paris, has been described as the Original Sin of the Arnaulds.[5]

Nevertheless the Jesuits were back by 1603. They worked in education and spiritual direction and as confessors to kings. Their schools at this time were regarded as modern: they taught Latin effectively, Greek, it is said, rather less so, and modern subjects were readily admitted to the curriculum. On the other hand, they neglected French and put small boys onto Latin from the outset, although the children obviously had only a feeble grasp of their own language. The Jesuit plays, usually in Latin, were famous throughout Europe; they helped boys to speak well and to carry themselves well in a society where manners and deportment were important. They soon had almost a monopoly on education and they did not take kindly to the Oratorians when they founded their schools. Naturally, the *Petites Ecoles* of the Port-Royalists, which were set up in the late 1630s, were equally unwelcome.

The Jesuit influence in the sphere of spiritual direction was pervasive. They confessed courtiers, nobles, the gentry and the upper bourgeoisie who were happy to send their boys to their schools. In this work the Jesuits were faced with considerable problems. The lives of many of their penitents were far from edifying. The Jesuits' aim was to keep such people to something like regular practice and it is not surprising that, confronted with certain moral dilemmas, their judgement was not always prudent. The lax casuistry of which they were accused by Pascal was not the monopoly of the Jesuits, though because they confessed so many more than anyone else, they were natural targets. That they went beyond the bounds of the permissible is shown by Innocent XI's condemnation in 1679 of a whole list of their laxist opinions. Pascal, however, was correct in his main accusation that the casuists practically sabotaged the overriding importance of the gospel teaching on charity. The Abbé de Saint-Cyran himself, writing before Pascal, turned against casuistry (although he himself had once been a practitioner) as he saw the great moral imperatives replaced by dubious reasoning. There was in fact a strong animus against the casuistry among the clergy at this time, including Bossuet, who remarks somewhere on the disgust he felt after having to read some of the casuists' manuals. What we would regard as rigorism was not a peculiarity of the Jansenists.

It is difficult to speak with fairness of the role of the Jesuits in politico-religious questions of the time. Their function as royal confessors laid them open to every kind of accusation of intrigue and wire-pulling. How far these accusations were justified it is difficult to say. Few, if any, were impartial about the Jesuits and even modern historians have not been entirely free of prejudice. That they were the sworn enemies of the Jansenists goes without saying, and they maintained that they were the first to be attacked. Yet it cannot be denied that the Jesuits played a role of the first importance against the Jansenists. But even in this they were not alone. Vincent de Paul was in the field before them; it was he who organised the first joint approach of the French bishops to Rome seeking a condemnation. However, neither the bishops nor the parish clergy *liked* the Jesuits. Not only were the clergy Gallican but they felt that the Jesuits with their special 'faculties' from the pope to hear confessions and to set up churches were a threat to their own position. The exaltation of the religious life over that of the pastoral clergy was gravely offensive to them. Hence the popularity of Saint-Cyran's vehement polemic against the Jesuits which appeared in a series of pamphlets under the name Petrus Aurelius. Once again, it can be seen that the anti-Jesuit stance was not peculiar to the Jansenists.

The Jesuits are too often thought of as complaisant confessors of the great, although they tried, through their 'congregations' of young laymen, artisans, journeymen and craftsmen, to reach out to the less privileged members of society. These congregations (sometimes known as sodalities) had an enormous vogue in western Europe and they enabled innumerable men to lead a spiritual life which would not otherwise have been available to them. But the system was unduly regimented, tended to be inward-looking and could be said to have been somewhat elitist.[6] The congregations were also associated with the 'secret' Compagnie du Saint-Sacrement which was suppressed by Louis XIV.

In a great age of mysticism the Jesuits also made their contribution. Père Louis Lallement, whose spiritual doctrine, no doubt thanks to Bremond, has had a certain vogue in modern times, was a true contemplative and formed a whole group of Jesuits when he was in charge of the tertianship (a kind of second novitiate after ordination) from 1628 to 1632. Among those who received his teaching was Jean-Joseph Surin, who gained an unhappy notoriety through his involvement with the Ursulines of Loudon but who (and in spite of an astonishing variety of psychological disorders), was a mystic of a high order. His teaching, born of his experiences and the graces of contemplation, can be found in his *Catéchisme spirituel* and in his *Lettres spirituelles*. That he was unbalanced – and few of the 'spirituals' of the seventeenth century seem to have been wholly balanced – that he was imprudent and indeed naive, that he became afflicted after the Loudun affair with aphasia, amnesia, dyslexia and temporary anorexia, not to mention other psychological disorders that looked very much like possession, did not prevent him from maturing a very profound mystical doctrine. It is to be noted too that both he and Lallement took a pessimistic view of human nature, and they insisted on the need for extreme mortification if the subject was to proceed to mystical prayer; excesses in mortification ruined Lallement's health and probably contributed to Surin's disorders.

Lallement and Surin were rather special cases and there were other Jesuits who, through their mission work in France and through their activity as spiritual directors, were able to discern genuine mystical gifts in people as far distant socially as servants and great ladies. Men like Rigoleuc, Guilloré and others need to be remembered and set against the all-too familiar picture of intriguing Jesuits and lax confessors. The religious scene in seventeenth-century France was extremely varied and a complete and balanced account of it would be very difficult to draw up. Even Bremond's *Histoire littéraire du sentiment religieux en France* is neither wholly balanced nor complete.

It is even more difficult to assess the state of the Christian life in the lower strata of society. First, there is the question of the clergy. Although there were many learned priests, doctors of the Sorbonne and the like, they were usually to be found in Paris or big cities like Rouen. But even they had no pastoral training. At the beginning of the century there were no seminaries at all. One or two attempts were made in the early decades but seminaries came into existence only gradually, first through the activity of Bérulle's oratory and Adrien Bourdoise's small establishment at St Nicolas-du-Chardonnet in Paris, and then, and most important of all, Jean Jacques Olier's foundation in 1641, of the seminary of St Sulpice, also in Paris. But the seminaries of the time were very different from their nineteenth-century successors. At St Sulpice it was assumed that a man had already acquired a theological degree and the purpose of his entering the seminary was to prepare him spiritually for ordination and to give him some minimal initiation into the pastoral life. He stayed a year, perhaps two years, never longer. What the training of other priests in places remote from the capital was like it is more difficult to say. Some parish priests 'took in' one or two students and gave them enough theology for ordination. In the first decades of the century ignorance was undoubtedly one of the greatest defects of the parish clergy and that ignorance, as we know from the experiences of Vincent de Paul, was sometimes all but complete. Priests hardly knew how to celebrate Mass or administer the sacraments. If Adrien Bourdoise insisted rather fussily on externals, the right kind of clerical dress, the right sort of deportment inside and outside the church, and if he was unduly concerned about rubrics and ceremonial, it was because all these things were wanting.

Of pastoral zeal there was little enough. Until the priests of the Congregation of the Mission, the Jesuits and the men trained by St Jean Eudes and others began their popular missions up and down the country the people were largely uninstructed and uncared for. Many had simply been abandoned and whole areas that escaped the attentions of the missionary priests have remained dechristianised to this day. But much was achieved and the situation in the second half of the century was a good deal better than it had been.

Whether and how often people saw their bishop is not clear. Visitations were carried out but usually by archdeacons or other officials and it has not been established how often the Sacrament of Confirmation was given. Too many bishops spent their time in Paris and whenever Louis XIV wished to call one of the famous Assemblies of the Clergy he had no difficulty in getting a good turn-out. The bishops themselves were often faced by powerful corporate bodies like diocesan chapters who insisted on their rights, and the bishop was not always made welcome. Their ability to appoint parish priests was also limited. A proportion of the parishes could only be allocated to men with university degrees and landowners could exert influence.

As for the people, their practice was very much what it had been in the Middle Ages. The country was still Christian and there was a high attendance at Mass on Sundays and feast days but there was little sense of community participation. Some pursued their own devotions, the illiterate told their beads or just looked on. The literate occupied themselves with books of devotion like the Hours of the Blessed Virgin and perhaps a few with one of the *Manières d'entendre la Sainte Messe* (How to attend Holy Mass) when they became available. These books followed the action of the Mass and provided more or less suitable prayers and commentary. The worshippers stood or knelt wherever the fancy took them. They received holy communion rarely, perhaps once or twice a year, unless they had come under the influence of the Jesuits and their congregations. Death, especially for infants, was an ever present and greatly feared reality. God was a God of justice rather than of mercy. Extreme unction, i.e. the anointing of the sick, was associated with death, and even Louis XIV seemed to think that a person who had not been anointed stood a very poor chance of salvation. Worship and religious practice were largely formalist; all that was necessary was to go through the motions. It was this religious formalism that Saint-Cyran opposed and it was for a religion of the heart that he and others worked.

However, in the latter part of the century there was what can only be called a pastoral liturgical movement that went beyond the Gallican revision of the liturgical books. Translations of the Mass and other parts of the liturgy, with commentaries, began to appear. Their whole thrust was towards an understanding of the liturgy and a more meaningful participation in it. How far these translations touched the illiterate or those who could only read with difficulty is another matter. The poor, and there were many of them, would not have been able to afford them. Humble people nourished their devotion on pilgrimages and the keeping of the many feast days of the time, as they had done in the Middle Ages. But these practices were often open to abuse and superstition and many bishops tried to suppress them.

There was of course all the relentless moralising of writers and preachers; there was little that could be said to be encouraging or joyful in any of it. The same could be said of the architecture of the age, the so-called French Baroque. What churches of the epoch remain are heavy and sombre. The dome of the Val-de-Grace in the rue St Jacques is surprising and exciting but the interior nowadays is dark and almost threatening. Richelieu's church, in his example of town-planning (located at Richelieu precisely), is light in the interior but the handling of the stone-work is heavy. There was, of course, the richly decorated royal chapel at Versailles, though the Mass was sometimes smothered by instrumental music and the courtiers sat with their backs to the altar, facing the king in his tribune.

The French school of spirituality, it has been said, was marked by the spirit of the age which was imbued with a certain Augustinian pessimism. Bérulle's view of human nature was sombre and Gibieuf held pessimistic views of the original corruption of human nature. The repetition of the words *néant* (nothing) and *anéantissement* (annihilation) in the works of Bérulle is daunting although he supplied the corrective with his emphasis on the incarnation and the adoration of an all-loving God. There was, we are

21

told, 'a too fearful attitude towards the majesty of God and [even] the Blessed Sacrament and a rigorist tendency in morals and asceticism'. St Francis of Assisi's joyful acceptance of nature, the sun, the birds and music was wanting. This spirit of the age was present from the beginning of the century and cannot be attributed to Jansenism though it made its acceptance all the easier. As Bremond remarked, theology apart, it was already there.[7]

One of the more startling features of the religion of the time is that the Christ of the gospels seems to be largely absent from it. Even Lancelot, a subdeacon (he never proceeded to the priesthood), the principal master at the *Petites Ecoles,* with a good knowledge of Greek and Latin, confesses that he had not read the New Testament until he was over twenty. There was much quoting of the scriptures in Jansenist writing. M. de Saci translated the Bible and there can be no doubt about the reverence in which the Jansenists held it. The nuns themselves always had more or less apt quotations on their lips to meet and comment on various eventualities. They had a profound reverence for the Blessed Sacrament but, even so, the humanity of Christ seemed to be swallowed up in the divine. There was a touch of monophysitism in much of the writing of the time. So sound a theologian as Bossuet in his *Méditations sur l'Evangile* omits the whole of the public life of Christ and goes from the Sermon on the Mount to the Passion. It may be because of this lack of evangelical emphasis that much of the piety of the seventeenth century lacks warmth. It was left to the humble Visitation nun, Margaret Mary Alacoque, who was without any intellectual pretensions, to supply the corrective later in the century. Whatever is to be said of her visions and locutions, her real importance lies in her rediscovery of gospel values. In somewhat sombre fashion the Port-Royalists accepted devotion to the Sacred Heart of Jesus and it was not until the eighteenth century, when the Jansenists had become sectarian fanatics, that there was opposition to what they called the new devotion.[8]

One of the puzzles of the age is the state of the religious education given to children. Jacqueline Arnauld (Mère Angélique), the daughter of a wealthy family, received hardly any at all and yet from the age of five she was destined for the religious life! After she had established the reform at Port-Royal she, the Ursulines and others undertook the education of girls, and that provided at Port-Royal was regarded as being particularly distinguished. Private tutors, however, still remained common in noble families and the education the girls received was often good. Madame de Sablé, with whom La Rochefoucauld discussed his *Maximes*, Madame de la Fayette, his intimate and author of the germinal novel *La Princesse de Clèves*, and, above all, Madame de Sévigné, are all witnesses to the intelligence and culture of women in the highest circles of society, even if Madame de Sévigné must be considered something of an exception. Her range was enormous. In her letters to her daughter she could go from St Augustine to Descartes, from Corneille to Racine and from them to Nicole's *Essais de Morale*. She could discuss the ins and outs of Molinism and Jansenism, in light-hearted fashion it is true, and expect to be understood. She protested that she was not devout but she showed a genuine concern for her spiritual well-being. On the other hand, there were ladies of the court whose spelling, even in an age when spelling was still uncertain, was atrocious and whose knowledge of religion seems to have been small. Bossuet, it has been said, in his sermons to the great always showed himself to be conscious of having to 'instruct' them.

For boys, of course, there were the numerous schools of the Jesuits and, on a much smaller scale, those of the Oratorians. The boys went to these schools at a rather early age, and though the secular instruction was good, the religious teaching seems to have been more questionable. It was the age of the catechism and no doubt the boys in the Jesuit schools were taught either from Bellarmine's catechism or that of Peter Canisius. In the middle of the century the Sulpicians made strenuous efforts to instruct the young, especially the under-privileged. They issued 'The Instructions to be given to Footboys during Lent', a somewhat mobile congregation, it is to be supposed.[9] Even the education given to Louis XIV's Dauphin does not seem to have been very intelligent. The poor boy was not very bright and yet his tutors, under the supervision of Bossuet, stuffed him with all sorts of information he could never have absorbed. Bossuet wrote his long and boring *Histoire Universelle* for his royal pupil. He begins with creation, gives a summary of Old Testament history (with special reference to the kings of course), the main facts of the life of Christ and the origins of the Church and winds up with a chronicle-type history of emperors and kings. If the Dauphin ever tried to read it he would have been stunned by its sheer quantity. All the tuition was interspersed with periodic beatings by underlings in the presence of the Royal Tutor.

The *Petites Ecoles,* which operated from the late thirties until they were suppressed in 1662, were in advance of anything of their time. They introduced the boys to Latin and Greek through French, obviously (to us) the only sensible thing to do. The religious education was somewhat intense. The masters were chosen for their moral as well as their intellectual qualities and the religious education was as careful as the secular. The basis of their instruction seems to have been the catechism drawn up by Saint-Cyran, which is more a series of statements than mere questions and answers and, in spite of attempts to proscribe and condemn it as Jansenist, it is difficult to find in it any Jansenist doctrines. A contemporary describes how it was used:

> For Catechism we had the one with the title *Théologie Familière,* printed by royal privilege and the approbation of the Doctors. The principal points of the faith and the truths of the gospel were explained to us in a simple manner that was proportioned to our mental ability. Our masters inculcated in us a fear of God, an aversion from sin and a great horror of lying. Also, I can say that I have never known more sincere people with whom one could be completely open....[10]

When the boys were at Port-Royal-des-Champs the liturgy of the monastery, in which they took part according to their age and ability, was there in the background all the time. On Sundays and feast days someone, often Lancelot it would seem, would read to them from lives of the saints or from other suitable books. They were also allowed indoor games on these occasions but otherwise their noses were kept close to the grindstone. They were constantly supervised and, apart from walks on Sundays and some other days there was (as far as we can tell) no exercise at all. By English standards the atmosphere was a little suffocating and lack of contact with ordinary society (which was regarded as morally dangerous) cannot have been beneficial to the general formation of the boys. However, the comparatively small numbers who passed through the schools seem to have been happy enough. They were certainly loyal.

All these schools were for families of the well-to-do and it was not until the end of the century that Jean Baptiste de la Salle brought about something of a revolution by his foundation of schools for poor boys and training colleges for those who were to teach them. If there was a rise in literacy in the eighteenth century it was no doubt thanks to him.

Another source of instruction was the preaching of the time, though this was a feature of the second rather than the first half of the century. Bossuet did not begin to preach (in Metz) until 1652, and he ceased to do so when he became tutor to the Dauphin. Bourdaloue, who was five years younger than Bossuet, began preaching in 1666 and continued after the older man had retired from his activities at court.[11] There were others, like the Oratorian Massillon, who was a moralist like Bourdaloue.

In addition, there were the more popular discourses of Jean Eudes, which he preached far away from Paris to humble congregations; his sermons were an important element in his missionary campaigns. The priests of the Congregation of the Mission did similar work. They were simple, direct and kept close to the Gospel. All this preaching and much more had a considerable effect on the people, and the religious situation at the end of the century was a good deal better than it had been at the beginning. But all was not well. Although it is difficult to trace, there seems to have been an erosion of the faith which would reappear only in the eighteenth century. The *libertins*, free-thinkers, were known in the first part of the seventeenth century and only Pascal seems to have taken them seriously. Bossuet was a great traditionalist and did not foresee that the very basis of the faith he proclaimed with such fervour would shortly be called into question. In this Fénelon was more perceptive.

It is more difficult to discover what sort of preaching took place at Mass and Vespers on Sundays in ordinary parish churches. Many of the clergy in Paris and other big cities were educated and theologically well informed. They were capable of preaching and we know that M. Du Hamel, the parish priest of St Merri, in the fashionable Marais quarter of Paris, did so with great success. The many people who heard him said that there was nothing so fine as 'the *prône* of M. Du Hamel and the instruction of M. Feydeau' (one of his curates).[12]

The *prône* was in the morning and the 'instruction' was in the afternoon. The former was a survival of the medieval 'bidding prayers', which by this time was a fairly flexible formula. It had consisted of intercessions for various categories of people from the pope downwards, and for the dead, but also included simple instructions on the Lord's Prayer, the Creed and the virtues and vices. By the seventeenth century in France it had become a sermon, or could be used as an occasion for a sermon, more familiar in tone and form than the grand *oraisons* of the famous preachers like Bossuet for whom the sermon had become almost a liturgy in itself. The instruction was of the catechetical kind and Feydeau used it assiduously for years to propagate his Jansenist views – and got into trouble for doing so. Late in the century there was Duguet, first an Oratorian and later a vehement opponent of the Bull *Unigenitus*, who had an enormous success with his instructions when he was a young man. In the cities, then, there was a good deal of instruction and people showed their appreciation by attending in great numbers. What happened in rural parishes, untouched by the missions, is another matter.

However, the dominant Gallicanism of the time which seemed to be a strength *vis-à-vis* Rome proved to be a weakness in the pastoral sphere. As the absolutism of Louis XIV increased the bishops had less and less liberty of action. When the king insisted on his right to the *régale*, the revenues of certain vacant sees, he came into serious conflict with Pope Innocent XI, who resisted him and refused to institute bishops who were royal nominees. At one time there were thirty-five vacant dioceses and the problem was only solved by Innocent's successor, Alexander VIII. Then in 1682 came the famous Four Articles which summarised the Gallican Church's position. The first rejected the deposing power of the pope, long a dead letter, the second repeated the doctrine of the Council of Constance (1414-17) that General Councils are above the pope, the third affirmed 'Gallican liberties', namely 'the rules, customs and institutions received in the Gallican Church', which covered canon law – it was by virtue of Gallican canon law that the marriage between Napoleon and Josephine was annulled in 1809.[13] The fourth article, while conceding a principal role (*praecipuas partes*) to the pope in matters of faith, refused to accept his teaching as irreformable without the subsequent assent of the (Gallican) Church.

At the high point of conflict with Innocent XI, Louis had summoned an Assembly of the Clergy, 'practically naming its members, among whom was the timid Bossuet',[14] to state the case of the Gallican Church. Agreement with the Four Articles was at first imposed on all lecturers and professors and candidates for degrees, but when the king later wanted to come to some accommodation with the papacy over the appointment of bishops he withdrew this requirement. But the Articles remained on the 'statute book' of the Church and, later, in the Organic Articles, Napoleon tried to reimpose them. In any case, neither the bishops nor Louis were consistent in their opposition to the papacy. When the king had decided to destroy Port-Royal he acquired from the pope the necessary authorisation, and when the bishops wanted papal support they sought it, in one way or another.

Such was the background to the Jansenist conflict. In the beginning and before Jansenism can be said to have existed, there were those like Saint-Cyran and Mère Angélique who were above all concerned with the interior renewal of the Christian and they wished to bring about a renewal of the Church. In this they are to be grouped with Bérulle, Vincent de Paul, Olier and the rest. French seventeenth-century Christians, at least at their best, were seeking a real contact with God, what might be called an experience of God, as the many mystics of the time showed. There were others who were content neither with the 'easy devotions' of some Jesuits which, in the phrase of Bossuet, seemed to be no more than 'putting cushions under the elbows' of the would-be devout, nor with formal celebrations of the liturgy which left the heart untouched. Hence the interest of many, including Jansenists, in promoting a devout celebration of the liturgy. But the Jansenists destroyed any good they might have done by their opposition to their own bishops and to the papacy and by their intellectual stubbornness. Only they were right and all the rest of the world was wrong. In the latter part of the century, there is an observable hardening of their positions. Port-Royalists came to reject mysticism; even the revered writings of Saint-Cyran were 'edited' to remove anything that suggested mystical prayer, and towards the end of the century Pierre Nicole assisted Bossuet in getting rid of the 'mystical invasion' that had marked all the earlier part of the century.

If the condition of the French Church at the end of the seventeenth century was considerably better than it had been at the beginning it was because of the many forces at work which produced the improvements. Among them were the Jansenists who, however detestable the doctrines of Jansenism, drew many who were and remained ignorant of those doctrines, to a more serious style of Christian living. One of the great defects of the Jansenists, however, was that they were unduly inward-looking and unconcerned about the mission of Christ, whether to the neglected Christians of their own country or the pagans abroad. It is one of the bitter ironies of the situation that while the Jansenists were quarrelling with the Jesuits about grace, the latter were dying for the faith in North America.

Perhaps on the credit side can be put their educational efforts which, for the age, were enlightened, their translation of the Bible and their spiritual direction by which they contributed to the formation of a devout and informed laity. Heavily on the debit side was their moral rigorism which showed itself in their unrealistic demands in the matter of the sacraments of penance and holy communion. It is this more than anything else that is associated with the word 'Jansenism' – though it was the eighteenth-century Jansenists who emphasised it and turned it into a very harmful tradition that lasted long after Jansenism was dead. In a broader perspective, they were turned towards the past. Rather like Tertullian, they wanted a 'pure' Church which, of course, meant an elitist Church. On the other hand, the Jesuits, St Vincent de Paul and others were concerned to meet the needs of the day. Whatever the faults committed, they were forward-looking and, in the long run, it must be said that the future was with them. The very fact that one has to explain what Jansenism was is a sign that it died a death a very long time ago.

2

JANSENISM

The greatest, and most damaging controversy that afflicted the French Church in the seventeenth century was Jansenism.[1] It began as a controversy about grace, what theologians call actual grace or the grace that God freely gives to enable human beings to enter into salvation. It may seem remote from Christians of today and wholly irrelevant to non-Christians. How then are we to see it now? Is it possible to get the whole matter in perspective?

For Christians there are two orders, the order of creation and the order of salvation or redemption. These orders are not mutually exclusive. At some indiscernible time in the past the human race, encapsulated in Adam (the human being, *anthropos-homo*), fell out of favour with God or, rather, abandoned him and cut himself off from him. By so doing he damaged the harmony in himself and destroyed his relationship with God. How was he to get back into the order of salvation? Was it possible for him to be rescued, to be redeemed? Only God could do this, for to exist in the divine order of salvation is to be raised from the self-wounded condition of the human creature, and that can only be the work of God. As creatures, made by God, and totally dependent on him for our natural existence, we have no *claim* on him. Grace is not integral to human nature, it is not a necessary element of it, it can only be given – and received. As we are dependent on God in the natural order, so we are totally dependent on his 'faithful love' for restoration to the order of salvation and reconciliation with him.

This is the teaching of the whole Bible from the first obscure promise of salvation in Genesis 3 to the climactic work of redemption wrought by Jesus Christ in his passion, death and resurrection.

Since then, all who approach him in faith (itself prompted by his grace), and are initiated into his life by baptism, confirmation and the Eucharist, are in the order of salvation, though they have to make their way as pilgrims through this world until the promised consummation when they will see God face-to-face and will be fulfilled as complete and whole human beings, experiencing an unutterable joy.

That, briefly, is the Christian vision and, in view of the radical importance of the issues at stake, it is not surprising that Christians have reflected on, debated and argued about the freedom of the will, about grace, about the ways of God with human creatures, about predestination. It has been a peculiar concern of the Church in the west since the monk Pelagius (thought by some to be Welsh) and his follower Celestine taught (or appeared to teach) that human beings could save themselves by their own efforts. Christ's life was an example and all that was required to emulate it was personal discipline. This teaching was fiercely contested by St Augustine in the last decades of his life, and his writings proved to be the source of endless controversies which began after his death in 430. The Christians of southern France, where most of the bishops were themselves monks, found some of his conclusions too rigorous and were accused of holding that the first movements of mind and will towards 'justification' or righteousness were within the scope of the human will. This view was condemned at the Council of Orange in 529 (later endorsed by the pope), which also set out in balanced fashion the Church's teaching on grace, free will and predestination. Nonetheless, the debate went on, sometimes acrimoniously, through the Middle Ages, and even the calm synthesis of St Thomas Aquinas did not satisfy everyone. The reforming Council of Trent took up the teaching of Orange, but by this time Luther's teaching on justification by faith alone had penetrated most parts of Europe. Calvin, who came after him, claimed to be a disciple of Augustine and produced an extreme doctrine of predestination.

These events re-stimulated the debate among Catholic theologians and for some years there was a good deal of vehement controversy. Clement VIII tried to sort the matter out by calling together a company of theologians, the *Congregatio de Auxiliis,* but he did not live to see its end. His successor Paul V continued the work, but no conclusion satisfactory to both parties (broadly Dominican and Jesuit) was reached, and the pope brought the meetings to an end. All he could do was issue orders that opposing parties were not to call each other heretics and that there must be no further publications about the matter. His injunctions had only a partial success.

In more recent years the whole debate about grace, at least for Catholic theologians, has ceased, not because they do not see the importance of the matter but because there has been a return to a far more biblically based theology. They have seen that all questions of original sin, grace and free will must be referred to Christ and his saving work. We cannot even begin to see the meaning of original sin until we see it in the light of Christ's redemption. Increasingly, theologians have come to realise that grace is not simply a *something (*an *aliquid)* but rather a living in Christ who, given faith, lives in us. In short, there has been a return to the Pauline and Johannine theology of grace.

How was it that the controversy about grace, free will and predestination came to be revived in the seventeenth century? Cornelis Jansen, a professor at Louvain University, continued the age-old controversy with his *Augustinus* which appeared in 1640. After years of study of the works of St Augustine, especially his later polemics against Julian of Eclanum, he thought he could put an end to the controversy. He accepted the agreed doctrine that for every good work that makes for salvation God's grace is necessary, but the question for him was whether the will remains free under the movement of God who wills that a person should be saved. Augustine had raised the question and *seemed* to hold that grace, called efficacious by later theologians, impelled the consent of the will.

When all is said and done, that was the nub of the matter. Under the influence of grace, did the will remain free? There was also the question of predestination. Were all to be saved or only those who received efficacious grace? The matter had been debated for centuries and the Calvinists had come down on the side of pre-destination: only those whom God had decided should be saved would be saved and to them alone was efficacious grace given. The rest were consigned to eternal damnation. The teaching of the Church was and always had been that God did not will that any-one should be lost, and that is the plain teaching of the New Testament. But there was another factor. The Church had declared that Augustine was the *Doctor gratiae* and Jansen unreasonably assumed that *all* the teaching of Augustine was the teaching of the Church. So, in secret, he set out to expound the true teaching of Augustine, refuting the Pelagians, the so-called Semi-Pelagians and the Neo-Pelagians, that is the Jesuit Molina and his followers. To a certain extent the *Augustinus* was an anti-Jesuit tract but Jansen also rejected the careful analyses of the medieval scholastics who, he argued, had corrupted the true doctrine of Augustine. Jansen was appointed Bishop of Ypres in 1636 and died in 1638, his book fin-ished but unpublished. A letter of submission to the Holy See was found among his papers, though it was not published with his book in 1640. An edition appeared in Paris in 1641 and its thir-teen hundred pages in folio had at first a considerable success. But during the next few years there were violent disputes, the Sorbonne opposing Jansen and also, of course, the Jesuits. Eventually seven propositions, later reduced to five, were extracted from the *Augustinus* and sent to Rome for judgement. In all this controversy Antoine Arnauld had taken a leading part in the defence of Jansen. He questioned whether the propositions (except the first) had been taken verbatim from the *Augustinus*, and it was his contention that it and the other propositions could be interpreted in an orthodox sense. The first condemnation from Rome came with the Bull *Cum occa-sione* in 1653 in which the Five Propositions were attributed to

Jansen, though without particular emphasis. This devastated Arnauld and in the vehement controversy that followed he began, apparently with the help of Pierre Nicole, to work out the fateful distinction between the *droit* and the *fait:*[2] the propositions were *rightly* condemned as heterodox but in *fact* they could not be found in the *Augustinus*. A small assembly of bishops under the guidance of Mazarin (now the First Minister after Richelieu) had further recourse to Rome and the new pope, Alexander VII (said to be in favour of the Jesuits), declared in 1656 that the Five Propositions were in the *Augustinus* and had the sense intended by Jansen. A formulary was imposed to this effect which had to be signed by all the clergy but nothing was done to implement it. What then was the content of the propositions?

1. Without grace, some of God's commandments cannot be kept even by the righteous by their own efforts, however much they wish and try to keep them; they lack the grace that makes them possible.
2. In the state of fallen nature interior grace is never resisted.
3. In the state of fallen nature interior freedom (of the will) is not necessary for merit or demerit; all that is needed is freedom from coercion.
4. The Semi-Pelagians admitted the necessity of interior, prevenient grace; they were heretics in that they believed that such grace could be resisted by human will.
5. To say that Christ died and shed his blood for all is the error of the Semi-Pelagians.

In the first, the equivocal term is grace. For Jansen it meant efficacious grace which, as the second and third propositions show, was irresistible. A freedom that was not 'coerced' was sufficient for Jansen to maintain that the will was 'free'.[3]

In fact, underlying all of the first three propositions is the denial of the will in any understandable sense. The Roman authorities saw very clearly that this was the heart of the matter. If the will is not free, then salvation is impossible for all, for we cannot be saved without the free consent of the will. That, in fact, was Augustine's teaching. To paraphrase it, it is God who saves but he will not save us without or against our consent. Jansen's trouble, however, lay further back. For him fallen human nature was hopelessly corrupted by original sin which gave an irresistible penchant for self-love (*concupiscentia*) and all that was not God. He called this a *delectatio victrix* (overwhelming pleasure) which needed a *gratia victrix* (victorious grace) to overcome it and, indeed, to overwhelm it. It is odd that this aspect of Jansen's teaching did not receive any specific mention by the Roman authorities.

That, in brief, was the doctrine, but as stated in the Five Propositions it was constantly contested by the Jansenists, led by Arnauld. Apart from the first, which *could* be interpreted in an orthodox sense, they maintained that the others were not in the *Augustinus* or, if they were, that they had been torn out of context. There may have been something in the second point. The learned Franciscan Luke Wadding, who was a member of the Roman commission, refused to agree to the condemnation. What was unfortunate was that no Roman document ever provided references to the contexts from which the propositions were drawn. It was this factor which led to the interminable and acrimonious disputes which afflicted the French Church for the rest of the century.

Jansenism, then, was first a theological opinion that was born in the Low Countries. When it was introduced into France it was defended by Antoine Arnauld. When Rome condemned the propositions Arnauld had recourse to the distinction of the *droit* and the *fait*. He was not anti-papal in any doctrinaire way and he wanted to remain loyal but he was a sharp-minded theologian; he had read the *Augustinus* and he was convinced that the Five Propositions did not represent fairly or, perhaps, accurately, Jansen's teaching. As to the *fait* he held that it was quite within the limits of orthodoxy to differ from the pope and, out of deference to him, he held that it was in order to keep a respectful silence. But it is necessary to say something about the general position at that time.

Though accepted by some, the infallibility of the pope had not yet been defined as a doctrine of the Church. In the Gallican Church it was widely contested and one reason for the unpopularity of the Jesuits was that they held it and tried to propagate it. Furthermore, there was widespread disagreement among theologians on whether the infallibility of the *Church* (gathered in General Council, for instance) extended to facts. Arnauld and his followers were not alone in holding that it did not. Their position, therefore, was compatible with orthodoxy as it was then understood. Though some of his writings were put on the Index of Prohibited Books Arnauld was never in fact declared a heretic by Rome. The real point at issue was obedience both to the bishops and the pope and it is fair to say that Arnauld never sincerely gave this. He and his followers set up their judgement against that of their lawful superiors.

It was in this way that Jansenism came to be identified with French Jansenism and that most of the trouble and controversy took place in France. Yet it is one of the odder aspects of the whole affair that, as the years went by, the argument was not so much about Jansen's teaching as about the lawfulness of withholding assent to the statements of successive documents and formularies that the heretical teaching was in fact in the *Augustinus*. In later years Arnauld himself seems to have lost interest in Jansen's doctrine and to have adopted the Thomist teaching on efficacious grace. The Thomists taught predestination to glory, which was Augustine's *donum perseverantiae*, the final gift of grace that ensures salvation, but they rejected predestination to damnation. They held strongly the New Testament teaching that Christ died for all and that the salvation gained for us by Christ had to be personally appropriated by faith and the sacraments. That is an over-simplification of a complex matter but is sufficient to show how orthodox Thomism differed from Jansenism. The rival system was that of

Molina, a Spanish Jesuit of the sixteenth century, who wrote his *Concordia liberi arbitrii cum gratiae donis* in 1588. He held that the freedom of the will was not sufficiently respected in the Thomist system, according to which grace had the inherent 'power' to assure the consent of the will. Molina's view was that God gave grace but that it became efficacious by a human act of free will. His theory was fiercely attacked by the Thomists and was Jansen's main target. Since the Jesuits (with some modifications) were the main propagators of Molinism Arnauld became their untiring opponent in France. He believed that Molinism attributed too much to human nature which led to an improper independence of God. This, combined with a humanism inherited from the Renaissance, led in turn to a moral laxity of which the casuists were the disreputable exponents.

Hence came what is arguably best referred to as moral Jansenism, with which Jansenism has been identified throughout the centuries. It was marked by an extreme austerity, a distrust of human nature, a great consciousness of sin, a rigorism in the practice of the sacrament of penance, and a disposition to keep people away from frequent communion because they were not worthy. Lying behind all this was a certain image of God. Jansenist writers constantly stress the justice of God. Since human beings have no claim on him for grace or salvation God could choose this one and reject another and in all his doings he was *just.* God was high, remote, unaccountable, terrible, and the love of Jesus Christ played too little part in the soteriology of the Jansenists. The *Deus terribilis* and the merciful Jesus never seem to meet.

There was also what might be called political Jansenism or, more exactly, the intervention of the secular power in a theological dispute. This was begun by Mazarin in the 1650s at the time of the Fronde,[4] when the Jansenists were suspected of involvement with those who were promoting civil war. Mazarin saw in Arnauld and his followers a dissident group who could be dangerous to the state. He later indoctrinated the young Louis, who had never forgotten his humiliating experiences during the Fronde, with these ideas, and when the king attained his majority and took power into his own hands he determined to suppress Jansenism and to get rid of Port-Royal, which he regarded as a nest of conspirators. In his campaign he constantly sought the assistance of Rome, quite inconsistently with his Gallican views, and used successive archbishops of Paris to achieve his purpose. In the last years of his life he succeeded in getting his way first by destroying Port-Royal and then by persuading the pope to issue a final condemnation in 1713 in the Bull *Unigenitus*. In fact it failed in its purpose and after Louis' death in 1715 it provoked appeal after appeal against it. Its numerous opponents, called Appellants, resurrected the old cry for a general council. To this, they said, they would give obedience, though it is debatable whether they would in fact have done so. It was at this time that Jansenism began to become a sect, radically Gallican and even 'Presbyterian'. This kind of Jansenism, which had no interest in the theology of Jansen, became very bitter and moved steadily towards schism, which was brought about by the constitutional clergy of the French Revolution.

In the seventeenth century, in spite of its alleged daunting rigorism, French Jansenism appealed to a considerable number of people, many of whom gathered round Port-Royal which was regarded as the centre of a spiritual elite. It was certainly an elite but in the eyes of less enthusiastic witnesses it was not so much a spiritual elite as an Arnaldist stronghold. In the monastery there were five Arnauld sisters and others who were cousins or family connections. The community also regarded themselves as a spiritual elite. Hence their haggling in later years about who should be their spiritual directors and confessors. Only those who were of the 'right kind' were acceptable, that is those who shared their preconceptions and their somewhat precious way of going about things.

But there were not only the Arnaldists in the monastery, there were others among the 'solitaries' outside it. Among them were Antoine Le Maître, distinguished advocate and spectacular convert, his brother, and eventually his cousin Le Maître de Saci. In addition to these there were members of the nobility who built houses around Port-Royal and gave the whole establishment a certain cachet. There were the Duke of Luynes, the Duchess de Longueville (a relative of the king yet at one time involved in the Fronde), and the Comtesse de Vertus. There were learned men among them like Pierre Nicole (who was said to have read everything) and, when he was not in hiding, Antoine Arnauld made longer or shorter visits. The rumour went round that at Port-Royal there were a dozen sharp pens at the ready to refute all comers. An exaggeration of course, as was the story which reached the king's ears that there were no less than two hundred men at Port-Royal who, from his point of view, could only be disturbers of the peace. Two or three old soldiers had been multiplied to make two hundred.

The attraction to the life of and around Port-Royal is undeniable and it was as difficult for people of the seventeenth century to understand as it is for us. Why didn't the 'solitaries' join a religious order? There were some in various stages of reform which were no longer decadent. But several of the solitaries were too old and some were eccentric, pious 'drop-outs', some distinguished like the Marquis de Sévigné who, it seems, did not wish to give up their liberty. De Sévigné was in fact a great benefactor of the monastery. The great ladies had certain obligations in the world and were either too old or too infirm to enter a religious order. It needs to be said too that in spite of St Francis de Sales and his *Devout Life*, the notion that men and women could lead an authentic life outside the cloister was still regarded as somewhat strange. After all, it is only in our own time that it has been accepted that lay people can live a dedicated spiritual life in the world.

It can be said in favour of the solitaries that they sought a way of Christian living that they could not find elsewhere. At Port-Royal there was a broad pattern of life into which the solitaries fitted themselves according to their abilities. There was regular prayer, the Divine Office, study for those capable of it, manual work – gardening and the like – and the gathering in of the harvest in which those who were able took part. In addition, there was the availability of spiritual direction which they sought and needed. From 1648 and after 1669, when the interdict had been removed, there was always in the background the austere beauty of the monastic liturgy, attested by many visitors over the years. At a time when the liturgy was overloaded with ceremonial or was celebrated in a cold and formal manner, the liturgy of Port-Royal stood out in its simplicity and devoutness. Voices only were heard in church and the music was plainsong. The solitaries (and visitors) joined in the worship on Sundays and the great feast days, in the penitential processions at Rogationtide and the joyful ones at Corpus Christi. The solitaries also recited the Divine Office in their (often humble) dwellings, acting as a sort of relay to the nuns in their chapel so that the praise of God could continue through much of the day and night. Otherwise their spiritual nourishment came from the reading of the Bible (not very common at the time), from the Fathers of the Church and from the spiritual classics of the past. In an age of many devotions, at Port-Royal there was much devotion.

These remarks have their point in trying to make an assessment of Port-Royal. It was its general ethos that remained in the memory of many devout persons long after Port-Royal had been destroyed. The great pity is that this spiritual tradition was distorted and eventually ruined by what can only be called intellectual arrogance and theological pig-headedness.

3

JEAN DUVERGIER DE HAURANNE
Abbé de Saint-Cyran

No man of his time has been the subject of so many contrary and sometimes contradictory judgements as Jean Duvergier de Hauranne, usually known as the Abbé de Saint-Cyran, an obscure monastery of which he was commendatory abbot. He was a holy man who dominated souls and seduced them into heresy. He had direct and all but infallible intuitions of God's will, yet made deep professions of his nothingness and humility. Educated as a boy and theological student by the Jesuits he became their severest critic and might be described as a *malleus Jesuitarum,* a hammer of the Jesuits. A defender of the Church, especially of the episcopate, and professing a love of the Church, he was a heretic and, with his friend Cornelius Jansen, a heresiarch who brought to birth the abominable doctrine of Jansenism. Reputedly very learned, his mind was confused and he never managed to organise his erudition. While appearing to lead a pious and withdrawn life he indulged in savage criticisms of those who disagreed with him. With the air of a prophet he made cryptic pronouncements that impressed only his adoring disciples. He was concerned for the reform of the clergy but lived most of his life as the beneficiary of an abbey of which he was not abbot. For all his professions of piety his temper was uncertain and his behaviour unpredictable.

Henri Bremond, who was hostile, was unable to make up his mind about Saint-Cyran: 'His whole life was a continual failure, made the more bitter by a few successes, the desolating emptiness of which he could not but recognise.' He was 'prodigiously preoccupied with himself' and 'there were clearly morbid indications in his character'. He was a psychopath because of his heredity.[1] Yet he can conclude that Saint-Cyran 'stopped this side of mysticism but his deeper life was full of God'.[2] It must be said that a man of whom such differing judgements have been made is a puzzle and it may seem futile to attempt to penetrate the enigma. But Saint-Cyran is worth study because he did in fact exercise a considerable influence during the years between 1620 and his death in 1643, and it would be unjust to say that his influence was wholly for the bad.

There has been a good deal of writing in recent years about Jansenism in general and Saint-Cyran in particular and this makes a more balanced assessment a little easier. It is a long time since Sainte-Beuve wrote his *Port-Royal* – to him must go the credit of discerning for the first time that Saint-Cyran was not a charlatan but a remarkable man in spite of his eccentricities and absurdities.[3] More recently the great scholar Jean Orcibal planned and carried through to completion a monumental study in five volumes, *Les Origines du Jansénsime,* the second volume of which, comprising nearly seven hundred pages, is wholly devoted to Saint-Cyran. All writers in the area since then have been indebted to his work. Tempers are calmer now and it should be possible to approach both Jansenism and Saint-Cyran in a more objective way.

In spite of the assertions of some writers, perhaps misled by the 'de', there was nothing aristocratic in the ancestry of Jean Ambroise Duvergier de Hauranne. The family appears at Bayonne in the fifteenth century as butchers but by the sixteenth century they had moved up the social ladder considerably. They had become very wealthy wholesale merchants still concerned with cattle but no longer with the slaughter-house. Jean Duvergier *père* had made his way rapidly and had what is described as a brilliant career in the city council, being elected as an alderman (*échevin*) while still quite young. He seems to have been more literate than many of his fellow councillors since he was commissioned on several occasions to speak and write for the council. It seems likely too that he had a wider knowledge of south-western France than his colleagues, for his business took him to Dax, to the Limousin and to faraway Poitiers. Like others of his status in the town he was not over-scrupulous. On one occasion, and it was probably not the only one, he managed to smuggle into the town seventy oxen and four hundred sheep, thus evading the tax due on them.

This may not have been too difficult as Bayonne and its council were dominated by the Duvergiers, the Sorhaindos and several other families who were all interrelated by marriage. In other words, the town was run by a wealthy oligarchy. No one else could oppose them and members of these families seem to have behaved much as they pleased. There was in fact a certain tradition of violence in the Duvergier family. One whose behaviour must have become intolerable was imprisoned twice; another is described as 'the principal swashbuckler of the town at the time'[3] and was, unbelievably, a priest and treasurer of the cathedral chapter. Yet another, also a Jean, though indicted for various crimes of violence, strode about the streets, sword in hand, openly defying arrest. It is not improbable that Jean Ambroise inherited something of the family tradition of violence. Later in life he sometimes had diffi-culty in repressing the *bouillonnements* (the boilings-up) of his nature. This may account for the violence of his controversial writ-ings and his savage remarks about people.

The Duvergiers were intensely ambitious, as is shown by their rapid rise to dominance in the town. Jean Ambroise very soon showed that he was determined to shine, though not in the sphere of action. His ambitions were spiritual and intellectual, it being his aim to master the whole range of ecclesiastical sciences. He wanted to *know*, and as the years went by he became very learned and freely contradicted those who disagreed with him. When people accused him later of dominating the souls he was directing they may have discerned something of this urge for power which Duvergier tried hard to repress. He rejected several offers of bishoprics because he

had set his sights on something higher, nothing less than the renewal of the Church in France.

The social power of the oligarchy is revealed in their political
stance. They were hostile to the aristocratic governors of the region
and were successful in their attempts to reduce their power. At the
same time, they were intensely loyal to the Bourbon king, Henry
IV, when he ascended the throne. Bayonne, the Béarn and Navarre
were close to each other. Henry was of their world, they knew him
personally and Jean Ambroise inherited this tradition. Inevitably
they were anti-Ligueurs[4] who opposed the Bourbon succession and
wanted to capture the throne for the Guises.

This attitude partly accounts for their religious stance. Although
there were Protestants in Bayonne, like the Lalandes who were
related to members of the oligarchy, there was no bloodshed in the
town during the very bitter Wars of Religion. The Bayonnais are to
be grouped with those referred to by historians as the '*politiques*'.
They knew they were strong enough to prevent a Protestant take-
over and they detested the fanaticism of the Ligueurs. What they
wanted was peace and a situation that would allow them to pursue
the all-important business of money-making. This peace was maintained largely thanks to their loyalty to Henri Bourbon.

As far as their religious life was concerned, the Bayonnais were
conventionally pious, they went to church and no doubt once or
twice a year they received holy communion. But 'the spirit of gain'
dominated their religion.[5] They were ready to milk the Church as
occasion arose for in their view it was a very wealthy institution.
They were anti-clerical in the sense that they would stand no non-
sense from the clergy and they had no scruples in resisting Maury,
who was both a bishop and an aristocrat. Fortunately, he died while
Jean Ambroise was a child and this fact would make a considerable
difference to the boy's future career. The Duvergiers and the rest
disliked monks and religious whom they believed to be both rich
and ignorant. They seem to have had a particular dislike of the
Jesuits, perhaps because they thought of them as a new-fangled reli-

gious order which they could not accommodate in their very tradi-tionalist way of thinking. The town needed a school but they would not have the Jesuits, the experts of the time, and they screwed money out of the chapter to get one founded. It was not a very good school – some five masters in succession proved to be unsatisfactory and had to be sacked.

This was the background of Jean Ambroise's childhood and youth of which unfortunately little is known. He was born in 1581, a son of his father's second wife and one of a brood of thirteen children. He was evidently a younger son and, although the family was well-to-do, provision for younger sons always caused some difficulty. Jean Ambroise's father decided that he was to be a beneficiary of the Church's wealth and had him tonsured at the age of ten. This was the first step on the ecclesiastical ladder, though it was not regarded as committing the boy to ordination. What was more important, it also meant that he could be provided with a benefice, but for this he had to wait until the death of Bishop Maury in 1593. In the meantime, he was sent to school, however unsatisfactory it may have been.

There is one important element of Jean Ambroise's upbringing of which nothing is known. His mother remains a shadowy figure but it is likely that she was more sensitive than her husband's fam-ily. His father was a successful and able man but it is difficult to imagine that he had any of the finer graces; Jean Ambroise showed a quality of intuitive intelligence that he is more likely to have inherited from his mother. Later on, when he was beginning what for the family was an unusual career in scholarship, his mother showed some understanding while he busily pursued his study of the Fathers of the Church with his friend Cornelius Jansen. He also had a strongly affective side to his character and that too may have come from her. He was kind and helpful to at least three of his nephews and when he had received his commendatory abbey he surrendered all his claims on the family estate without difficulty. He never forgot his family or his home town and in response to requests from that quarter did all he could for it. He was not the inhuman monster some like to imagine him to have been.

Since the local school could not take a bright boy very far his father looked around for something better. The Jesuits had founded a school at Agen in the Guyenne which was reputed to be the best in south-western France and Jean-Ambroise was sent there at the age of fourteen. He received a good grounding in Latin and Greek and, as the Jesuits prepared students for university entrance, was probably initiated into philosophy. Since he did proceed to the university he was presumably successful in his studies but two events occurred which affected his future. His father died in 1586 in his mid-fifties and the family evidently thought that provision must be made for the son to continue his studies. What exactly happened is not recorded but about two years later Duvergier was made a subdeacon, one year below the canonical age of eighteen. As a subdeacon he could be presented with a prebend which carried with it an income. The second event was the appointment of Bertrand d'Eschaux as Bishop of Bayonne. He was an intimate of Henri IV, one of his counsellors and his almoner, and this made him acceptable to the oligarchy. Whether or not it was his influence that made possible the presentation of a prebend to Duvergier is uncertain. The bishop did not take possession of his see until 1599, and then by proxy, but the king had nominated him some four years earlier so that he may have been able to exert some influence in the interim. In any case he was to have a decisive influence on Duvergier's future.

In 1598 or 1599 Duvergier went to the University of Paris and was matriculated in the Faculty of Arts to read philosophy. The course was not inspiring, consisting as it did of a 'servile commentary on the logic, ethics, physics and metaphysics of Aristotle'.[6] To this was added some study of Euclid and a little science. Duvergier proceeded Master of Arts in 1600. Normally he would have joined the Faculty of Theology and graduated as Doctor of Theology after a long and gruelling course. There must have been consultation with Bishop d'Eschaux for he persuaded Duvergier to take his theological course with the Jesuits. Jesuit-educated himself, the bishop had a great regard for them. He seems to have suggested that since the course was only four years long and as, in any case, they taught sound doctrine, Duvergier would do better to go to them. In some ways the advice was unfortunate; Duvergier was to find later on that study with the Jesuits had prevented him from taking his doctorate at Paris. Moreover, since the Jesuits had been temporarily expelled from France, Duvergier had to go to Louvain where the Jesuits had a college which, however, was not an integral part of the university.

Nonetheless, the college had a high reputation. One of the staff members was Lessius, a Molinist, regarded as an expert on grace and predestination who got into trouble on that subject with his own superiors in Rome. The teaching of scripture was in the hands of the famous Cornelius à Lapide who wrote a many-volumed commentary on the entire Bible. He was an immensely learned Hebraist, and from him Duvergierer received an initiation into Hebrew. The *Summa Theologiae* of St Thomas Aquinas was the basis of the theology course but the lecturers had considerable freedom in their treatment of him. Nonetheless, Duvergier acquired a lifelong esteem for St Thomas whom he distinguished from other scholastics who in his view were mere logic-choppers. What is a little surprising is that the full course on moral theology and casuistry was taught only to Jesuit students. The rest received an introduction lasting only one year. Even so, Duvergier learnt enough to make an unfortunate use of it in later years.

He was undoubtedly one of the brightest students and he ended his career with the Jesuits with what is described as a brilliant defence of theological theses, a task usually given only to the best student. At the Sorbonne it would have earned him the licentiate and the doctorate that automatically followed. One observer of the defence was Justus Lipsius, classical scholar, Professor of Latin at Louvain University (where he never gave a single lecture) and a friend of the Jesuits (who had finally converted him from a zig-zag course from Lutheranism to Calvinism and back again to Catholicism). He was greatly impressed by Duvergier's performance and sent him a warm, indeed flattering, letter of congratulation. In the course of it he suggested that Duvergier might do well to turn his attention to the more positive side of theology, the Fathers and Councils of the Church. This advice had an effect, for that is what Duvergier would do in the next ten years or so.

Like many another student Duvergier felt drawn to Paris and its university. There he made useful contacts, attended the lectures of Duval, the spiritual director of Madame Acarie, and was befriended by Gamaches, the professor of moral theology. When, however, he attempted to repeat his Louvain success he ran up against opposition. The Sorbonne was opposed to the Jesuits and there was a rule that anyone who had studied with the Jesuits might not graduate in theology. While this cannot be considered a personal affront to Duvergier it seems to have turned him away from an academic career. He returned to Bayonne, received a canonry at the cathedral and, thanks to the influence of the bishop, began to move on the fringes of the not very reputable court circle. Some were evil livers, others were *libertins* and not one could have been called a devout Christian. The king, aware that the Wars of Religion had seriously damaged the cultural life of the country, tried to raise the tone among this unpromising lot. One of his entourage, the Comte de Cramail, liked to stimulate discussions, and the king, entering into the spirit of the thing, posed what might be called a case of conscience: what should a loyal courtier do if the king after defeat in battle had to take to the open seas with two or three of his followers and was in danger of starvation? Would it be lawful for one of them to commit suicide to provide meat for the king?! Duvergier seemed to be a very bright young man and Cramail asked him to write a reply. This was *La Question Royale* which was a largely pagan exercise in casuistry in which the author displayed his learning. Duvergier's answer was affirmative. The king was the corporate head of his people, without him they could not exist, therefore the preservation of the king's life was a necessity. This, Duvergier sought to prove, with a great display of learning drawn from Aristotle and even St Thomas, and adopting their view of the corporate state. How serious he was must be a matter of speculation; later his defenders called it the *jeu d'esprit* of a young man. That he had a profound loyalty to the king cannot be doubted. About a year later, in 1610, Henri fell to the knife of an assassin (alleged to be the agent of the Jesuits!) and Duvergier wrote a long poem in baroque Latin as a tribute to the king. In later years, when he had become the enemy of the Jesuits, they dug up *La Question Royale* to show that he could indulge in a kind of casuistry that was quite disreputable. The defence then was that it had never been intended for publication; that it had been published was the responsibility of the Comte de Cramail. One feature of this time is that the notoriously debauched life of the king does not seem to have concerned Duvergier.

His life at this time had more than one dubious aspect. Somewhere about 1609 he was sent on a secret mission to England accompanied by a dissolute spy. Nothing seems to be known about this expedition. To whom were they sent and what were they supposed to discover? After the Gunpowder Plot of 1605 the Catholics were hard-pressed, fines were imposed and houses were searched, but by 1610 things had quietened down. On the political front Henri may have wanted to know the intentions of James I in the Clèves-Juliers affair. The Catholic duke had died and the succession was disputed between the Protestant and the Catholic powers (Austria and Spain). James was hesitant. He was expected to support the Protestant claims but did not want to alienate Spain. Henri was ready to invade but was assassinated before he could do so. It is a pity that there seems to be no record of Duvergier's time in England, nothing to tell us of what he thought of the country and its people. If he had met any, he could only have spoken to them in French or, possibly, Latin. In Henri's court circle, which included Cramail, there was a George 'Critton' (i.e. Crichton),

Regius Professor of the Collège de France at Paris, and from him Duvergier could have acquired some information about Scotland and James I.

All this, however, was but an interlude. What was more important for Duvergier's life was his meeting with Cornelis Jansen, then a young man who had only recently graduated at Louvain. After his long and arduous course he had come to Paris for a change of air (though the air of Paris at the time was anything but salubrious) and perhaps to make contact with the university. He was a tall young man, somewhat gauche, painstaking and earnest, who probably felt somewhat out of place in the sophisticated city. How he and Duvergier met we do not know but it would seem that a community of interest drew them together. Both discovered that they wanted to explore the earlier tradition of the Church and it looks as if Justus Lipsius' suggestion to Duvergier was having effect. At the invitation of the latter, they shared the same lodging and began their studies. But Paris proved too noisy and distracting and Duvergier invited Jansen to go back with him to his home in Bayonne. They were able to occupy a family property called Camp-de-Prats just outside the town and there they settled down to an intensive course of study on the scriptures, the Fathers and councils of the Church. This went on from about 1611 to 1614. Duvergier's mother, who seems to have taken this all very calmly, once remarked to her son that he would injure the health of his friend by so much study. It may have been the other way around for Jansen had an enormous capacity for systematic work. He and Duvergier compiled dossiers, now called *fiches*, of passages from Church literature on all the subjects that interested them. Orcibal, however, has made clear that at this time neither had any special interest in St Augustine or in the question of grace and predestination. Like other young men they discussed the renewal of the Church and this was later built up into a conspiracy to overturn the Church!

Nor was their study uninterrupted. In 1612 Jansen was appointed what we would call headmaster of a school founded by the Bayonnais, the sixth in succession after five others had proved unsatisfactory. Duvergier seems to have moved about the country a good deal and by 1613 he is found in Poitiers with Louis de la Rocheposay, bishop of that place, to whom he had been introduced by his patron, Bishop d'Eschaux. His stay was short and he was back at Bayonne in 1614, the year that Jansen returned to Louvain to take up an academic post there. Jansen had become deeply attached to Duvergier and tried to keep in touch with him though his friend did not always answer his letters. But there is one letter of Jansen's, dated 9 March 1617, in which, in somewhat ungainly French, he reveals his affection for him. He speaks of the great affection Duvergier had always shown him, an affection he would do nothing to damage. He knows that Duvergier's nature is such that he would never do anything inconsistent with their friendship, anything that would ever be to the detriment of the interior bond by which God had bound them together for so long. He wanted to keep that bond whole and entire all the days of his life.[7]

This letter throws light on both men. The picture of Duvergier as an almost inhuman ogre who was irascible, bossy and given to contradicting is evidently wide of the mark, at least when he was young. He showed great kindness to Jansen who in character could hardly have been more unlike him. He befriended him in an alien Paris and, as well as inviting him to his home, he provided a living for him with the headmastership of the school. Jansen, who was poor and from a poor family, had none of the airs and graces of the cultivated Frenchman. When he returned to Louvain his relationships with his colleagues were not always easy. He was or soon became somewhat secretive and yet Duvergier penetrated all this and saw something of the worth of the man. It was not the last time that he would show an ability for the discernment of character.

Louis de la Rocheposay was learned in the classics but had little theology and, as a bishop, he felt he ought to improve his knowledge. Accordingly, he invited Duvergier to come and live in his house at Coussay and read one question of the *Summa Theologiae* of St Thomas with him every day. Duvergier stayed with him for some five years though his time was interrupted by visits elsewhere. This period was painful yet important for his subsequent life. He gained a certain notoriety with his *Apologie pour M. de Poitiers* in which he defended him from taking up arms against a threatened attack of a Huguenot force which fortunately never materialised. In a sense the book is split down the middle. Duvergier knew the Christian tradition, none better than he, and he gives the book a veneer of religiousness, though the examples of valiance are drawn from the Old Testament, and he exalts the natural virtues. Indeed, he relativises Christian laws which, according to him, differ according to different times! Courage and the resort to arms are necessary to the well-being of the state and at times also to that of the Church. He adopts a thesis of the time that certain noble characters (*généreux*) can be classified as a type of demi-god and they are allowed do things that are forbidden to lesser folk. Bishops belong to the highest order and if they take up arms this is perfectly legitimate.[8] Here it seems Duvergier was indulging in some flattery of his patron. The book was apparently riddled with a corrupt casuistry on the subject of duels, usury and simony! In any case it was an anachronism – even if a few years later Richelieu led the troops at the final assault on La Rochelle, presumably wearing the hat of the king's first minister. It was Duvergier's last attempt of the kind and, like *La Question Royale*, was in total contradiction of what he would shortly do.

While he was at Poitiers he met Richelieu, then a very young and inexperienced Bishop of Luçon. Poitiers, partly under the influence of Rocheposay, had become something of an intellectual centre. There were many cultivated people living there, among them lawyers who in those days were learned men interested in literature. Richelieu was glad to leave his neglected and deplorable diocese and from time to time seek more congenial company. including Duvergier. Their relationship became close. Duvergier assisted Richelieu in various ways, keeping him informed of what was going on when the young bishop was exiled from the court, corresponding with him regularly and seeing to the publication of his *L'Instruction Chrétienne* which Richelieu, with the assistance of Dr Richard Smith,[7] wrote for the benefit of his ignorant clergy. When Richelieu became chief minister in 1624 it might have seemed that Duvergier's career was made. Richelieu did indeed offer him a bishopric but Duvergier had taken the measure of the man and refused. He knew that Richelieu would wish to dominate him and use him as a tool, as he did everyone else.

While still at Poitiers Duvergier came to know and to form a close friendship with Sebastian Bouthillier, whose family had long been connected with the Richelieus. Bouthillier was a really devout priest and he had a decisive influence on Duvergier. It was he who taught him what it meant to be a priest and he initiated him into mental prayer, of which Duvergier had been ignorant up to this time. He may also have influenced him to be ordained priest, after so many years as a subdeacon. However, that step had, in any event, become necessary, as Rocheposay had presented him with a canonry at Poitiers and the local canons did not welcome him at all. Duvergier thought that ordination would help his cause. Rocheposay also presented him with the priory of Vouneuil which was not yet vacant! That too made life unpleasant for Duvergier. Finally, the bishop presented him with the abbey of Saint-Cyran, a miserable and unhealthy monastery in the midst of marshes on the edge of the river Indres which, however, provided him with a sufficient income for the rest of his life. But Bouthillier also appreciated Duvergier's worth and when he took possession of his see as Bishop of Aire in 1623 he invited his friend to his diocese as Vicar General to help him in its renewal. Most unfortunately, Bouthillier died within the year, and Duvergier thus lost a friend who would almost have saved him from some of his later extravagances.

While at Poitiers Duvergier met another man who, without either knowing it at the time, would lead him in a direction which would eventually dictate his future life. One day Bouthillier brought Robert Arnauld d'Andilly to Duvergier and introduced them briefly: 'This is M. Robert Arnauld', he said, 'This is M. Duvergier'. These two very different men took to each other immediately. Robert Arnauld, the eldest son of the powerful legal family of that name, had been elaborately educated in the classical learning of the time. While still young he was introduced to the court and later on he became a *conseiller d'état*, a kind of mentor to the dissolute Gaston d'Orléans, the king's brother, who intrigued against Richelieu.

The relationship between the two men was close and somewhat over-heated. Duvergier's letters to Arnauld were written in a fantastic style, convoluted and at times almost untranslatable. He pours out his affection, straining the analogies between divine and human love to the limit and beyond. If they had been written today suspicion would have fallen on the nature of the friendship but both men were morally beyond reproach. Arnauld, however, remained a good friend until Duvergier's death. It was he who introduced him to his sister, the Abbess of Port-Royal, and that is how he became involved with that community and the whole Arnauld family. It was at this time too that Duvergier met Pierre de Bérulle, the founder of the French Oratorians, and Charles de Condren, who was to succeed Bérulle as General.

Richelieu, Bouthilliers, Arnauld, Bérulle... it is a distinguished list. Duvergier, now the Abbé de Saint-Cyran, was moving in a new world and Arnauld wanted to push him even higher. In 1621 Saint-Cyran went to live in Paris where Arnauld introduced him to court circles. He received offers that would have led to high honours and a bishopric. He refused in turn the office of Almoner Royal (first from Marie de Medici and then from Henrietta Maria, the Queen of England), the tutorship of the young Henri de Guise, and the role of spiritual director to the Calvairiennes who had split from the prestigious royal monastery of Fontevrault. If, as he believed, he was the man least suited to solitude, he found that he was not at all suited to the society of the court. As he said in a letter to Robert

Arnauld, he was tired of being a performing dog. Although he usually wrote badly his conversation was sometimes brilliant and it is not difficult to imagine the not very cultivated courtiers hanging on his words for a new flash of wit.

The truth is that Duvergier's ordination to the priesthood in 1618 had marked the beginning of conversion. Although it seemed opportunist at the time, he took the matter very seriously and prepared himself for it with great care. It seems that henceforth he saw his role as that of a man who would do what he could for the renewal of the Christian life in the Church in France. He would continue his studies tirelessly over the years that followed. In all of this Bouthillier had a decisive influence on Saint-Cyran and his meeting with Vincent de Paul in 1622 opened up another opportunity. Vincent's own experience had shown him the deplorable state of the parish clergy. He determined to do what he could to improve this situation and he initiated the fourteen-day retreats for ordinands. Saint-Cyran helped him to obtain the property Vincent needed for his work and continued his support for years.

In view of what was said about Saint-Cyran in his lifetime and what has been written of him since, it is important in an assessment of his character to point out that men like Bouthillier, Bérulle and Vincent de Paul, all perceptive and distinguished, appreciated Saint-Cyran's qualities and valued his friendship. They were not likely to be taken in by a psychopathic charlatan. It would seem that people then were more tolerant of eccentricity than were nineteenth-century biographers but, what is more important, Saint-Cyran's friends saw in him a deeply spiritual man even if, like Vincent de Paul, they regretted some of his later excesses

Meanwhile Saint-Cyran had not forgotten Jansen. In 1621 he visited him in Louvain for about three months[9] and in 1625 Jansen stayed with him in Paris. Since 1619 Jansen had been reading St Augustine and he was amazed and enchanted by what he found in his works on the subject of grace. For him it cut through all the Scholastic debates on the subject and he was convinced that he had arrived at the truth. He shared his enthusiasm with his friend, and because the theology of grace was very contentious and no doubt because public debate had been forbidden by Rome in 1607, they decided to keep quiet about it. They continued their discussions by correspondence and, since letters were sometimes opened *en route* or never reached their destination, they devised a code to deceive ill-wishers. They invented a whole series of bizarre names and terms among which 'Pilmot' stood for grace. This was later blown up to mean a plot against the Church.

Since his own lifetime Saint-Cyran has been regarded as the arch-Jansenist who contaminated the nuns of Port-Royal. His mind is not at all clear on the subject and we cannot do better than follow the delicate analysis of Jean Orcibal, who knew more than anyone else about the relationship between Jansen and Saint-Cyran. Referring to the long correspondence between them from about 1617 to 1636, Orcibal called it 'a dialogue of the deaf':

> Both were disciples of St Augustine of Hippo but they represented two families of different minds. They read him in different ways. Jansen was an intellectual, he was searching for a theological solution to a precise academic problem of which he saw the actuality. Duvergier's preoccupations were, on the contrary, practical, and even these were somewhat vague. For him the return to Augustinian spirituality was the way whereby the primitive Church could be made to flourish in the seventeenth century. This was the 'grand design' that Sebastian Bouthillier had worked on in Rome, and he doubtless had understood Duvergier better than the professor of Louvain.[10]

At the same time it was Jansen who had led Saint-Cyran to the late anti-Pelagian works of Augustine which Jansen himself had read many times. A small Louvain edition of them was available which Saint-Cyran acquired and later distributed to others, notably the young Antoine Arnauld. In some of his writings (unpublished in his lifetime) certain Jansenist theses can be detected, but they are derived from the works of St Augustine and should be described as Augustinian rather than Jansenist. Saint-Cyran had other interests. He was concerned with the spiritual life, was known to be a skilful spiritual director and he saw in Augustine's doctrine on grace as the basis of humility, total dependence on God, which, with all spiritual directors, he regarded as the bedrock of the spiritual life. As a pastor of souls he was interested in psychological states and he was credited with considerable powers of discernment. Such an interest was totally foreign to Jansen. Finally, Saint-Cyran never read the *Augustinus*. When he received a copy in prison his eyesight was so bad that he was unable to read the closely printed volume. He glanced through the tables of contents and into the different parts of it and expressed himself to be disappointed. It lacked 'unction', a grave charge with him; it had nothing to offer to those who were trying to lead a spiritual life. But perhaps more by hearsay than reading he learnt something of the contents of the book and he urged Antoine Arnauld to defend it. Rather like a theological Helen, Arnauld launched a thousand pamphlets.[11]

While at Poitiers Saint-Cyran had already met Pierre Bérulle, founder and first General of the French Oratory and later Cardinal. He was a man of extraordinary spiritual penetration who produced a mystical theology, a real theology which left its mark on the French Church for the rest of the century. He was profoundly concerned about the condition of the clergy but he realised that amelioration was not just a matter if discipline. From his long ponderings and studies he worked out a theology of the Church as the sacrament of Christ who is its high priest. All comes from him – Church, sacraments, priesthood – and he is the model of the ministerial priesthood. But this not merely in an external or moral sense. The priest has to reproduce in himself the 'states' of Christ. As Christ was consecrated in the incarnation the priest is consecrated by ordination. As Christ was poor, stripped of every earthly advantage, the priest must seek to reproduce this condition in his own life. As Christ in his life and by his passion, death and resurrection, gave perfect worship to God and was caught up in loving contemplation of the Father, so the priest through his liturgical ministry, as well as his private prayer, must be an adorer of God. All must come from the depths of his being where Christ is present and where the Holy Spirit dwells.

The contemplative life had almost disappeared, and was being revived in the household of Madame Acarie, which was a centre for theologians and spiritual people, among them Bérulle. He had a strong desire to promote the contemplative life and, with her encouragement and urging and in the face of many difficulties, he managed to bring some Carmelites from Spain and establish the first Carmel in Paris.

All this and much more appealed to Saint-Cyran. He was impressed by Bérulle's personality and, above all, his spiritual doctrine, and for some months he spent long hours with him almost daily. They had a mutual concern for the renewal of the Church and Bérulle shared with Saint-Cyran the difficulties he was having with the Jesuits, partly over the Oratory's founding of schools. More importantly, they exchanged views about the deeper things of the spiritual life and the accord was so complete that Bérulle relied on him to see his *Grandeurs de Jésus* through the press and entrusted to him the correction of his *Vie de Jésus*.

But the influence was not all one way. Bérulle admired Saint-Cyran's great learning and drew on it as he needed. His own turn of mind was for the abstract and he expressed his thought in ways others found difficult and rather heavy. Saint-Cyran had a keener psychological mind and he helped his friend to 'translate' his teaching into more palatable terms. Even so, Bérulle's teaching made its way slowly throughout the first part of the seventeenth century and was later filtered through the minds and actions of men as various as Vincent de Paul, Jean Jacques Olier and John Eudes.

In addition, Saint-Cyran supported Bérulle in his difficulties over his 'Vow of Servitude' to the Blessed Virgin Mary which he wanted to impose on the Spanish sisters he had imported from Spain. Bérulle also maintained that he was and must remain their spiritual director. This led to conflict with the Carmelite friars who rejected the 'Vow' and contested Bérulle's claim to be spiritual director. In another matter, Saint-Cyran rallied support for the founding of an Oratorian house in the Low Countries and he played a decisive role in the election of Charles de Condren as General after Bérulle's death.

Although he lived quietly, by the middle of the 1620s Saint-Cyran was well known in Paris to people of importance and there is little or no evidence that anyone thought him odd or eccentric. Nor, up to 1625, had he shown any animus towards the Jesuits. Then appeared a book arrogantly and absurdly entitled *Somme Théologique*, in emulation of the *Summa Theologiae* of St Thomas. Its author was a Jesuit, Garasse. The tone was flippant, the learning superficial and the book of dubious orthodoxy in many places. Its irreverence shocked Saint-Cyran, who regarded it as playing to the gallery of the sceptics and *libertins*. To make matters worse, the book was intended to be some sort of riposte to Bérulle's *Grandeurs de Jésus*. Saint-Cyran decided to do battle and, drawing on the considerable collection of material in his notebooks, he proceeded to pulverise the unwary Jesuit, in three volumes. He was completely victorious. *Somme Théologique* was condemned by the Sorbonne and Garasse, who had been 'writer-in-ordinary' to the Jesuits, was relegated to the provinces where he passed the rest of his life in edifying fashion. The attack was also a declaration of war and Saint-Cyran was now identified with the anti-Jesuits.

From Bérulle Saint-Cyran had learned of the eminent dignity of episcopacy and priesthood or, as we would say, the true nature of the office. In an age when the Church was full of careerists, royal patronage and innumerable ordinations of men without any sort of vocation, it was an important and necessary emphasis. Both Bérulle and Saint-Cyran regarded the ministerial priesthood as the 'order' founded by Christ – hence it was superior to religious orders founded by men. The bishop, as the representative of Christ, had a jurisdiction that required obedience from the religious in all pastoral matters, including the hearing of confessions, even if they had received special faculties from Rome. As is well known, the battle was joined in England when Richard Smith was appointed Vicar Apostolic there. The religious refused to recognise his authority in the matter of faculties for confession and other matters.

Similar, though less intense trouble was also brewing in the United Provinces (Holland). To defend episcopacy and his now deceased friend Bérulle, Saint-Cyran launched into a series of vehement and sometimes virulent pamphlets against the Jesuits under the assumed name of Petrus Aurelius. These, eventually published in a book entitled *Petri Aurelii Opera*, had a wide circulation. The National Assembly of the Clergy offered him a large sum of money, which he refused and, although his pseudonym was not breached, the Jesuits suspected him of being the author. Among other things he attacked their liking for pagan authors, their propagation of external devotions and their relaxed casuistry. This last influenced both Antoine Arnauld and Pascal.

In a sense it was the parting of the ways. Saint-Cyran henceforth would be their unrelenting critic and they repaid him in kind. When his identity later became known the Jesuits scoured his record to discover any scandal concerning his earlier life but all they found was *La Question Royale*. Saint-Cyran *had* mixed with dubious company and it would not have been surprising if he had been morally contaminated, but the Jesuits could find nothing. In subsequent years they knew very well that he was closely associated with the leading French Jansenists, notably Antoine Arnauld, and he did nothing to mollify them.

Over the centuries many have said that Saint-Cyran was closely associated with Port-Royal and had initiated the community into Jansenism and other peculiar practices. Here dates are important. The reform of Port-Royal began in 1608 and Saint-Cyran had but one brief contact with the monastery in 1625. He became spiritual director and confessor to the nuns in 1635, was arrested and imprisoned in 1638 and first set eyes on the *Augustinus* in 1641. It would be rewriting history to accuse Port-Royal of being a Jansenist monastery before 1641. It was a house of strict observance. Mère Angélique placed great emphasis on poverty, and the life was austere. If Angélique was a Jansenist then so too was St Bernard.

As mentioned above, Saint-Cyran came to know Robert Arnauld in 1620 and through him he learned something of the family. However, it was not until 1625 that he had any notable contact with the monastery and then concerning the question of Angélique's mother joining the community. Always a conventional Catholic, in her later years Mme Arnauld had become devout. Her husband had died, several of her daughters had already entered the monastery and she felt drawn to the monastic life. But she was still hesitating and Angélique seems to have been somewhat pressing. Saint-Cyran was asked to intervene.[12] One of his letters shows considerable insight. He thoroughly understands Mme Arnauld's hesitation. She was drawn to the life but she was getting on in years and understandably was doubtful about the radical change of life that entering the monastery would entail. Writing to Mère Angélique, Saint-Cyran dissuades her from bringing pressure to bear on her mother or even from seeming to do so. Madame Arnauld, he feels, intends to join the community but she must be allowed to do so at her own time and in her own way. This advice was in line with his usual course of action: he tried to discern the movement of the Spirit in the soul and he knew this took time. In this case he was resisting Angélique's impetuosity and in the end he proved to be right.

In the years that followed, until 1633, Saint-Cyran was a busy man and Port-Royal was by no means at the centre of his preoccupations. He was still seeing a great deal of Bérulle, whose *Vie de Jésus* he was working on. His circle of friends and acquaintances was steadily widening and his reputation as a spiritual director was growing. Père Joseph de Tremblay, Richelieu's *éminence grise,* had taken under his wing a group of nuns from Fontevrault who had broken away from the abbey to begin a reformed way of life. They became known as the Calvairiennes. As is well known, Père Joseph had many irons in the fire and had to be absent for some months. He asked Saint-Cyran to give the nuns spiritual direction while he was away. He was so successful that when the Capuchin returned he found the nuns so much under Saint-Cyran's influence that he took umbrage. This led to a definitive break. Saint-Cyran had made a dangerous enemy. His friendship with Vincent de Paul continued, though the latter began to be concerned about some of his friend's *outré* sayings.

The rift between Richelieu and Saint-Cyran also began to show itself. Saint-Cyran ranged himself with Bérulle and the party of the *dévots* who thought that France should ally herself with the 'Catholic' powers, the Habsburgs of Spain and Austria, in the interests of regaining Europe for the Catholic faith. Richelieu saw them as a danger to the integrity of France. Between them, from the south and the east and the north, they encircled France. The counter-balance must be with the Protestant powers. In the ensuing political tussle Bérulle and his party lost and Bérulle died in 1629 in what was called disgrace. His death was a great loss to Saint-Cyran. His influence could well have saved him from his later excesses and helped him to achieve a better balance in his life. As it was, Saint-Cyran was ranged against Richelieu who after 1630 became all-powerful. But the break was not yet definitive.

The course of events that led to Saint-Cyran's deeper involvement with Port-Royal is complicated. Briefly, Sebastian Zamet, Bishop of Langres, had begun to take an interest in the community in 1627. Their fame as a reformed house had spread and Zamet saw it as a base for the propagation of his ideas. With little regard for the Benedictine-Cistercian tradition of the monastery he sought to impose on the community post-Tridentine devotions, perpetual adoration before the Blessed Sacrament, grand and rather hothouse ceremonies with flowers and incense and elaborate habits for the nuns. He accordingly established a convent near the Louvre with the intention of attracting ladies from the court. But trouble came first from another quarter. For some time the Oratorians had been visiting and preaching at Port-Royal – among them was the saintly Charles de Condren, a contemplative with a very metaphysical turn of mind. He was a disciple of Bérulle's, of course, but he developed certain aspects of his teaching that rather distorted it. Under his influence and that of some of his colleagues, Mère Agnès, a younger sister of Angélique, was moved to write down a series of meditations on the Blessed Sacrament. At first reading they are certainly disconcerting, somewhat awkwardly expressed exercises in abstract mysticism . The humanity of Jesus Christ seems to be swallowed up in his divinity. The relationship between the incarnate Christ and God is obscured; it is as if the incarnation had not taken place. But it was a purely private document, written entirely for Mère Agnès herself. Unfortunately copies were made, as was the habit of the time, and one or more got out to the wider world. The *Chapelet Secret*, as it was called, was condemned by the Sorbonne and the Jesuits.

Zamet was very embarrassed and, being no theologian himself, he did not know what to do. He had heard of Saint-Cyran and now he turned to him. Saint-Cyran read the document with great care, decided it could be interpreted in an orthodox sense and realised, as others did not, that the *Chapelet* represented the prayer of a deeply contemplative nun. She used expressions which could be equated with those used by some of the classical mystics. Saint-Cyran himself wrote a defence of the *Chapelet* (which remained unpublished) and, through Jansen, obtained theological approval for it from the University of Louvain. This was endorsed by Rome though the authorities there said that it was not to be circulated.

Zamet's gratitude was profound and he immediately invited Saint-Cyran to act as spiritual director and confessor to the nuns. Thus began Saint-Cyran's association with Port-Royal, brief in duration but profound in effect. For some years, in reaction to the easy and formal confessions which he believed too many practised and which were fostered by the Jesuits, Saint-Cyran had adopted a different way of doing things. In this he was harking back to the discipline of the early Church (at least of the fourth and fifth centuries) when there was a long period of 'penance' and exclusion from holy communion until the penance had been concluded with public reconciliation. He also set great store by the rigorous practice of St Charles Borromeo in the sixteenth century but failed to take into account that the saint had been engaged in cleaning up a very corrupt diocese. Saint-Cyran also looked for external signs of real penitence in those he confessed. Before receiving absolution they must fast, give alms, withdraw from the world and show a real 'unction', or devotion. This he called '*renouvellement*'. The spiritual condition of the penitent must be near perfect before he or she could be admitted to communion.

This became Saint-Cyran's practice at Port-Royal and the sisters, who were deeply impressed by his personality and the depth, as they saw it, of his spiritual teaching, were enraptured. After some resistance by a few, they adopted the practice enthusiastically. They wanted several '*renouvellements*' and, although Saint-Cyran did what he could to restrain their ardour, some went to extremes. On one occasion Mère Angélique refrained from communion for six months to make sure that she had done an adequate amount of penance and so that she should not make her communion in a state of imperfection. It seems that Saint-Cyran himself did not realise that what was suitable for certain people living in the world was not suited to a community of dedicated women who were already living a very mortified life. Paris at the time was full of pious tittle-tattle and news of these extraordinary procedures got around. In addition, people lighted on some of his statements about the efficacy of absolution which, he said, following Scotus, was only a declaration that a penitent was forgiven. He was accused of unorthodoxy.[13] It was another nail in his coffin.

However, as stated above, Saint-Cyran's role at Port-Royal did not last long. Zamet grew jealous of his influence with the nuns and Saint-Cyran withdrew after a disagreement with him. But the impression he made on the nuns was lasting. It appears in one way or another in the sayings and letters of Mère Angélique, in the letters of Mère Agnès who at first did not take to him, and even in the writings of Mère Angélique de Saint-Jean who could hardly have known him personally. He gave the community a certain stamp that was held against it for years. The nuns, who constantly recalled all they owed him, did nothing to mitigate the situation. When to this was added his independence and his refusal to be subservient to the great, Port-Royal was considered to have been made in his image and likeness.

Although Saint-Cyran appeared to be almost a hermit, living first in the cloister of Notre Dame and then in other lodgings near the Carthusians in the rue S. Jacques, he was much sought after. Among his friends, acquaintances and admirers were noblemen, courtiers, soldiers, great ladies, lawyers – especially those connected with the Parlement of Paris – scholars of Paris and Louvain and men of letters. He also had friends among the best of the bishops and priests of the time who were concerned with the renewal of the Church.[14] Saint-Cyran evidently had an attraction that the printed word cannot convey. These people were sane and intelligent and they evidently thought that he was worth cultivating. It does not seem to be recorded that they found him odd or rebarbative. Their regard is, I think, some testimony to the quality of his personality. It also has to be said that Saint-Cyran did not seek such company; it was Robert Arnauld who was his all too active and self-appointed publicist.

All was not well, however. The earlier relationship between Richelieu and Saint-Cyran was wearing thin. The cardinal had wanted to make him his own man, as he did everybody. He had offered him benefices and, again, a bishopric, he had tried flattery and, on one occasion, as Saint-Cyran approached he said to his entourage, 'Here comes the most learned man in Europe' (although there was probably a touch of sarcasm in this). But Saint-Cyran rejected the benefices and was unmoved by the flattery. Gradually he found himself impelled to oppose the ways and policies of the all-powerful First Minister. Richelieu, for his part, saw that the man was dangerous and on one occasion remarked that he had fire in his belly. As Jean Orcibal wrote, 'by his [Saint-Cyran's] moral authority, by his many relations with the court, nobles, the *parlementaires*, the bishops and the party of the devout,'[15] he had become a danger to the cardinal's power.

Several events occurred which became points of conflict. One was the marriage of the king's brother, Gaston, to Marguerite of Lorraine (not yet part of France) which put the succession in jeopardy. By the law of the Church the marriage was undoubtedly valid but Richelieu press-ganged the theologians of Paris to declare that it was invalid as it had not received the assent of the king. Although Saint-Cyran said nothing publicly and wrote nothing about it, it became known that he did not agree with Richelieu. Then, when the cardinal floated the notion that the pope should make him Patriarch of France and the West, Saint-Cyran, with a number of bishops who refused to be terrorised, was naturally opposed to it.

A more personal matter also became a cause of hostility not only for Richelieu but also for the Chancellor, Séguier. Antoine Le Maître, an Arnauld, son of Catherine Arnauld and her loose-living husband, Isaac Le Maître, became the most notable advocate of his time at the early age of twenty-one. He attracted the attention of Séguier who became his protector, concerned to promote his career. Séguier saw the young man as his future successor. At the age of twenty-six Le Maître had thoughts of marriage but was discouraged by his aunt, Mère Agnès. Three years later he was present at the death of Robert Arnauld's wife and he was so moved by the ministrations and ardent prayers of Saint-Cyran that he rushed out into the garden and wept, giving full vent to his feelings. As he walked up and down in the moonlight he decided to give himself to God.[16]

Le Maître put himself under the direction of Saint-Cyran and told him of his intention to leave the Bar and go into retirement immediately. At once Saint-Cyran realised that the moment was critical for himself. He knew that Le Maître's decision would cause uproar and that he would be blamed for it. But he also felt that he could not refuse his counsel. Wisely he advised delay. Le Maître must continue pleading until the courts closed in August and he must take time to reflect on what he was proposing. He must wait on the movement of the Spirit. That was the course Le Maître took and when the law term came to an end he went to live with Saint-Cyran, with whom he remained for a few months, later becoming a 'solitary', first at Port-Royal in Paris and then at Port-Royal-des-Champs with one of his brothers. During August he sent two letters, one to his father and one to Séguier. The first was pompous and somewhat censorious, excusable perhaps in the light of his knowledge of his Father's appalling treatment of his mother. The second disturbed Séguier on several counts. Le Maître was undoubtedly a coming man, everything lay open to him and here he was throwing all his chances away. When he read in the letter that Le Maître was retiring from the world, that he was not going to enter a religious order or seek ordination, which could well lead to a bishopric, Séguier was puzzled, disconcerted and annoyed. When the content of the letter got about Paris the reactions of many others were similar and they blamed Saint-Cyran. Richelieu was not pleased. Le Maître was a brilliant man, a future public servant who could have been very valuable to the state.

Le Maître's letter to the Chancellor became generally known in December 1637. Less than six months later Saint-Cyran was in prison. But it was not a simple case of *post hoc, propter hoc.* Richelieu had been gathering material on Saint-Cyran for some time. Like the Tudors, he had learned the uses of propaganda and, like Walsingham, he made extensive use of spies, one of whom was the Abbé de Prières. Richelieu of course knew of the correspondence between Saint-Cyran and Jansen. To add fuel to the fire the latter wrote a pamphlet in 1636, the *Mars Gallicus,* which was a strong denunciation of Richelieu's foreign policy. Jansen was an enemy, a subject of the king of Spain and, by association with him (although by this time their correspondence had ceased), Saint-Cyran had also become an enemy.

One of the matters that irritated Richelieu was what seems to us the tedious dispute about contrition and 'attrition'. Was sorrow for sin out of love of God necessary in the sacrament of penance? Or was attrition, sorrow inspired by fear of God and his punishments, sufficient? Saint-Cyran held the former view, as his practice had long implied and as he had taught explicitly. He insisted that his view was that of the Council of Trent. Richelieu held the latter view and was, frankly, piqued. He felt that his theological competence, which was minimal, was being called in question.

Another irritant was Saint-Cyran's habit of making enigmatic and provocative remarks. The Church had not existed for six centuries! What exactly he meant by this is not clear. He seems to have thought that since the days of St Bernard the Church had become corrupt and, possibly, that the system as it was had to be destroyed before it could be renewed along his lines. He voiced his views to Vincent de Paul and, in a long conversation with the Abbé de Prières at the Abbey of Maubuisson, he broached 'the most delicate subjects with a scarcely credible imprudence'.[17] Among his views were that the Council of Trent was no more than a gathering of Italian and Spanish bishops, that the early Church was superior to the contemporary Church, and that Scholasticism fostered intellectual pride. He also aired his opinions on the sacrament of penance. All this the Abbé collected and duly conveyed to Richelieu.

It is clear that Saint-Cyran disliked his interlocutor and despised him for his lack of learning and his ignorance of theology. He was out to shock him. He does not seem to have realised that the man was a hostile gossip or that he would share these juicy morsels with his associates in Paris. As Bremond remarked, Saint-Cyran was incredibly preoccupied with himself or, perhaps more kindly, that he was preoccupied with his own opinions. He did not take the measure of the Abbé de Prières or realise that potentially he was a dangerous enemy.

By 1638 Saint-Cyran had many enemies: Zamet, the Jesuits – he was known to have said that the society ought to be destroyed for the good of the Church – the Capuchins, notably Richelieu's *éminence grise*, as well as several lay people. His indifference to the susceptibilities of some who had hitherto been well-disposed towards him alienated them and he lost their support. Poring over his books in his lodgings and writing ceaselessly he became very opinionated. He had never experienced the cut and thrust of academic life, had never held any public office, even that of parish priest, and his knowledge of ordinary Christians was limited. He confessed few and they were either religious or lay people like Le Maître who were already determined on a serious spiritual life. While Vincent de Paul was organising his Sisters of Charity to care for the poor and orphans, Saint-Cyran talked grandly of charity but did little to help them. By now he was surrounded by a whole range of enemies and Richelieu sought only an occasion to pounce.

This he found in the publication of a book entitled *De La Sainte Virginité* written by an Oratorian called Seguenot. It seems, among other things, to have contained a mishmash of Saint-Cyran's thought of which it was but a caricature. Seguenot was unknown to Saint-Cyran, who knew nothing of the book, but Richelieu and others chose to think that he was behind it. Seguenot took up Saint-Cyran's views on priesthood, religious vows, the relations between philosophy and theology, the irresistibility of grace (certainly not Saint-Cyran's view) and the insufficiency of attrition. Worse still, the book was full of inaccuracies and unorthodox statements.[18] It was delated to the Sorbonne on 3 May 1638; on the 7th Saint-Cyran's enemies joined forces and the Jesuits circulated manuscripts containing lists of maxims that were attributed to him. On a bright May morning, the 14th, police surrounded the house at an early hour and at 6.00 a.m. they entered and arrested him. Offering no resistance, Saint-Cyran said he was ready to go wherever the king should send him and he was carried off in a coach to Vincennes. On the way Robert Arnauld met him and asked where he was going. Saint-Cyran replied that he was being taken to Vincennes and he pointed to his escort. Then he asked if Arnauld had a book with him and he handed him a copy of the *Confessions* of St Augustine. So he was taken to prison and thrust into a dungeon of that grim place.

All this was accompanied by a minor reign of terror. The Oratory was threatened, the rumour went around that Mère Angélique was to be arrested and the few solitaries at Port-Royal were dispersed. Every effort was made to give the impression that there was a conspiracy and that Saint-Cyran was at the heart of it. As the news broke people thought that something very serious was amiss and they suspected that Saint-Cyran was guilty of grave heresies. Even those well-disposed towards him were thrown into confusion and for a time thought that he had been in the wrong. Such was the effect of Richelieu's propaganda. But as they recovered from the shock they muttered the word 'martyrdom', and then and forever afterwards Port-Royal regarded him as a martyr for the truth.

Although the language is exaggerated there is no doubt that Saint-Cyran underwent real physical and spiritual suffering. Thrust into the dungeon, deprived of the Eucharist, or of any spiritual care, for a time he experienced some sort of spiritual darkness. He came near to despair, very like that which Mère Angélique de Saint-Jean would experience in her confinement in the convent of the Annonciades years later. The rigours of these first months of imprisonment certainly damaged his health, which never recovered – many had died before him in Vincennes. It seems all too likely that his death was precisely what Richelieu wanted. Nothing was alleged against him, there was no trial and rumour and accusations were given free reign. But seventeenth-century prisons were by no means hermetically sealed and, as Saint-Cyran's friends learnt of his plight they recovered their nerve and rallied round. Bishops, nobles, great magistrates, Vincent de Paul and even Richelieu's sister, the Duchess of Auguillon, publicly showed sympathy for him and at one time or another made representations to the cardinal. Although the current of opinion was now running strongly against him Richelieu remained unmoved.

The reasons for Saint-Cyran's arrest and imprisonment have been debated from that time to this. Some have alleged that a main cause was the difference of theological opinion between him and Richelieu on the matter of contrition and attrition. However, Richelieu was above all a statesman with a secularist mind and such a divergence of views would not have been sufficient to move him to act, however much his theological vanity may have been piqued by this turbulent priest with peculiar views. But the matter did take on a political relevance when the need for true contrition was urged on the notoriously scrupulous Louis XIII by, of all people, his Jesuit confessor. Such a doctrine of contrition could be dangerous in ways Saint-Cyran had never imagined and, of course, he had nothing to do with the matter. What was of crucial importance to Richelieu was that over the years Saint-Cyran had rejected his approaches and he held a view diametrically opposed to his own regarding Gaston's marriage – and that was a political matter. Finally, and after the early years before Richelieu came to power, Saint-Cyran had quietly but steadily resisted him. Honours and benefices had all left Saint-Cyran unmoved. He would be no one's lackey.

Month by month went by, no charge was brought against the prisoner, and there was no trial, though futile attempts were made to gather evidence, however dubious. Charles de Condren, with whom Saint-Cyran had had a serious difference of opinion a year or two earlier, refused to appear before a secular judge. Vincent de Paul defended his friend and set against his provocative statements all the good he had done for the Church by his actions. Zamet's written statement against him was so vague that it was dismissed by Richelieu with contempt. Nothing heretical could be found in the forty manuscript volumes which had been seized after Saint-

Cyran's arrest. Little was left to Richelieu but an examination of the prisoner and he appointed Dr Lescot, his own confessor, to do the work. The examination went on for some days and produced little in the way of result. Saint-Cyran affirmed his submission on the Council of Trent, put some of his more questionable statements in context and denied that he had made others. Lescot, who was something of a careerist and apparently not highly regarded as a theologian, decided to concentrate on the question of contrition/attrition. After a good deal of hesitation Saint-Cyran eventually wrote to Chavigny, the governor of Vincennes and a former friend, and said that he would go so far as to condemn those who condemned contritionism. He wrote out the whole of his deposition and Vincent de Paul got a message through to him telling him to write to the very end of each paper so that nothing could be added by Lescot or anyone else! It was all in vain. Saint-Cyran's friends had thought that if he showed a little flexibility and gave way on the matter of contrition he would be released. It was now clear that although no charge of substance could be brought against him Richelieu was determined to keep him confined, which he did until his own death in 1642.

It is highly likely that Saint-Cyran's imprisonment did more to increase his prestige at the time and for a long time afterwards than anything he had done or written while he was free. Once the conditions of his imprisonment were improved through the kindness of Chavigny, who provided him with a room and access to other prisoners, Saint-Cyran was able to recover his spirits. Gradually friends were allowed to visit him and he then began a correspondence with various people outside the prison. He wrote letters of spiritual direction to a number of people, though since he was under constant supervision it was not easy to do this. He either wrote when the guards were otherwise occupied or Robert Arnauld d'Andilly, when he visited him, took down letters at his dictation and smuggled them and the others out of prison.[19] After his death these and other letters were published and were much read for many years to come. It was through them that Saint-Cyran gained a reputation as a spiritual director and it was as such that Sainte-Beuve chose to define his role in the life of the Church at the time.

As we have seen above, Saint-Cyran's first conversion came at the time of his ordination under the influence of Sebastian Bouthillier. Overlapping that, both before and after, there was his association with Bérulle whose personality, spiritual depth and doctrine made a lasting impression on him. It was from him too that he acquired his high notion of priesthood. But he also had a profound admiration for St Francis de Sales whose teaching he communicated in his own way to others. As a spiritual director Mère Angélique, who for a short time had been directed by the saint, regarded Saint-Cyran as his successor. Unfortunately, Saint-Cyran had too little of Francis's *suavitas,* whether for his own good or that of Angélique. Yet, in spite of his stiffness, his harsh judgements and his rigorism, Saint-Cyran had been growing in spiritual depth all the time. His devastating experience in the dungeon of Vincennes marked the beginning of a second and definitive conversion. No more do we hear of strange utterances, though of course he was too old to put aside all his eccentricities and his preoccupation with his own notions. The new spiritual maturity was apparent in the many letters he wrote to a wide range of readers. This late spiritual maturing needs to be taken into account in any assessment of the man.

Unhappily he never lost his anti-Jesuit animus. While in prison he urged Antoine Arnauld to write against one Habert, whom both regarded as a creature of the Jesuits, and who was denouncing the *Augustinus* in a series of vehement sermons. That his mind had not changed at least on certain topics is revealed in his letters to Arnauld: He was ready to die in prison or elsewhere for the truth about grace.... 'If we ruin that, we ruin every Christian truth and particularly about penitence, vocation to the priesthood, the faith itself and all the rest.' After the publication of the Bull *In eminenti* (1643) he told Arnauld that he must write again: 'If you keep silent the stones will cry out'.[20] A man of course can undergo conversion and much of the old Adam can remain. On the night of the feast of St Clement, 23 November 1654, Pascal had his mystical experience which, as far as these matters can be judged, was far more profound than Saint-Cyran's and changed his whole life. Yet, twelve months later he would begin that series of contemptuous and often unjust and uncharitable condemnations of the Jesuits in what we know as the *Lettres Provinciales*.

After the death of Richelieu in 1642 renewed efforts were made by Saint-Cyran's friends to obtain his release. Persons in high places counselled delay in the interests of face-saving and he wasn't freed until 6 February the following year. He was a broken man: he had been gravely ill several times while in prison, his eyesight was failing and he was generally enfeebled. His friends took him about to visit people and these, of course, included the nuns of Port-Royal. But his first visit was a fiasco. The dear sisters were delighted to see him but some of them got 'choir giggles' and Saint-Cyran was not pleased. The second visit however was all that it ought to have been. Then he addressed Antoine Le Maître, surrounded by the solitaries and, for a man so weak, spoke at great length to them.

When he had settled down in his old lodgings he immediately began writing again, this time against the Calvinists. Inevitably he worked slowly and can have achieved only very little. For the last two months of his life he was obviously unwell and an apoplexy took him away on 11 October 1643.[21]

His funeral was at S. Jacques du Haut Pas (which still exists) in the rue Saint Jacques and was attended by a very distinguished gathering, including one princess, dukes, nobles, members of the haute bourgeoisie and others. It was almost an apotheosis or an anticipated canonisation and his anniversary was celebrated not with a Requiem Mass but with the Mass of a Confessor in white vestments! Richelieu was dead, Louis XIII was dead and his son Louis XIV was a child. The Saint-Cyranists now had no fear. It would be nearly two decades before the new king would begin his long and unrelenting campaign against Port-Royal and the Jansenists.

Saint-Cyran's memory lived on, notably at Port-Royal where he became almost a cult-figure and a prophet. Miracles were alleged to have occurred at the touch of his relics. But he lived on also in his writings, most of which were published after his death though there remains a considerable quantity of unpublished manuscripts. Four volumes of his *Lettres spirituelles,* much 'edited' by Robert Arnauld, appeared in 1645 and 1647. Others containing his ideas on priesthood, *Lettre à Guillebert sur le Sacerdoce* and *Pensées sur le Sacerdoce,* appeared as late as 1744. Certain features of his prayer can be discerned from his *Lettres* and other writings, as they are by Bremond who saw Saint-Cyran as fundamentally a man of prayer.

There was the prayer of the lowly (*la prière des pauvres),* the total availability of the humble to the interior movements of God in the soul. Before God we are like beggars, displaying the wounds of our sins and weaknesses and letting them plead to God for us. This comes from St Augustine, but also from the Psalms, for it is a profoundly biblical notion. Saint-Cyran was soaked in scripture (in the Vulgate version); its phrases were often on his lips as were those of the liturgy.

Quoting from his *Oeuvres chrétiennes* Bremond singles out two samples of St Cyran's teaching on prayer:

> Jesus Christ did not underestimate the importance of charity [in the soul] any more than he diminished [the power of] the word of truth. There is an interior quiet that is as pleasing to God as every kind of good work and occupation; and there is a silence which is as pleasing to him [as many words].

This seems to be an echo of Augustine's Letter to Proba, evidently reflecting on Romans 8:26-27:

> Only the Holy Spirit can enable us to pray, in the measure that he is in us and *grows* in us.[22]

For Saint-Cyran the dominant virtues were not fear and penitence but 'silence, flexibility and docility to the inspirations of

God'. Bremond saw Saint-Cyran as basically a contemplative; perhaps it was for that reason that he turned away from holding office
and mere erudition and theology. No doubt, continues Bremond,
his prayer did not rise to the heights of the great spiritual people of
his time; he 'stopped short this side of pure love' because he was too
preoccupied with himself. He concludes, however: 'There remains
the great servant of God whom St Jeanne Françoise de Chantal
revered, the fine religious genius which, if it did not fulfil its
promises of evident election, nonetheless retained in its witness to
invisible realities that special accent which no human art can coun-
terfeit and which so strangely moves people's hearts.' (This from a
writer who did not like Saint-Cyran!) The better Saint-Cyran, the
one that matters, was 'above all and almost uniquely a solitary, a
contemplative [*meditatif*] and a man of prayer'.[23]

One possibly surprising feature of Saint-Cyran's character is his
concern for the young. While in prison he instructed the young son
of a gaoler and sent him away to be educated. The *Petites Ecoles*
were initiated by him even before he was confined in Vincennes.
He wanted to save boys from the crudities of the schools of the
time and to help them grow in grace and virtue. His contribution
to the schools was necessarily limited by the years of imprisonment
but before that and at the request of Jerome Bignon, one of his
'converts', he wrote for his boys a kind of catechism called *Théologie
familière ou Brève Explication des Principaux Mystères de la Foy*
(1637). It was written in straightforward language of the sort suited to boys of cultivated and well-to-do bourgeois families. As the
title suggests, it covers the principal mysteries of the Faith: God,
the Fall, redemption, incarnation, the Church, grace, charity,
prayer (commentary on the Lord's Prayer) and the sacraments. It is
noteworthy that he has no less than thirteen answers on charity and
only five on grace. His outlook is traditional and patristic, rather
than medieval or post-Tridentine, and his answer on the Church
prompted his enemies to take exception to it. He described the
church as the *congregatio fidelium* (the assembly of the faithful),

which seemed to his enemies to be Protestant, although it has a respectable ancestry in Gregory the Great, among others.[24] Saint-Cyran completes his teaching on the Church by considering it as the mystical body of Christ 'formed by the Holy Spirit who was sent to perfect his disciples'. For him the Church was the spirit-filled body of Christ and this teaching is carried through to charity: we must love other Christians because they are our brothers and sisters who, with us, make up the body of Christ.

We naturally look for heterodox statements on the matters of redemption and grace. His statement on the former at first seems to be all-inclusive: 'It was necessary for Christ to die to accomplish the final work for the redemption of the human race *(pour le rachat des hommes)*'. However, the Jews of the Old Testament who did not hope in the Messiah and the pagans are excluded. If this seems shocking to us we should recall that this was common teaching at the time. Indeed, Protestants held that Catholics could not be saved and vice versa. Saint-Cyran was not anticipating the Fifth Proposition. Further, in a way that was not all too common at the time or, indeed, until much later, Saint-Cyran saw that the resurrection was intimately related to the redemption. It was necessary that Christ should rise again to communicate his (divine) life to us and 'this he did by giving the divine Spirit the very day he rose again...'.

On grace there is really nothing very alarming. It is a gift of God communicated to us by Christ to enlighten our minds (a favourite notion of Saint-Cyran's), to fortify the soul and to enable us to do what God wants of us. Echoing the Second Council of Orange and the Council of Trent, Saint-Cyran says that we are totally dependent on God and that we need his continual assistance if we are to persevere. When he considers more closely *why* we need grace his language seems to be Jansenistic but is in fact Augustinian. While we are in this life there is in us 'a corruption of nature that Scripture calls concupiscence' which drives us to do things that go against the law of God (cf. Romans 7:15-20). The grace of God enables us to overcome that tendency. Nowhere is there any mention of the irresistibility of grace, nowhere do we find the terms *gratia victrix* or *delectatio victrix.*

When he comes to prayer he is fairly conventional, repeating Augustine's view in his Letter to Proba that prayer is basically desire. But like the Port-Royalists and their followers throughout the century he shows a great esteem for liturgical prayer. In the context of vocal prayer he speaks of the overriding excellence of the liturgy: we should have a particular devotion to the Divine Office and the sacrifice of the Mass is the most excellent of all forms of prayer.

His treatment of the sacraments is for the most part conventional but there are always touches of his own. Following the patristic tradition, he sees confirmation as the 'completion' or 'perfection' of baptism, but for him the heart of the matter is charity. As well as the gifts of the Holy Spirit given in the sacrament, confirmation perfects the charity originally communicated in baptism and therein lies all its strength.

In his treatment of the Eucharist he is thoroughly Tridentine. He speaks of transubstantiation (without, however, using the word), but he seems to endorse the annihilation theory (probably under the influence of Charles de Condren) when dealing with the change of the elements. The substance of the bread and wine are 'taken away' (*ostés*) to give place to the body and blood of Christ.[25] However that may be, the purpose of the Real Presence is to continue on earth the sacrifice of the cross so that Christ here and now may communicate to us the fruits of his sacrifice.

Saint-Cyran had a profound reverence for the Eucharist and this goes some way to explain his very demanding practice of the sacrament of penance to which he devotes a long section. The communicant must have a sincere desire to love God *perfectly* 'since this sacrament is a proof of the great love God has for us and is the means chosen to form with us a perfect friendship'. This perfect love of God must be striven for in the sometimes long discipline of penitence which he imposed on those penitents who were willing to undertake it. They must experience an inner impulse which is formed within them by the Holy Spirit who enables them to have a true detestation of sin and turns their heart to God. Even this is orthodox enough but he wanted penitents to manifest this experience by fasting, alms-giving and withdrawal from the world. It must be a *felt* experience; that would be the guarantee that the penitent had conceived a perfect love of God in his heart. In this sense penance was a necessary condition for the reception of Holy Communion. People must be in an advanced state of charity and Saint-Cyran, always an untidy thinker, did not connect this with his other teaching that the Eucharist is the great sacrament of love, the sacrament that communicates love and makes up for defects in the act of repentance. In any case his theory was wildly unpractical. Not everyone can express penitence by tears or the expression of fine sentiments. How are people who have to earn their living to withdraw from the world? In fact Saint-Cyran confessed very few people. He never sat for long hours in a confessional listening to humble Christians who found it difficult to confess their sins at all. In any case he did not like doing so and when people came to him and he saw that they would not or could not undertake his discipline he confessed them as any other priest would have done.

Yet the *Théologie familière* has certain virtues. There is a deep sense of God, a profound devotion and clear insights into many matters of doctrine. Though genuinely theological, everything is expressed in non-technical language. A sign of its popularity is that it went on being published until 1693.

In the 1643 edition the second part of the book is entitled *Le Coeur Nouveau* and is illustrated with an altar. At a time when altars were becoming very elaborate this one is very simple, perhaps like the one at Port-Royal. It is covered with a frontal and there is a dossal of the same material, across the middle of which are embroidered the words: *Dabo vobis cor novum* (Ezekiel 36:26 – 'I will give you a new heart'). After the word *vobis* is a drawing of a heart that looks very much like representations of the Sacred Heart, a devotion which the Jansenists later rejected. The text expresses much of what Saint-Cyran was trying to teach. The Christian life required a complete change of heart, a constant interior renewal. In the 'Little Treatise' that follows, addressed to persons living in the world and to married people (which echoes St Francis de Sales' *Introduction to the Devout Life*), Saint-Cyran lays great stress on the central importance of charity, love of God and, flowing out of that love, love of others. For an understanding of Saint-Cyran's seemingly austere outlook, this is an important emphasis.

The first two treatises of the *Coeur Nouveau* are concerned with Mass: *Explanations of the Ceremonies of the Mass* and *Exercises to hear it well.* These are indications that Saint-Cyran was concerned that people should understand and follow the action of the Mass intelligently but also that their hearts should be engaged by it. His commentary on the Mass is notable in that he eschews the allegorical 'explanations' of it that were still common at the time and in places reveals his patristic learning. Thus he accepts St Cyprian's interpretation of the mixing of the wine with water: it is a symbol of the union of Christ with his people. He is also aware that the presentation of the gifts (or offertory) required a procession of the people who brought their gifts to the altar. Although his rigorism about the reception of Holy Communion is well known – he envisaged the communicants receiving it during the Mass – his practice was not always the custom at the time. Finally, for him the Eucharist is the action of the whole body of Christ, the High Priest, of whom the priest is the minister.

In the picture of the altar mentioned above there is a crozier-like staff from which is suspended a vessel containing the Reserved Sacrament. This custom had been common enough in the Middle Ages in France and England and survived into his own time, as it did at Port-Royal.[26] The last of the 'Little Treatises' was concerned with that matter: 'Reasons for the Ceremony... of suspending the Blessed Sacrament... over the High Altar'. Saint-Cyran lists some twenty-four reasons for the custom! The most interesting is that for him it is a symbol of both the passion and the resurrection. The

Sacrament suspended above the altar recalls the gospel saying of Jesus that when he is lifted up he will draw all to himself (John 12:32). It is a symbol of the Lamb who was sacrificed and who, in the Eucharist, is offered at every moment, as he will be offered to the end of time. But it also represents the risen and glorified Christ 'for it is by the communication of his life in glory that he draws all to himself'. Finally, it is a sign of the ascension strengthening our hope that we shall follow him and it is a 'figure' of the second coming of Christ, of which the Eucharist is the pledge, when he will gather the living and the dead (cf I Thessalonians 4:16-17). Whatever may be thought of the details, it is an example of a very condensed theology expressed with considerable simplicity. Emphasis on the resurrection and ascension in conjunction with the redemption witnesses not only to Saint-Cyran's learning but also to his theological understanding of a tradition that goes back to the Fathers of the Church.

It is not known when this 'Little Treatise' was written or to whom it was addressed; it is permissible to think it was written for the nuns of Port-Royal who were committed to perpetual adoration of the Blessed Sacrament by about 1630.

Saint-Cyran's short pieces are some of his best writings. As has been said above, he wrote much but published little. His style was usually poor, convoluted and obscure. But in conversation he had the gift of paradox and made good use of aphorisms, some of which were recorded and, as Sainte-Beuve remarks on more than one occasion, they seem to have been echoed by Pascal. Saint-Cyran once said: 'All in all the whole world is no more than a hospital filled with the sick who are for the most part unhappy.' Pascal said something very similar: 'The natural conviction of Christians is illness.' Of the tedious and very self-conscious stylist, Guez de Balzac, Saint-Cyran remarked: 'M. de Balzac is like a man before a beautiful mirror which reveals a spot on his face. He is so enchanted with the beauty of the mirror that he does not think of removing the spot'.[27]

Saint-Cyran was a speaker rather than a writer and some of his sermons in front of the grille at Port-Royal were so moving that not only the nuns but the Oratorian Fathers who were present were enthralled. Claude Lancelot, his faithful disciple and memorialist, once asked him to help him write out a text of a sermon preached there on Good Friday. Saint-Cyran replied that he could not remember what he had said. He had been speaking *ex corde,* from the fullness of his mind and heart, apparently spontaneously, but in fact out of the depths of his lonely ponderings on the mystery of redemption.[28]

It may be thought that this portrait of Saint-Cyran is unduly favourable. But in the past he has too often been presented as an egotistical ogre whose influence was wholly bad. He was in fact a very vulnerable human being, handicapped by a tortuous temperament, derived from his peculiar ancestry against which he was reacting during the entire second half of his life. He did not follow his forebears in their physical violence and worldly ambitions but a tendency towards inner violence was only dispelled in his last years. He had ambition but it was directed towards spiritual achievement and if he never became what he sought to be, his 'failure', in Bremond's term, is the lot of most mortals. If, as Bremond suggested, he stopped this side of mysticism, how many have achieved that? And if, as Bremond could also say, 'his deeper life was full of God', that is high praise indeed. His opinions were often unbalanced, even bizarre, and his sayings and his writings are sometimes absurdly exaggerated. He worked too much alone and it was unfortunate that his friends Bérulle and Bouthillier, who understood him and could have done something to keep him on an even keel, died young. Perhaps it is not an oversimplification to say that his primary aim was to develop in the Catholics of the time a deeper interior life in an age when religious practice was too often formal and conformist. This is evident in his 'Little Treatises' which were addressed to ordinary people. Although he had a gift of spiritual discernment it is strange that this failed him in his direction of the nuns of Port-Royal in the matter of the *renouvellements* when he showed a lack of prudence and firmness. In his cryptic utterances he was inconsistent and admitted that he said one thing to one person and another to another. In the first case, he sought to please and in the second, he could be simply provocative and contradictory to a man like the Abbé de Prières who irritated him and whom he despised. These and many more inconsistencies simply cannot be reconciled, and even John Orcibal, who did so much to rehabilitate Saint-Cyran in his lengthy life of him, had to call his last chapter 'Les Deux Saint-Cyrans'. He remains and perhaps must remain, something of an enigma, yet men like Cardinal de Bérulle as well as many lay people who esteemed him highly, seem to have discerned more acutely than we can the worth of this strange character.[29]

Note A: Saint-Cyran and his Principal Biographer

Saint-Cyran's posthumous image suffered at the hands both of his enemies and of his friends. The nuns of Port-Royal more or less canonised him, treasuring his words throughout the century, and this affected their attitudes and actions. If he spoke of martyrdom they applied his words to themselves when 'persecuted' by the king and the archbishop, thus acquiring a persecution complex. If Bérulle had spoken about his difficulties with the Jesuits and his dismay with certain procedures in Rome, these sayings were remembered by Mère Angélique and conveyed to Antoine Le Maître who wrote them all down. Saint-Cyran, the friend of Jansen, must have been right and they could not, therefore, accept that Jansen was a heretic. In their pious enthusiasm they distorted his teaching and his memory. They treasured his relics and believed that they worked miracles of healing. These matters did not remain unknown to contemporaries or to posterity.

But it was Claude Lancelot, the *over*-faithful disciple of Saint-Cyran, who projected the image that remained with historians for centuries. Of very humble parents, Lancelot was for many years a member of the community presided over by Adrian Bourdoise at S. Nicolas du Chardonnet in Paris. Never more than a subdeacon, he became fascinated by what he could learn of Saint-Cyran who, in 1637, took him under his wing and had him made sacristan at Port-Royal. In the five years Saint-Cyran was in prison Lancelot had no personal contact with him but he was with him in the seven months of 1643 until his death. However, the impression of St Cyran's personality and teaching remained with Lancelot for the rest of his long life. For years he collected reminiscences from those who had known Saint-Cyran intimately, he listened to conversations and he asked questions. Scholars as different from one another as Sainte-Beuve, Bremond and Orcibal have pronounced his account authentic. Apart from some dates and confusion about certain events, what Lancelot wrote was correct. Nonetheless his *Mémoires touchant la vie de M. de Saint-Cyran*, which were finished by 1663, is hagiography, not objective biography. Therein lies its weakness. For Lancelot, Saint-Cyran was a hero, a holy man, a saint, and everything he did and said must be treasured and written down. As Orcibal wrote, 'he had a superstitious respect for each and every action and word of Saint-Cyran'.[1]

In addition, M. de Saci put at Lancelot's disposal all the documentation collected by friends, including Saint-Cyran's nephew, Barcos, and his unpublished letters. He was well equipped for his task and the honesty with which he completed it is shown by the fact that he intended his account to be read by these people and the close circle of friends who had known and revered the subject of the memoirs. He never intended them for publication and that may be taken as some excuse for his retailing of petty and sometimes ridiculous details. The book was not published until 1738, much edited, and thereby hangs another tale.

Thanks to the literary detective work of Bremond and Orcibal, we now know that the Jansenist who did the editing made numerous alterations, suppressions and corrections and added long justi-

---

1. *Jean Duvergier de Hauranne, Origines* III, Appendices etc. p. 15.

fications of theological positions. From a comparison of the book with the manuscripts in the Bibliothèque Nationale and the Bibliothèque de Port-Royal, Orcibal is able to list twenty-five such changes from the original text – and the list may not be exhaustive. All the alterations were made to protect the reputation of Saint-Cyran and to build him up as a Jansenist saint. Thus Saint-Cyran was often accused of illuminism, the conviction that he *knew* the will of God, not only for himself but for others as well, and that he was directly inspired by the Holy Spirit. All references that bear on the matter are suppressed. Others concern such petty details of his behaviour as that he recited the Office while someone was sewing his cuffs, or that he said the Rosary just to fill up vacant times in his day. Saint-Cyran being questioned by Lescot, who conducted his examination in prison, is compared to St Paul before his pagan judges, and one Maundy Thursday Saint-Cyran allowed his disciples to liken him to Christ. Praise of the *Augustinus* and statements on grace and attrition are simply omitted.

Reprehensible as these 'corrections' are, their suppression is understandable. Lancelot was excessively pious and Saint-Cyran was his hero and he thought that every tiny detail could only enhance his reputation for sanctity. Bremond, who disliked Saint-Cyran, calls them distortions (*déformations*) and warns historians against using them without due caution.[2] So it was that Lancelot, writing with the best of intentions, did his hero a good deal of harm. Another defect is that he knew nothing of Saint-Cyran's early life; this may be the fault of Saint-Cyran himself who wanted to forget all about it and told Lancelot very little. Furthermore, Port-Royal and the later Jansenists also distorted his image. He held various views of which they disapproved and presented him as one of themselves with all the fanaticism that overtook them in the eighteenth century. 'The Jansenists and their adversaries were agreed in making Saint-Cyran the head of a new party',[3] their party. It is only since the pioneer research of Jean Orcibal that it has been possible

2. Op. cit. III, p. 19 and HSLR, iv, p. 40, n.
3. Orcibal, op. cit, p. 33 and Bremond, op. cit, iv, pp. 82-83.

to see Saint-Cyran as he was, warts and all. I have omitted the pious habits, customs and doings of Saint-Cyran.

Note B: Saint-Cyran and Jansenism

At one time it was assumed that Saint-Cyran was a Jansenist in the full sense of the word, i.e. that he accepted and taught the whole doctrine of Jansen. After Orcibal's prolonged examination of Saint-Cyran's writings this is not certain, even if his true position is not wholly clear. That there was much which appears Jansenistic in what he wrote is certain, and Orcibal has a whole long chapter on Saint-Cyran's *thèmes jansénistes*,[1] but his conclusions show that influences on Saint-Cyran were very various. We know that in his meetings with Jansen in 1620 and 1625, when Jansen had only begun his intensive reading of Augustine, they discussed the matter of grace, but between those years and 1628, when Jansen began to prepare his *Augustinus*, there were no more meetings and, as has been said, their correspondence was something of a dialogue of the deaf. In all these years Saint-Cyran had other interests and concerns and he was constantly with Bérulle. Both of them were principally concerned with the deepening of the spiritual life and Bérulle saw in the traditional doctrine of grace the basis for the total dependence of the human being on God. This was also and explicitly Saint-Cyran's view. Hence one of his favourite sayings, taken from Augustine, that the Christian is like a beggar before God.

In a much more elaborate way this is reflected in the works of Bérulle. In the *Grandeurs de Jésus*, for instance, 'he was much more concerned to emphasise the role of divine grace in the Christian life' than with constructing a theology. He considered that 'in the deplorable state to which the sin of Adam has reduced us we have no right to anything but nothingness .... All that is within our power is to sin. There remains but one way of escaping the domination of the Demon.' We must 'put all our liberty in the hands of Jesus for the more we belong to him, the freer we shall be'. Similar

---

1. *Origines*, V, pp.81-135.

statements can be found in Saint-Cyran's writings and for him, as
for Bérulle, this was the 'solution', as far as there could be one, of
an efficacious grace that determines the will yet leaves it free. It is
very different from Jansen's view. Bérulle continues: 'Thus it [the
grace or God himself] will unite us to Jesus by a bond that is
analagous to that which unites the Son to the Father in the Holy
Trinity'. It is fused 'with the instinct we have to return to God, an
instinct that God has imprinted on our hearts which, in spite of the
Fall, is consonant with our origin'. This too was congenial to Saint-
Cyran's thought. Like Bérulle, he was deeply attached to the person
of Christ and he went beyond Scholastic distinctions to the reality
as he saw it, namely that grace unites us to the Father through the
Son. Fundamentally, Saint-Cyran saw grace as love, or even as the
Holy Spirit, rather like Peter Lombard in the twelfth century. Grace
is God's love that carries us to God, and that, it seems, was the
source of his concern about the presence of 'contrition', love of
God, in the sacrament of penance.

Although he retained an esteem for St Thomas Aquinas, St
Augustine was for him, as for Bérulle, the one 'who spoke a language that was as powerful in its effect on the heart as on the mind'.
He was the 'protector' of God against humankind and 'he knew
perfectly well how to exalt the glory of the Creator above the lowly
condition and ruins of the creature'. Bérulle continues: 'Jesus
Christ did everything for grace, St Augustine gave everything to
grace, and woe to those who make a schism in grace', dividing grace
from Christ. Bérulle was probably writing against Molina and his
fellow Jesuits.[2]

Saint-Cyran, of course, did have some 'Jansenist' notions. He
held the theory of the salvation of the few which, with others of the
time, he thought was gospel teaching. 'Many are called but few are
chosen', was a text he quoted more than once. He probably also
believed that unbaptised infants were deprived of the vision of God

1. For all the above see J. Orcibal, *Origines*, III, pp. 80-82; *Origines*, V, *La Spiritualité de Saint-Cyran*.

and suffered pain. But this he found in Augustine and he read the very rigorous views of the Irish Franciscan, Florentia Conrey (Conrius), who certainly held that view. As for predestination, his attitude was pragmatic. He told those whom he counselled not to bother their heads about it. If they were coming closer to Christ and doing the will of God, that was all that mattered. If he urged Antoine Arnauld to defend the *Augustinus* it was because he thought the very nature of grace was in jeopardy and that the Molinist theology limited God's power and infringed his liberty. The Thomists said something very similar.

4

ANGÉLIQUE ARNAULD
Reformer Abbess of Port-Royal

I
The Early Years

The career of (Jacqueline) Angélique Marie Madeleine Arnauld was not entirely untypical of the religious life of the early decades of seventeenth-century France but in many ways it was unusual. Thrust into the monastic life at the age of eight she made her novitiate in the abbey of a great lady who was disreputable in her own life and the sister of one of the king's mistresses, yet she became the reforming abbess of the crumbling monastery of Port-Royal. Though destined to be a cloistered nun, she experienced the seamier side of life, not only the immorality of the age personified in the Abbess of Maubuisson, but the lies and deceit that hoisted her into the office of abbess at the age of eleven. She came to know a whole range of people, from saints like Francis de Sales and Jeanne Françoise de Chantal, to the loose-living friar who was the occasion of her conversion. In the last years of her life Port-Royal became the centre of the Jansenist controversy and she died knowing that her monastery was under threat.

Much is known of her: several people wrote about her, she wrote many letters and, under pressure, she reluctantly wrote part of her autobiography which she abandoned when she reached 1638, though she lived until 1661. There are many inconsistencies in her character which can be traced to her unfortunate upbringing, but she stands out as a remarkable woman in an age filled with strong and colourful personalities. Contrasted with the well-ordered religious life of today, her intrusion (for it was no less) into the abbacy of Port-Royal seems all the more bizarre and inconceivable.

Jacqueline was the third child and second daughter of Antoine Arnauld and Catherine Marion and she was followed rapidly by two more daughters. Both the Arnaulds and the Marions were well known legal families of the *haute bourgeoisie* and of the *parlement* grouping. They were represented on the Council of State, and were on good terms with the king, Henri IV. The newly-married Arnaulds shared a large house in Paris with Simon Marion, to whom it belonged, and since both he and Arnauld were prominent lawyers it is to be supposed that they were reasonably wealthy. Yet the presence of five daughters in the still young family filled the parents and grandfather with dismay. They had ambitions for the children: Robert, the eldest son, had been elaborately educated, but for the girls there was the question of dowries. Both Arnauld and Marion felt they could not face the expense of marrying off all five daughters. The eldest, Catherine, was eventually married to Isaac Le Maître, also a lawyer, but the next two must become nuns. The dowries could be small or, with a bit of wangling, might even be dispensed with. Abbeys and other benefices could be granted *in commendam* as the king determined, and the beneficiaries could draw the revenues, sometimes without the requirement of residence. Benefices were a source of income and Richelieu came to own a whole collection of them. If all went well the Arnauld girls could be provided for at little or no cost to the family.

It is something to the credit of the Arnauld parents that it was Marion and not they who took the leading part in selecting Jacqueline (later Angélique) and Jeanne (later Agnès) for the religious life. One day in 1698 Marion called the seven-year-old Jacqueline into his study and, lawyer that he was, he put a question that looked for an affirmative answer: 'Wouldn't you like very much to be a religious?'. Writing later she said she hardly knew what a religious was but she did not like the idea at all and her dismay showed in her face. So her grandfather continued 'But you won't be just a nun, I will make you an abbess and mistress over others'. She hated the whole idea, but after some reflection she turned to her grandfather and said, 'Yes, I will be a nun but only if you make me an abbess'.

Then it was Jeanne's turn; she was now six years old. Her grandfather would make her an abbess too, but even at this early age Jeanne was more reflective. She took two or three days to make her reply. Abbesses, she had heard, were responsible to God not only for their own souls but for those of their nuns. She felt she had as much as she could do to look after her own. At this Jacqueline intervened: 'Oh, I want to be one and I will see they do their duty'. And she turned to her sister and told her she was silly not to want to be an abbess: 'See that they keep their rule and you will get by'. The main characteristics of the two girls were already evident. Jacqueline would command and Jeanne would be the contemplative.

The next phase of the proceedings throws a vivid light on the state of the French Church at the time. It was one thing for Marion to say he would make his two granddaughters abbesses; it was another to find abbeys for them. The king would have to be approached but a vacancy or a resignation would first have to be found or engineered. One of Marion's friends was Edme de la Croix, Abbot of Citeaux, and he knew of an ancient, half-ruinous and very run-down monastery in the Chevreuse valley, not far from Versailles (then no more than a royal hunting box). The Abbess was Dame Jeanne de Boulehart and Abbot de la Croix got to work on her. She proved to be reluctant; she had hoped to have one of her relatives succeed her. After a good deal of persuasion she consented to have Jacqueline appointed as her coadjutrix. The king was approached, he gave the necessary brief, Jacqueline was rapidly 'clothed' in the monastery of St Antoine of Paris and application was made to Rome for the papal bull of appointment. It was refused on the grounds that Jacqueline was only a 'novice'.

Meanwhile, the Benedictine Abbey of St Cyr had fallen vacant and Jeanne Arnauld was provided to that, apparently without difficulty. It does not appear that any application was made to Rome.

For a few weeks the two girls were together at St Cyr and then Jacqueline was swept off to Maubuisson to do her novitiate in a Cistercian monastery presided over by Angélique d'Estrées, the sister of one of the king's mistresses. The abbess had twelve illegitimate children whom she kept with her in the monastery where she educated them according to their rank. What scenes Jacqueline witnessed or what she knew about and what she thought of it all we do not know. She always preserved a total silence about her two years at Maubuisson. We do know however that the king regularly visited his mistress at the monastery and there were other gentlemen about the place.

However, wherever she was in these early days, Jacqueline won the hearts of those around her. Mme d'Estrées treated her kindly and perhaps protected her from the worst of what was going on around her and in her other monastery (for in addition to everything else she was a pluralist). She took the girl to Amiens where she was confirmed, taking the name of her patroness, Angélique, (by which she will be known henceforth).

This event opened the way to a further approach to Rome. A month later the child was solemnly professed and her grandfather and father could draw up a new document saying that Angélique was a professed nun of Port-Royal who was *seventeen* years old, though in fact she was only nine. This (and other documents) were all duly witnessed in legal form and in the one sent to Rome it was unblushingly stated that 'no deceit, fraud or unlawful agreement [*pacte*] had been entered into the affair'. But Rome was suspicious and it took pressure from the French ambassador and a cardinal to obtain the longed-for appointment.

Thus Angélique became abbess-coadjutrix of Port-Royal. That, however, was not the end of the alarms and excursions. Dame Boulehart's health began to fail in the summer and in early July her condition became desperate. The Arnaulds and their friends were afraid of some last attempt to thwart the pope's and the king's decisions and Angélique was hastily brought (without telling Mme d'Estrées) first to St Cyr and then, when news came of Dame Boulehart's death, to Port-Royal. There was no opposition and at the age of eleven Angélique entered peacefully into her office as full abbess. She never forgot these events. Although she had been professed at the age of ten and some present at the ceremony remarked that she did not know what she was undertaking, she always insisted that she knew very well and that, in spite of all the illegalities, she felt bound by the vows she had taken. For some years during her adolescence the whole experience was the source of much misery to her.

Angélique had much to suffer in the years that lay ahead and her upbringing at home did nothing to make the course of her life easier. It took years for her to overcome the damage that was done to her by her grandfather and, in a different way, by her mother. As she remarked in the brief autobiography which she eventually wrote under pressure, her mother did not love her. Mme Arnauld had wanted a son and although she was a good woman, with, however, only a superficial understanding of her religion, she never seems to have shown any affection. About 1595 a son, Antoine, was born, and his mother loved him passionately. But, alas, so did Angélique. She wrote, 'He was the loveliest child you ever saw, bright and with good looks'. Angélique loved to look after him and play with him: 'He could not live without me'; but her mother allowed her to be near him only 'on sufferance'. She was much alone and even her sister Jeanne (later Mère Agnès) was not a companion to her at this time.

The children of course lived at home, a great gloomy house, where they received the first elements of their education. Their governess was a Mme Pichotel who seems to have been strict. When Angélique childishly (and understandably) misbehaved during Vespers on a Whit Sunday Mme Pichotel whipped her when they got home. Afterwards she said to Angélique that she did it to make her remember for a long time that she had been naughty and not properly reverent in church. She did!

Whether Mme Pichotel was in charge of religious education is not clear. All that is recorded is that one day a Book of Hours with an account of the Passion came into Angélique's hands. She read this and wept. It was almost certainly her first introduction to the gospels. About the same time – she was now aged seven – she was prepared for and made her first confession, though her first communion would not follow for some years. The confessor in his instruction to her in the confessional told her to ask God for forgiveness, so when when got home she went out into the courtyard, knelt down, joined her hands, looked up to heaven and prayed for pardon. Nothing very remarkable in that, but both incidents are evidence of a budding religious sense, typical of a child, which never left her. Of Angélique's secular education we know little. Mme Pichotel was in charge of it and she evidently taught her and the other children to read and, no doubt, to write. Later in life Angélique, who was an assiduous letter-writer, wrote a vigorous prose, only occasionally getting herself tied up in knots.(As she often wrote at night by the light of a candle this may have been due to haste and tiredness.) She quoted the Vulgate on several occasions and must have learnt some Latin at some time or another, perhaps at Maubuisson when she was a child there. In any case there is no doubt about her intellectual vigour. She was a member of the Arnauld family, a very intelligent lot with all the learned background required of lawyers at the time.

However, before Angélique's life as abbess could begin another religious event was to take place. Her father had hesitated about having his ten-year-old daughter blessed as abbess until Dom Edme de la Croix, who seems to have been the evil genius in all this affair, urged that she should be blessed and at the same time make her first communion. For the second time no one thought of preparing her for it and she would have gone unprepared if a poor cobbler of the abbey had not handed her a book that seems to have met her need; she read it 'with great attention'. For the blessing and the first communion Angélique's mother organised a great party. She invited some three hundred guests, among them Mme d'Estrées from Maubuisson 'who queened it in the choir', Mme Desportes, abbess of St Cyr where Agnès was, and Mme Carnazette, abbess of Gif, another Cistercian monastery. The ceremony of blessing and Mass went ahead, Abbot Edme presiding. Perhaps it is thanks partly to the books she had read that Angélique maintained an extraordinary degree of recollection. As she was to write later she had a 'vivid impression of the presence and majesty of God and of Jesus Christ'[1] whom she seemed to think she saw. No doubt these impressions were quickly dissipated by the '*belle fête mondaine*' that took place in the monastery afterwards. As the centre of attention she may well have enjoyed herself. She was nothing if not resilient and, after all, she was still only a child.

Angélique was thus left to face her future. We do not have to speculate on what she thought; we can gather it from what she did and what she very gradually began to realise was her fate.

When Angélique was installed at Port-Royal, her parents looked at the monastery buildings with dismay. They soon realised that repairs would have to be made and, as an elementary precaution (which proved fruitless), they had the walls around the monastery rebuilt. Mme Arnauld also saw to the interior arrangements of the house. She appointed Dame Jumeauville from St Cyr as 'business' manager, and one of the community, Dame Dupont, as prioress. The latter was good to Angélique, deferring to her rank but apparently without the ability to form her in the religious life, and Angélique liked her, always insisting on going to bid her good-night. The religious observance was better than one would have thought. The nuns, though not Angélique, recited the office in church, matins being at 4.00 a.m., though what they made of it is another matter. If, like the nuns of Maubuisson, they knew no Latin, it must have seemed an unintelligible rigmarole. In any case, none of them had chosen the religious life and they amused themselves as best they could. One, with a bad reputation, had to be sent away and another was severely mentally handicapped. There was no common life, each nun having her own *peculium* (personal pension), which must have been very small indeed, and they ate apart. The work of the house was done by secular servants who robbed their employers, giving them as little as possible from the produce of the monastery lands and selling the rest for their own benefit. Mme Arnauld and Dame Jumeauville put a stop to that but, as the total income of the monastery was only 6,000 livres (parish priests often had more), there was not much to live on anyway. If, in Angélique's judgement, the nuns were poor creatures, they were respectable and were grateful for what the Arnauld family was doing for them. As always, Angélique won their affection.

Angélique spent much of her time playing and for company she had perhaps two or three *pensionnaires,* girls living in the house, ostensibly to be educated. From time to time she sent the old monastery coach to St Cyr to fetch Agnès, to whom she was becoming more attached, and another sister, Anne Eugénie. Angélique liked the open air and went on long walks with them beyond the monastery property. When it was raining she stayed in and read the *History of the Romans* and other books that she would later regard as frivolous. In these ways the hours and days were filled and she seems to have been reasonably happy but, as she wrote in her autobiography, she had 'a horrible aversion to the convent' and 'disliked all the exercises of religion'.

Even in these early years she realised her vows were invalid and that she could have renounced them, but the thought of her family, their dismay and the scandal that would be caused held her back. But this was not the only consideration. As she said, although she knew her vows were legally invalid, she felt that she had vowed herself to God. In this way she felt bound though the sense of the bond would be seriously weakened as she grew into adolescence. For years she felt uncertain of herself, she constantly sought guidance, and she was always looking for an assurance she never achieved until long years after her 'conversion'. There was yet another tension. She realised quite early that she had strong maternal instincts, first manifested in her love for her little brother Antoine. She wanted to marry and have children and it was a bitter irony to her that her elder sister who *wanted* to be a nun was thrust into an unhappy marriage while she was forced into a monastery. She did not know that she would one day find full scope for her motherliness in a way she had never imagined.

As puberty approached Angélique became aware of feelings and desires she had never experienced before and her little world began to seem unbearably confined. She looked beyond the monastery walls where there were those at hand ready to tempt her. A not very reputable monk living somewhere in the monastery invited a neighbouring abbess to come and see the young nun. She came with two nuns and two gentlemen, and they insisted on entering the monastery in spite of Angélique's reluctance. Although there was no canonical enclosure she knew that the visit was wrong and said so. But once allowed, it would be repeated. Angélique, in turn, made and received visits. Obviously the situation was potentially dangerous. As Angélique approached the age of fourteen she realised what was happening to her. She speaks of being 'horribly aroused', and had become conscious of her sexuality, though she always remained chaste. There was gossip which came to the ears of her mother who, as soon as she was free of child-bearing, came to the monastery and gave her daughter a dressing-down. She took it well, though afterwards she reflected ruefully that the life she had to live was not of her choosing but had been forced on her by her parents.

There ensued a period of boredom when she read Plutarch's *Lives* – favourite reading at the time – and this was followed by bouts of melancholy alternating with moments of incipient piety. All very adolescent, but Angélique was a strong character with strong feelings and her sense of frustration grew. First, she had an urge to throw everything up, whatever her family might think, and rush off to La Rochelle where she thought she would be safe with her Huguenot relatives. Perhaps it was a momentary temptation but it was as close to sin as she ever got. Feeling ever more frustrated, she fell into a deeper melancholy and then contracted a severe fever, possibly induced by the very unhealthy and marshy valley of Port-Royal, but there was also a psychosomatic factor. In all her early years as abbess, even after she had begun the reform of her community, similar symptoms recurred. When her nuns resisted her desires for regular observance in the matter of poverty and the common life she became downcast and remained so until they came round to her way of thinking. It seems certain that she was unconscious of this feature of her character, which can be seen as the manifestation of an ardent and very determined personality.[2]

Angélique became so ill that her mother took her back home to Paris and looked after her tenderly for months. She put her bed in her own room, she summoned physicians (who seem to have been little more effective than Molière's) and she employed a nurse to be with her night and day. It was this assiduous care which enabled Angélique to see that her mother really loved her and it changed her whole attitude to her. But, strange to say, while she was cared for medically, at no time was any priest invited to give her the pastoral attention she so badly needed. We have to assume that during all the months that Angélique was ill or convalescent she never received Holy Communion. Nor, of course, was she anointed (given 'extreme unction', as it was then called), for it was then the highly undesirable custom only to give that sacrament almost on the point of death. Her prosperous and well-dressed relatives crowded into her bedroom from time to time and Angélique eyed them with a little envy. Her elder sister Catherine, with whom she had a close bond, came but could not raise her spirits. She languished all through August and September until October, when her condition began to improve and her parents sent her into the country, to Andilly, a property her father had inherited. She loved the place: 'I thought the house so beautiful and I would have been very happy never to go away. I thought one ought always to live in such lovely places.'

Angélique gradually recovered and began to get over her fits of melancholy. At this time, however, there were two incidents that might well have occasioned a relapse. Her parents began to suspect that she was thinking of the 'world' and, even, of marriage. One day her father presented her with a deliberately ill-written paper and said brutally, 'Sign it', without giving her time to read it. She cast her eye over it rapidly and realised that she was being required to re-affirm her vows. She dared not refuse but, as she said, she was 'filled with rancour and indignation'. Meanwhile her mother had gone to Port-Royal and searched through all her daughter's papers for love letters. She found nothing. Angélique must have been resilient to put up with such persecution.

In early December she was taken back to Port-Royal and, perhaps to provide someone towards whom Angélique could express her motherly feelings, her parents sent their little daughter Marie, a lively and intelligent child who had been much afflicted with smallpox, to keep her company. Although Angélique was far from well, much troubled in soul and feeling gloomy, the nuns welcomed her back with joy. Her other sister, Agnès was also living in the house and this must have been a consolation to Angélique. Port-Royal was beginning to fill up with Arnaulds.

Meanwhile things had been happening in her absence. Itinerant Capuchins had been calling from time to time to preach a sermon for which they received a meal or a night's lodging. One of them gave to Dame Jumeauville a book of meditations, *Pratique de l'Oraison Mentale ou Contemplative,* originally written in Italian by a Capuchin, Mattia Bellantini da Salo. Dame Jumeauville found it satisfactory and handed it to Angélique who liked it. This happened during the Lent of 1608, and around the time of the Feast of the Annunciation a Père Basile arrived at the monastery, asking if he might preach. It was late, 'the torches were being lit', but it was not yet dark. Angélique was in the garden and when she was told he was in the monastery she hesitated a little and then decided that he could preach before Compline, his sermon taking the place of the preliminary reading. (Evidently Angélique was attending choir now.) Père Basile preached on the incarnation, on the self-humiliation of the Son of God in the crib with the beasts, lowering himself to the human condition and putting on our human flesh even though 'all flesh is as grass…'. Angélique was swept away; after a few sentences she hardly heard the words, and she was touched by God: 'Through her sufferings of recent months God had led her into the desert and now his all-powerful voice was dispelling her sorrows and her anguish, inspiring in her a desire to serve him as a religious.' As she was to write later, 'I do not know what I would *not* have done for God if the grace he gave me had continued to move my heart'.[3] This was the beginning of conversion and at the same time a manifestation of what had been going on in Angélique's soul for some time. She still had a long way to go.

Ironically, Père Basile was a bad and unchaste priest who, in a few months time, would abandon his habit and his priesthood.

The Reform of Port-Royal

Angélique had experienced a conversion of heart but she realised that it was just a beginning. She was keenly conscious of her defects and, like any convert, she was full of generous movements of soul. She wanted to give herself totally to God, felt she ought to give up her office as abbess – an abiding 'temptation' until she was able to surrender it – and, indeed, to leave Port-Royal and go off to some austere and reformed house where she would be unknown and utterly obscure. More painful still, she could find no one to guide her and help her to understand what was happening to her. There was no one to speak to her of God or indicate what his will for her might be. These and other anguished thoughts raged in the mind of this young woman who was not yet seventeen. She kept it all to herself, speaking of her doubts and feelings to no one. All that the nuns noticed was that she now spent long hours in prayer and was preoccupied with her thoughts. In fact, all her desire was to reform *herself;* the notion that she should reform her community did not enter her mind.

The connection with the Capuchins had been kept up. One day a Père Bernard came to the monastery and Angélique felt she could open her heart to him. What exactly they talked about is not clear. He confirmed her desire for self-reform and probably mentioned the matter of the reform of the monastery. In a tremendous sermon to the community he told them that their way of life was relaxed and that they must change it. He spoke harshly and without any nuance, without any understanding of the situation of the nuns. The nuns were shocked and dismayed, not least Dame Dupont, who did not conceal her feelings. This friar, she said, would put ideas in Angélique's head about a far-reaching reform but she, Angélique, was young and would soon get tired of it and the result would be nothing but confusion. Angélique took the rebuke very well, accepting she was not sufficiently sensible to be in charge of a community. All she wanted to do was to go away quietly to a house of regular observance. It is to be feared that the latter desire was an illusion. Angélique was so strong a personality that she would have made an impact on any community.

The succession of events after her conversion is difficult to establish. Angélique moved slowly, made her views known to one or two people and the first she won over was her own servant, who soon became a lay-sister. The second was probably a girl who was not yet professed. The prioress continued her protests and, as she was a good nun though somewhat limited in her understanding of things, Angélique treated her views with respect. Meanwhile, Père Bernard continued to visit the monastery but now, instead of preaching provocative sermons, he talked to nuns individually. He seems to have had some success. On one occasion he brought a Père Pacifique, old, wise, 'not a preacher and holy', according to Angélique. Bernard had told him that the reform was well advanced but Angélique said that was far from the case and she repeated her intention of going away to be a simple nun. Pacifique approved but Bernard rushed in, furious, and said he would tell her father. This was her worst fear. There was also talk of writing to the Vicar General of the Cistercians, Masson, who would take the reform in hand. Angélique vigorously rejected this suggestion, first, because she knew that Masson would tell her father and, second, because he would impose on the community the famous 'customs' of the Order at that time. For these Angélique had nothing but contempt. In her mind they were nothing but unlawful relaxations of the Rule and her aim was precisely the opposite. In this, and though so young, she was typically an Arnauld. She would have the absolute best; there could be no compromise.

The problems that lay ahead were solved in a rather different way. Although Angélique had acquired one or two recruits she felt isolated and sad. With unexpected patience, she was content to bide her time. Meanwhile, she went about reforming herself in a very imprudent manner. She changed her fine habit for a serge one that was so rough that it rubbed her skin, to her great discomfort, and when there was no one about she poured burning wax over her arms and legs as a form of mortification. She probably fasted a good deal and prayed a lot. It should be said, however, that these extreme austerities lasted only for a time and the established Port-Royal never practised physical forms of mortification.

Angélique continued to be unhappy and suffered from depression, a possible long-term result of her illness from which she may not yet have fully recovered. Her mortifications and her depression could not be hidden from the community, however hard she tried to conceal them. There was an air of change in the house and news of Bernard's approaches to Masson had reached her father. He invited Angélique to come to Andilly in September for the grape harvest. Bernard urged her to. The house was not yet canonically enclosed and he suggested that her father should send to Rome asking for new bulls to remedy the faults of the first. With many misgivings

Angélique agreed to join the family and M. Arnauld came to fetch her, with her sisters, Agnès and Marie, and took them off to Andilly.

Angélique's fears were more than justified. She found that the family knew everything. Her mother was filled with dismay, her elder brother Robert, described as brilliant and already making his way in the governmental hierarchy, was vehement against his sister, her father had a violent row with her and took to his bed, saying that she would be the death of him. Whether or not that was likely, the effect on Angélique was to bring on her fever again and send her to bed too. Everyone spied on her and a servant reported that Angélique went to bed in her day clothes, even her stockings, and that she was covered with fleas. Why the fleas had not been spotted before is not explained, but since her two sisters were sleeping in the same room with her it is likely that they would have complained. Fleas are sociable and no respecter of persons.

All this was too much for Arnauld père. He invaded the bedroom and gave vent to one of his terrible angers, reduced Angélique to submission and her two sisters to tears. As the girls began to cry, he went like a madman from one bed to another, beside himself, not knowing what to do. Angélique pleaded her conscience and refused to give way.[4] M. Arnauld refused to admit defeat and summoned Dom Masson, who began quietly: she must leave things as they were and the 'innocent liberties' she had taken in making visits in the surrounding district were permissible. Then the interview became stormy. He raged against the Capuchins, they were babblers, hypocrites and bigots and all they wanted was to use Port-Royal as a source of income. He questioned Angélique closely but she gave away nothing of the plans she had in mind. Afterwards he said to her father, 'She is too sharp [*fine*], she would not tell me anything'. All she would agree to was to have nothing more to do with the Capuchins and to accept a Cistercian monk named by her. That was the sum total of all the tears, rages and expenditure of nervous energy that had gone on for weeks.

Angélique returned to Port-Royal, ill and sadder than ever. But with typical Arnaldian tenacity she held fast to her intention. Meanwhile her father had consulted Dom Masson again and he (not Angélique) chose a monk to preach for the feast of All Saints. Not all the Cistercians were frivolous, as Angélique had termed them, and this one proved to be in favour of reform and preached a moving sermon on the text 'Blessed are those who suffer persecution for righteousness' sake'. When his first recruit said to Angélique that, if she wanted, she could be among those who suffer for righteousness, she repelled the suggestion but found the word had gone to her heart. She decided to make a general confession to the monk, the others did likewise and 'he confirmed us in our intention to bring about a reform'.[5] The confessor was Claude de Quersaillou (or Kersaillou), presumably a Breton. He was enthusiastic but lacked prudence. He condemned Masson's laxity: if Angélique went wandering outside the monastery grounds she would be committing a mortal sin! The comfortable 'customs' were rejected but he positively encouraged Angélique to live as a nun and maintain her desire for reform. He managed to get rid of Dame Jumeauville, sending her back to St Cyr. She had served the house well but she constantly spied on Angélique and reported everything to her parents. With her out of the way, Angélique could continue her (imprudent) austerities and spend long hours in prayer, both by day and by night. These practices, combined with attacks of fever and low vitality, gave her a pitiful appearance which, of course, the nuns noticed. The months went slowly by until Lent. Then, on 18 March 1609 (the exact date is recorded) the prioress, Dame Dupont, and one of the 'ancients', asked her why she was so sad and observed that it was her sadness that was making her ill – a perceptive remark. Angélique replied that she had indeed much to worry her but they had it in their power to relieve her distress. As has been said above, Mme Dupont was a good and observant religious and must hàve had some influence on the others. She replied: 'Madame, tell us what you want us to do, for provided you are happy I promise you that we will do

everything to please you.'[6] It was a generous response and shows
that Angélique had won the affection of her nuns, who had probably held back from reform because they did not understand what
it would involve and were frightened of the consequences. As for
Angélique, she simply said that she wanted to establish the common life and do away with individual possessions. The prioress
asked her if she had reflected on the consequences which would
have an effect on the material situation of the house. Angélique
replied that it was better that they should save their souls by
observing their vow of poverty whatever the difficulties might be.
Dame Dupont and her companion accepted this with very good
grace and a date, the feast of St Benedict, was appointed for the
surrendering of private property and the establishment of life in
common. During the next two days Dame Dupont and her companion went around telling the rest of the nuns what had been
decided and, no doubt, persuading them to do what the abbess
wanted. They had considerable success. On the appointed day,
after a little address by Angélique, the nuns went back to their cells
and brought their little boxes and bits and pieces, to which
Angélique added her own. It was not an impressive pile but it was
an example of real self-sacrifice. This becomes all the clearer when
we read in the account of this incident that a nun who was deaf
and almost dumb and who had lived in the monastery since she
was six years old, brought her tiny treasures too, after asking as
well as she could what was going on. (She, we are told, was very
devout. She immediately approved and then continued her devout
life, praying long hours before the Blessed Sacrament, eventually
dying on Good Friday, 1634.)

Two nuns stood out, one of them with a little private garden
with a gate which she locked. After some time and counsel from
her Capuchin confessor she put the key in a letter and asked him
to take it to the abbess. It was a hard struggle, as she was evidently
much attached to her little garden. The other resisted for months,
disturbed the life of the house and gave way to 'a violent and scan-

dalous outburst' so that she had to be penanced. But she was irrec-
oncilable and eventually was sent away to another monastery. All
that was left was a little flock of some ten nuns, for the eleventh was
out of her mind. Even so, Angélique was filled with joy – as
Angélique de Saint-Jean reported, 'the Mother lost her fever'. It was
at this time too that Agnès came to live permanently at Port-Royal
and, after a trial period during which Angélique took her in hand
rather roughly – she thought Agnès was too fastidious – she in her
turn became abbess and a great source of strength to the community.

To Angélique the establishment of the common life was just the
first step towards making the monastery what it should be. She was
determined to establish enclosure not only to keep 'seculars' out
(including her own family) but to keep the nuns in. Since she was
still only eighteen and had no experience of organised and regular
monastic life, one wonders where she got her information. In the
Middle Ages and in unreformed France enclosure was not insisted
upon and, as we have seen, there were many relaxations of the Rule,
even among Cistercians. Later, she certainly knew the Rule of St
Benedict and the regulations of St Bernard but she can hardly have
been aware of them at this time.

First, she told her nuns of her intention to impose enclosure.
All, including relatives, were to be excluded from the house; the
nuns might see them only in the parlour in the company of another nun. When at Easter time there was a 'clothing' the house was
invaded by relatives and others and the nuns murmured; would
Angélique exclude her own people? She had her doubts. She did
not want any more confrontations with her highly irascible father
but Dom Quersaillou egged her on. She laid her plans like a general preparing for battle. The summer months passed peacefully
enough but she knew that her father would come down in
September after the courts had closed. She was too frightened to
write to him and wrote to her elder sister Catherine (Mme Le
Maître), asking her to make her intentions known to him. But

Catherine could not bring herself to face her father and passed on the message to her mother. She did not take the matter very seriously. Angélique would not do such a thing as exclude her father and she dismissed the whole matter. Then, about the middle of September, a messenger arrived with a message that her father and mother, with Catherine, Robert and Anne, would be arriving on the 25th. Angélique filled with doubts and apprehension, consulted Dom Quersaillou again, took her courage in her hands and wrote direct to her father. For once he took the matter lightly and determined to go.

The morning of 25 September came, with Angélique continuing to be fearful and her nuns more so. Then she made her final plans. All outside doors were locked and Angélique gathered all the keys in her own hands, afraid that one of the nuns might give way and open a door. The office had been said as usual, Mass was celebrated, the work of the house continued and the community went to the refectory for the midday meal though Angélique did not join them. She was in the church praying. It was there that she heard her father's coach approaching. She went to the main door on which her father began knocking. Usually it swung open immediately. This day there was nothing but silence within. Then Angelique appeared at the judas-window let into the door, her face 'whiter than her wimple'. M. Arnauld demanded that the door be opened; Angélique begged him to go to the little door nearby which gave access to the parlour where she would speak to him. He broke into one of his dramatic rages; he insisted, he pressed, he commanded, he raged and he went on hammering on the door until all the nuns were terrified. In the midst of all this noise Angélique simply went on saying that she would see her father in the parlour. Her mother rushed up to the door and poured abuse on her daughter, then Robert took up the tale; she was a 'monster of ingratitude, a parricide!, she was responsible before God for what she was doing, she would kill her father!'[7]

The noise and the altercations went on, terrifying the nuns.

One of them tried to get a key and even the servants washing pots in the courtyard blamed Angélique for her ingratitude to her parents. But, amazingly, she stood firm. For his part Arnauld thought to try a trick and demanded to see his two daughters, Agnès and Marie, thinking that the door would have to be opened to let them out. Angélique was equal to the occasion. She gave a nun a key to a side door that could not be seen from the main entrance and, before their father knew what was happening, the two girls were beside him. Robert rushed at them and urged them to bear witness to their sister's ingratitude. Agnès, with all the composure in the world, replied that her sister had done no wrong; she was obliged to do what she had done. The Council of Trent had ordered it. Robert exploded: 'So now they are prepared to quote Canons and Councils against us!'[8]

It was all too much, it could not last, and when the tempestuous rages had subsided, the Arnaulds realised they had been defeated. In her temper Mme Arnauld had made a rash oath never to enter the portals of the monastery again and her husband, exhausted, ordered the horses to be put into the shafts of the coach. However, he could not go away like that. He approached the Judas-window once more and at last listened to what his daughter had to say and agreed to go into the parlour. The drama was not yet over. When Angélique saw the ravaged face of her father, she fainted and lay there unconscious for a long time. M. Arnauld then began shouting for help but the nuns were so terrified that they thought the quarrel was beginning all over again. Eventually they plucked up courage and came to rescue their abbess, but she was so weak and overcome that when she had recovered sufficiently she could only lie on a couch the nuns brought for her. There then ensued a more reasonable discussion. Both had been very moved by what had happened and the love they had for each other began to take over. Angélique was able to explain what she felt she must do and something of a compromise was reached. M. Arnauld might visit the monastery to see to the material side of things, but surrendered his intention of controlling his daughter's life and his desire to intervene in the internal affairs of the house. As they were talking, Dom Quersaillou made his appearance. Robert immediately began abusing him and M. Arnauld gave the poor man such a dressing-down that he retired in confusion. He was an enthusiastic but imprudent reformer and M. Arnauld, noticing that he was rather young, made a mental note to get rid of him as soon as possible. As for Angélique herself, her niece Angélique de Saint-Jean recorded that her health never fully recovered from the physical and emotional ravages of this experience.

This was the famous *'Journée du Guichet'* (The Day of the Judas-window) which marked a turning-point in the life and history of Port-Royal. Angélique won the battle of wills by reasonableness and persistence. It is clear that she was always capable of acting firmly but gently. Restraint always cost her a great deal and all the conflicts of her early life seem to have been responsible for a sometimes puzzling insecurity. She was afflicted with scruples and felt the need for clear guidance from men she could trust. Her search for a director who would support her and counsel her went on for years and the next phase of her life is the story of the many different directors who tried to help her and did so in ways that she did not always realise what they were doing.[9]

II
Consolidation

The first phase of consolidation had begun without Angélique's knowledge. With all the information M. Arnauld had received, he realised that she was determined to give up her abbacy and go to another monastery. Accordingly, after Easter he and his advisers had made an approach to Rome to have her situation validated. The whole story, including its deceits, was told, and Rome was very shocked and proved difficult. First, the Roman authorities demanded the restitution of all the revenue that had been unlawfully received by the monastery since the death of Mme Boulehart. To this Arnauld replied that he had received nothing but had, indeed, been supporting the abbey out of his own income. The facts were established in France but the turning-point in the negotiations seems to have been the information that the young abbess had reformed her monastery. This impressed the pope and the necessary bulls were granted *gratis* on 23 November 1609, arriving in Port-Royal early in the following year. What Angélique thought of all this does not seem to have been recorded but her desire to resign persisted.

At this time she was more concerned about the instruction and spiritual formation of her community. A certain chain of events had led to the appointment of a Père Archange de Pembroke, an Englishman who had exiled himself on account of his religion. He was known to M. Arnauld, was wise and prudent and had been instrumental in the reformation of two or three other monasteries of women. Although he was a Capuchin, M. Arnauld approved of him. He treated Angélique gently and with much insight, entering into her difficulties (some of which were still coming from her family) and guiding her both verbally and in writing. But Angélique's mind and heart were in turmoil and, according to Louis Cognet, she experienced something like a dark night of the soul. She did not understand herself, she was torn between her affection for her parents and her ardent desire to serve God and give herself wholly to him. Archange's letters seem to be mostly concerned with this tension but he gradually initiated her into interior prayer probably by means of the *Treatise on Prayer* by Peter of Alcantara, who had been a valued spiritual adviser to St Teresa of Avila. Archange also introduced to the house a Dom Eustache de Saint Paul Asseline, a reformed Cistercian. Of him Angélique wrote: 'He was a good religious who had more lights than anyone else. It happens that he was the son of one of the great friends of my grandfather, known and loved by my parents. They were very happy to see me in the hands of such men of wisdom whom they trusted.'[10]

The Cistercian authorities, however, remained difficult, unwilling to surrender Port-Royal to the guidance of any other than their own men. They refused to accept as director to the nuns a learned and experienced secular priest, insisting on sending a monk described as 'foolish and ridiculous'. He certainly lacked common sense. When administering the last sacraments to a nun he preached a very long sermon, to the distress of the patient. He remained a thorn in the nuns' sides until the end of 1611. But Père Archange still managed to give direction either by letter or during rare visits, and he managed to introduce a secular priest, a Dr Gallot, who had been helping the Carmelites in the rue Saint-Jacques. He spent part of the time providing much-needed instruction to the nuns. Then Dom Eustache de Saint Paul came. He was very different from his predecessor and did much to deepen the nuns' spiritual life. Meanwhile Archange continued to write, and even if his style was flowery his letters had a solid basis 'full of doctrine with many scriptural quotations'. His main themes were, firstly, the will of God accepted with love as the way to the kingdom of love and everlasting life, and the imitation of Christ in the Pauline sense, the formation of his image interiorly (a very Bernardine emphasis) and, secondly, incorporation, understood as incorporation into the mystical body of Christ. These, says Cognet, remained the basis of Angélique's spiritual life.[11]

Another important element of Angélique's spirituality was her love of poverty. Hers was not the formal poverty of any religious community living under vows and she wanted to make it a reality in her own life and in the life of her community. First, she wanted to return to the ancient Cistercian habit and get rid of the rather bizarre garments inherited from the former regime. They seem to have been wearing a cross between a religious habit and the sort of clothes worn by great ladies. Its basis was an ample pleated robe over which was worn a long cloak or mantle. To this was added, presumably for the choir, a cowl with wide sleeves and a wimple, the whole topped up with what is described as a 'toque made of linen'. All were adorned with various worldly accessories. Their underclothes were of linen, then regarded as a luxury. Angélique would have none of that. She and her nuns must return to the primitive habit made of wool and wear the black scapular over it. Typically, she went too far and met resistance. Wool was too good, they must wear rough serge of the cheapest sort which was 'as yellow as wax', but when she said that their undergarments must be of similar stuff the prioress objected that it would not only be uncomfortable but would breed fleas. Angélique's reply was that they would have to wash them more frequently and the washing would make them softer. It is not clear how successful she was or whether this arrangement lasted very long. The later portraits of Angélique and other nuns show the usual Cistercian habit, covered by a scapular with a red cross on the front which was incorporated when they adopted adoration of the Blessed Sacrament. It looks quite elegant though very simple.

Angélique herself insisted on wearing a patched habit made up of 'forty pieces' and it seems to have been anything but clean. In addition, she decided to live in discomfort. She slept on an old palliasse and her only covering was an old and smelly blanket. She had of course the privilege of abbatial apartments but when nuns were ill (as they frequently were), and because at least part of the infirmary was unhealthy and unusable, she put the nuns into her own room. Then she slept in a small room which was no more than a passageway to other rooms and, eventually, the church. All this was exaggerated behaviour, but we must remember that she was still very young and in the first fervour of a 'convert'. At the same time, it illustrates a certain logical ruthlessness which was very prominent in the temperament and writings of her youngest brother, the well-known Antoine Arnauld.

While these matters might appear to be petty details of no great interest, set against them was the very positive side of Angélique's love of poverty. If she wanted to 'give up', she wanted even more to give herself, which she did unstintingly. Nuns who were her contemporaries at this time constantly testify to her concern for the well-being of her nuns and of her unfailing care for them, especially when they were ill. A story is told of how she found a poor lay-sister shivering uncontrollably with a fever. Angélique piled on bedclothes and, finding they were not effective, she herself lay in the bed with the sister to give her what warmth she could.[13]

Gradually Angélique's reputation spread outside the monastery and the local people came for help, food and medical care. Angélique had already learned how to bleed her nuns – a remedy frequently resorted to at the time – and other simple medical arts. She seems to have run a regular clinic, much appreciated by the poor, for whom there was no medical care. At the time of the first Fronde in 1648 the people arrived with their portable property, their cattle, their chickens and geese, and Angélique opened various buildings, including the nave of the church, so that they could be stored and saved from the marauding troops. Even the books of the 'solitaries' were put in the choir. The people themselves were sheltered as far as possible within the not very safe walls of the monastery. In all this turmoil Angélique moved about, organising, comforting and giving what assurance she could. She was rather like the captain of a besieged fortress.

Port-Royal was not a wealthy monastery and when M. Arnauld withdrew his financial help the nuns were very poor indeed. Although Angélique was very well aware of the situation she did her best for her nuns, though their diet must have been monotonous and probably insufficient. Port-Royal was very unhealthy, the buildings were inundated from time to time in the winter and in the summer the valley was a breeding ground for mosquitoes. Fevers were a constant feature of life and some nuns died of tuberculosis. But Angélique extended her love of poverty to a refusal to be over-concerned about money. When money did come in she rejoiced but she was always strongly tempted to give it away. Later on, when Port-Royal of Paris was established she ran into debt and this troubled her greatly; how the debts were paid off is not recorded. By this time, however, Port-Royal was becoming more prosperous, girls were sent there to be educated and postulants brought dowries, though Angélique never insisted on them and was regarded as somewhat odd for doing so. Her view was that if a young woman presented herself and showed during her probation that she would make a good religious she was admitted. Angélique's monastery was not to be the refuge of the unwanted daughters of the well-to-do.

From the beginning of the reform Angélique had seen the importance of the daily office as the framework of the day and as soon as possible returned to the ancient custom of singing the night office (Vigils or Matins) at 2.00 a.m. This was followed at dawn by Lauds, but it is only for a later period that we have information about the whole horarium. Writing towards the last phase of the history of Port-Royal, Moléon (Desmarrettes-Lebrun), a Jansenist sympathiser, gives a description of the whole liturgy. Matins was at 2.00 a.m., followed by Lauds, sung in the winter at 6.00 a.m. This was followed by a Low Mass and Prime. After that was the 'conventual Mass'. The community then went to the chapter house for the Martyrology, the Necrology and a reading from the Rule which the Abbess expounded once or twice a week. Finally, there was a chapter of faults. Terce followed at 8.30 a.m., then the High Mass and, at 11.00 a.m., Sext. The midday meal followed (though in Lent the nuns did not eat until after Vespers), and None was said at 2.00 p.m., though in summer this was at 2.30 p.m., no doubt to allow for a little siesta. Vespers began at 4.15 p.m. and lasted until 5.00 p.m. or 5.15 p.m. because the nuns sang 'very slowly and distinctly'. Moléon does not mention Compline.

However, he gives a number of other interesting details. The nuns sang the Office according to the usage of Paris (the secular office) except for the Psalter, which (after 1680) they took from the Monastic Office, saying all 150 psalms during the week. Of the Sunday Mass we are told that after the Creed the celebrant came down to the grille, blessed bread, announced the feasts and fasts of

Jono

Just a quick note to thank
you for all your friendship and
support. It's been a rotten few
days but it's good to know
there's someone like you who will
take time out to listen,

Cheers Mate I owe you.

God Bless.

the week and 'gave a little exhortation or explanation of the Gospel'. After that the sacristan went to the nuns' grille, received a box containing the requisite number of altar breads for holy communion and brought it to the altar. At the 'Agnus Dei' the nuns exchanged with each other the kiss of peace. On Sundays and feast days everyone received communion and 'no Mass is ever said in this church without one religious communicating'.[12] (This of course is a corrective addressed to those who said the nuns went to communion only rarely.)

Moléon also includes a description of the church at Port-Royal. It is large 'and in its simplicity and cleanliness inspires respect and devotion'. The high altar is not attached to the east wall and above it is suspended a ciborium covered with a veil, under which there is a great cross, and lower still a painting of the Last Supper after the manner of Champaigne (the portraitist of Port-Royal, where he had a daughter). On the altar there is nothing but a crucifix, the wooden candlesticks standing on the ground at its sides. The whole sanctuary and the floor are of fine craftsmanship and so well polished and maintained that they look almost new although, says Moléon, they are one hundred and fifty years old. There are four pictures, like the one over the high altar, on the walls of the church. All this would have been very much to the taste of Ricci, the notorious Bishop of Parma and Pistoia, who held his synod in the latter city about a hundred years later. It was in striking contrast to the increasingly baroque and rococo interiors of the urban churches of France at the time. The suspension of the ciborium over the altar derives from the Middle Ages and has survived at Amiens cathedral and Solesmes. As far as Port-Royal was concerned, this had nothing to do with infrequent communion, as Père Rapin SJ unjustly remarked. The nuns of Port-Royal went to communion as frequently as others, even nuns, and, as Moléon's account shows, the altar bread was consecrated at the Mass, as Benedict XIV was to order in the next century and as is the practice now.

The daily programme must have imposed a heavy burden on

the nuns, all the heavier to bear as there was constant illness in the house, due no doubt to an unbalanced diet. No one had heard of vitamins then! But one of the features of Port-Royal is that in addition to the choir offices, all the nuns, not only the lay-sisters, had to work. They took their turn week by week in the kitchen, which involved not only cooking but washing up and scouring greasy pots. As in a medieval monastery everything had to be made on the spot. A detailed description shows that the life of the nuns was very full. They had to make their own habits, shoes and linen, as well as the linen and the vestments for the church, the communion bread and the candles. They bound books, no doubt for choir, they made windows, lanterns, candlesticks and 'other necessary objects in tin'. All this they did in the intervals of the office and whatever time they could spare for reading. They took it all, say the Constitutions, in a spirit of penitence.[13]

Outside the monastery were the farm and the extensive lands with woods, some four hundred acres in all, and fruit and vegetable gardens. The nuns worked in these gardens but they must have had servants to do the rest. When, after 1648, the solitaries, the *'messieurs de Port-Royal'*, began to gather in some numbers, they took an active part in the work of the monastery, especially at harvest time, and in felling trees and chopping the wood for fires. During the Fronde it was too dangerous to go out into the woods and there was insufficient wood for the monastery kitchen and the fires of the house. As Angélique records, the weather was very cold but she saw this as a blessing for, what with all female servants gathered in the monastery, refugee nuns from less safe houses, cattle under the chapter house and all the out-houses full of all sorts of things, there was a real danger of disease. However, everyone kept well, and for this Angélique thanked God.

This community life developed only gradually. Events had already occurred which concerned Angélique personally. The bull validating her election contained a condition that she must make a new profession within six months of its reception. It had arrived early in January 1610 and time was running out. Angélique hoped against hope that her father would forget all about the matter but it was not to be. M. Arnauld got in touch with the Abbot of Clairvaux who decided that the profession should be renewed. Arnauld arrived unannounced at Port-Royal and told his daughter of the decision. She raised no objection openly but she decided to go about it in her own way. On 8 May she was duly blessed with full ceremony and renewed her vows, but with a mental reservation. She was happy enough to vow herself to poverty, chastity and obedience, but held back her assent to commit herself to the Cistercian Order. It was her old desire not to be abbess, to be rid of the responsibilities of the office and to become an ordinary religious in some obscure house. It was an illusion about herself and her abilities. As Sainte-Beuve observed, 'as long as she lived she governed and reigned'. If the life of the monastery was to flourish and the work was to be tolerable it was necessary to recruit new candidates. There is no information about this in the early years, but as the fame of Port-Royal spread postulants gradually came forward. Angélique, however, had her sights on her own family. In her view their salvation would only be secure if they were inside the monastery; the disastrous marriage of her elder sister gave her some reason to think so. In the years following the reform she recruited no less than four of her sisters and then, after her marriage affairs had been settled by legal separation, Catherine too came and was professed, as she had always wanted. Later still their mother entered also.

What methods Angélique used on three of her sisters is difficult to ascertain (one *wanted* to enter), but she certainly brought pressure on Agnès, the Benedictine. Since she had not taken over her abbacy she was at Port-Royal a good deal and in 1610 and 1611 she lived there almost permanently. She remained attached to her Benedictine way of life and, although in favour of her sister's reform, she did not care for its rough austerities. She was careful in her dress, and was much given to quiet prayer, but in Angélique's view she was self-centred and too attached to her own ways. While Agnès was living at Port-Royal her health became very bad, she was confined to bed for long periods and, though Angélique attended her with great affection, she spent much of her time trying to persuade her sister to give up St Cyr and join her Cistercian community. Agnès eventually gave way, survived a somewhat rigorous novitiate and became a close and wise counsellor to her sister. She was later elected abbess and was universally loved by the nuns in the community and by many outside it, as her letters to a great variety of people bear witness.[14] But even though Angélique felt the need of Agnès' presence, it is impossible to approve of the pressure she brought to bear on her.

Six sisters and her own mother, then, but this does not complete the whole story. To them must be added four nieces, daughters of her elder brother Robert, among them the famous Angélique de Saint-Jean who was to be a power in the community for some forty years. After her nephew's dramatic conversion one of his brothers and a nephew lived in lodgings attached to Port-Royal. With hindsight it is clear that this gathering of so many relatives around the monastery was unwise. In the minds of the people and, more dangerously, in that of the king, Port-Royal became identified with the Arnauld family, the *petit troupeau* (the little flock), as some called them. Everything that later came out of Port-Royal was attributed to the nuns who were identified with the solitaries, of whom Louis XIV was to say that he heard too much for his liking. When the troubles began in the 1650s Port-Royal appeared to be peculiarly vulnerable.

The Search for Spiritual Directors

The years that followed 1610 were marked by a gradual implementation of the reform. Although much had been done, Angélique was determined to establish complete conformity to the Rule. Although this prohibited the eating of meat it was still allowed three times a week. When Angélique proposed complete abstinence from meat she met with some resistance. The community was still small and the nuns had to work hard but Angélique would not be deterred and, following her usual practice, she decided to abstain and attempted to do so without letting anyone know. In the refectory her platter was brought to her covered with 'the skin of a sheep' (according to the record) and under it was no more than a small omelette. This peculiar disguise could not have deceived for long as the lay-sisters would have had to prepare the meal, and even in a 'silent' community news gets around. Eventually Angélique sought the advice of the Abbot General, who replied that it was not in his power to grant a general dispensation from a papal directive. Abstinence could be allowed for short periods and for particular persons. Not quite scrupulously perhaps, she put the matter to the community, though in what terms we do not know, and all accepted her ruling or 'interpretation' of the abbot's letter.

At one time her own health gave cause for anxiety. In February she was seriously ill from what was probably a heart attack. For some time her life was in danger and, to her nuns gathered round her bed, she spoke with great regret of the reform she had not been able to complete and exhorted them to continue her work and remain faithful to what they had begun. Then, at the beginning of Lent, Père Archange intervened. In a letter that reveals a good deal about him and Angélique he wrote, 'You tell me that you have been ill and are weak but you do not say whether you are in bed or not. However that may be, realise that you are *obliged* to break the fast and, with dispensation from your confessor, and if your physician thinks it necessary, you must eat some meat'.[15] Otherwise, he goes on characteristically, his letter, as usual, interspersed with scriptural references; Angélique should practise 'discretion', moderation, both towards herself and towards those in her charge for they are no more than 'tender little lambs'. She must not be in too much of a hurry or the whole flock will die one day. As for her weakness of spirit, of which she complains, it will be with her until the end of her life, as it was with the Apostle who prayed three times that he might be delivered from it. Archange saw very clearly that

Angélique was too impetuous, wanting to do everything at once, and he did what he could to restrain her. Later on, Francis de Sales would say much the same to her.

In Champaigne's well-known portrait she appears calm and recollected but it is doubtful whether she was always like that. She was an extrovert and, although an enclosed nun, she must always be doing. Yet, at the same time, she believed in prayer and wanted to fill her life with it. This is the probable source of the tension that was apparent until almost the end of her life. She reproached herself for her lack of interior calm yet she was constantly breaking out. Her sister Agnès, in one of her letters, refers to her booming voice, which must have shattered the silence of the cloister from time to time. It was the tension within her and a feeling of insecurity which drove her to seek spiritual directors who must, she said, be at once firm (no doubt to restrain her impetuosity) and understanding of her very personal needs. One explanation of her constant need for guidance was that she had had no novitiate worth talking about, no authentic initiation into the religious life, and at first had to feel her way almost alone. It may also be that in an age when mere women, even abbesses, were hardly thought competent to manage their own lives, she felt the need of a man, a holy man, of course, though it must be said that she had clear ideas of the sort of man she wanted. Père Archange was the wisest of her early advisers but it seems that he had more to offer than she took or, perhaps, was willing to take. Writing to Agnès he gives more than a hint that Angélique sometimes disagreed with him. He prefers Agnès' way of thinking for, though Angélique's 'lights are extraordinary as are her sentiments they dazzled me and my mind cannot stretch so far.... I would rather put this matter before God than talk about it'. To put the matter colloquially, he found Angélique a bit of a handful. Much later on, when Antoine Le Maître was collecting material for what became his memoir of her, she did not refrain from a somewhat critical comment about him: 'He was truly prudent and wise... if he had not been fed with the reading of the casuists he would have been a perfect religious. Nevertheless he was better for us at that time than anyone else... and his counsel was proportioned to what we could (then) do'. It is a little ungenerous and haughty. But the testimony is suspect. Many years had passed since Archange had been her director and how did she know that he had been fed on casuistry? Who told her? His letters to her were not concerned with the matter at all.

In these early years various spiritual advisers came to Port-Royal, among them Dr Duval, a theologian and professor at the Sorbonne who was connected with Mme Acarie's[16] circle. There were Cistercians of much higher quality than those who had served the monastery in the beginning, and in the light of what was to happen, it was ironical that there were two Jesuits, Père Binet and Père Suffren. Père Binet, later an enemy, was an adviser to Angélique's mother rather than to herself. Angélique thought well of Père Suffren: 'Père Suffren was good and alone stood out against the contradictions that those fathers [i.e. the Oratorians] brought to the establishment'. This refers to the trouble that occurred over the Institute of the Blessed Sacrament when the Oratorian influence was strong.[17] In one of the seven letters addressed to Angélique, Suffren speaks of the reception of holy communion which was to become such a bone of contention later on. In the light of that controversy, his remarks seem curiously unjesuitical: 'communion should be rarer but good and fruitful rather than frequent and without profit'.

Angélique's search for spiritual directors continued and it was by a strange turn of events that she was to find one who would do much for her and give her peace of mind and conscience at least for a few years.

A Stormy Interlude
What facilitated visits from spiritual directors was the fact that the community had moved from Port-Royal-des-Champs to Paris. Angélique's mother had long been reconciled with her daughter

and on her frequent visits she had come to realise how pitiful were the physical conditions of Port-Royal. The buildings were damp, flooded in the winter, and some parts were unusable. The nuns were constantly ill and some died of tuberculosis. It may also be that Mme Arnauld even now had some notion of joining the community. Her husband had died in 1619, several of her children were in the monastery and the others were grown up. About the year 1623 she began talking about a move and in 1624 she acquired a property in the Faubourg Saint-Jacques, then on the outskirts of Paris. She persuaded Angélique to move the whole community to the new house in 1625. Port-Royal-des-Champs was virtually abandoned, only a chaplain being left behind to provide services for the people.

The new quarters were extremely cramped and not very satisfactory. Barns had to be converted into dormitories, the refectory was so small that the nuns had to take their meals by turns and the choir was not big enough to hold the whole community.

Later, thanks to endowments, new buildings were erected, including a large chapel designed by the distinguished architect Le Pautre, which, however, on the instructions of Angélique, was kept as austere as possible.[18] Mass is still said in the chapel, now much reduced in size, on Sundays. Angélique had been reluctant to leave Port-Royal-des-Champs. She liked its remoteness and the silence all around it which reflected the silence of the cloister, a silence she kept so imperfectly. Once the move was made, she said she was happy, but she always had a longing for the old Port-Royal and, in 1648, she went back to live there.

Before Port-Royal had moved to Paris, however, Angélique's fame as a reforming abbess had become known. The Cistercian monks had begun to reform themselves and a sign of this was the election of a new Abbot General, Dom Boucherat. He had naturally become much concerned about the state of affairs at Maubuisson which continued to be notorious for its scandalous way of living. In Angélique he saw an agent of reform but before inviting her to go to Maubisson he first sent a monk-visitor to ask Mme d'Estrées to surrender her abbey. Her answer was to have him beaten up and imprisoned. He managed to escape, and believed that if he had not his life would have been in danger. Sterner measures were called for and the abbot invoked the secular arm. The provost and the police assaulted the place, scaling and breaking down the walls. They searched for the abbess everywhere and eventually found her in a remote room, lying half-naked on a mattress. They dragged her out protesting and screaming and put her in a convent for fallen women.

No doubt news of the affair reached Angélique and she was understandably reluctant to take on so thankless a task. The abbot ordered her to go. Full of misgivings (which in the event were fully justified), and taking with her two nuns and her young and already ailing sister, Marie Claire, she went back to the monastery which she had known as a child.

There is no need to spend time speculating on what lay before her. There was everything to be done and Angélique knew it. The situation was similar to but much worse than that which obtained at Port-Royal eighteen or so years earlier. There was little or no common life. Each nun had her garden with an arbour in which to entertain visitors, both male and female. There was no enclosure and on certain feast days the nuns despatched Vespers and Compline in haste so that they could go out into the country nearby and dance with monks from a neighbouring monastery. The choir offices were a scandalous farce. Animal-like noises were launched from one side of the choir to another and as the nuns knew no Latin they doubtless thought that this was no worse than making incomprehensible noises purporting to be Latin at each other. Angélique tried her charms on the older nuns who had known her as a child but without much effect. Very quickly she realised that the community could not be renewed without an injection of new blood and she received permission from the Abbot of Citeaux to admit postulants without dowries. Soon she had

123

recruited some thirty young women whom she began to form. She instructed them to take on all the most difficult and unpleasant tasks of the house and give an example of charity and forbearance. She practised what she preached and won the affection of the local people by attending to the sick and needy as she had done at Port-Royal.

But all this work was destined to be jeopardised. Angélique came to Maubuisson in February 1618, and in September of the following year, Mme d'Estrées descended on the house in force. She had escaped from her convent, had informed some of her relatives and proceeded to Maubuisson to reoccupy her abbey. With the Count of Sanzai and several gentlemen, Mme d'Estrées gained entrance through the collusion of a nun of the community and confronted Angélique and her nuns just before the hour of Terce. Evidently Mme d'Estrées had got up very early for once. At first the conversation was formal and polite: 'Madame', said the deposed abbess, 'I have come to thank you for the care you have taken of my abbey during my absence and I must now ask you to return to your own and to leave me to look after mine'. Angélique replied that she was unable to do so as she was there by the authority of the Abbot of Citeaux. Mme d'Estrées then said that she had lodged an appeal. Angélique, the daughter and granddaughter of distinguished lawyers, understood that sort of language and replied in kind: 'Your appeal is not yet voided; the sentence of deposition given against you retains its force both in my regard and in our Order. Here I can only regard you as deposed since I was established in this house by M. de Citeaux and the authority of the king. Perhaps then you will not take it ill if I sit in the seat of the abbess.' This she promptly did. Mme d'Estrées seems to have retired for a while for the nuns went to Mass and later to dinner in the refectory. Mme d'Estrées then sent a chaplain as a sort of envoy to deliver an ultimatum. Angélique rejected it and was surprised to see the Count of Sanzai and his followers appear in the church with drawn swords. One discharged his pistol. 'But', continues the narrative, 'I was not surprised and I replied again that I would not go and that I would only yield to force for then I could be excused in the sight of God.'

At this, all the young nuns seized her by her belt and 'pressed me so that I was almost stifled'. Mme d'Estrées' temper was mounting. She was incensed that she should be resisted by a mere *bourgeoise* and she went to tear at Angélique's veil. Then, 'my sisters who were lambs became lions... and a big girl called Anne of St Thecla, the daughter of a gentleman, went up to her and said, "You wretched woman. You dare to want to remove the veil of Mme de Port-Royal. I know you. I know who you are" ', and, at that, and in the presence of the men with the swords and pistols, she tore off Mme d'Estrée's veil and flung it on the floor. The party then had to use force. They took Angélique by the arms (she put up no resistance) and led her out to a waiting carriage. But the young lionesses would have none of that and they clung to the wheels while Mme d'Estrées, now beside herself with rage, urged the coachman to whip up the horses at the risk of the young women's lives. Angélique, still calm, got out, assembled her nuns and then, in a procession, two by two, they set off for the nearby town of Pontoise. When they arrived there the people cried out: 'Here are the sisters of the good Madame de Port-Royal. They have left the devil in their monastery. They have left the plague there. It's that infamous woman, that damned soul, who has chased them out.'

On arriving at Pontoise Angélique led her nuns into a church which turned out to belong to the Jesuits! People rapidly rallied round and made various offers of accommodation, but Angélique was determined to keep her community together. The vicar-general offered her his house, an offer she gladly accepted, and he found lodgings elsewhere. Even though the house was large it must have been something of a crush to fit all the nuns in. There they stayed and lived the religious life as best they could.

On another plane Angélique had been busy. She had managed to send a message to her family, knowing that they would soon find a legal remedy. Although the courts were closed her brother (later Bishop of Angers) soon obtained injunctions to arrest Mme d'Estrées and to reinstate Angélique. Armed police approached the abbey and Mme d'Estrées took flight. By this time it was 10.00 p.m., the police were joined by the clergy of the town and together they conducted the nuns back to their monastery. 'The night was changed into day', wrote Angélique, 'by the number of torches that each one carried. Each policeman, and there were a hundred and fifty of them, held a torch in his hand and a musket on his shoulder'[19]

Angélique stayed at Maubuisson for another thirteen months during which the king appointed as abbess Mme de Soissons, illegitimate daughter of the Count of Soissons. This may seem a strange choice but Mme d'Estrées was still threatening the house and it was thought that a member of a powerful family would be its best security. Angélique stayed on, a not very welcome member of the community, to initiate the new abbess into her duties. It was inevitable that the arrangement would not last and the final straw was the large number of poor subjects Mère Angélique had admitted to the community. It was time to go and, after obtaining the permission of the abbot and the consent of the community of Port-Royal, she made arrangements to leave. She asked her mother to organise carriages to transport the thirty nuns and sent them on ahead as she herself had business to do in Paris. Before leaving she told them that when they came in sight of the steeple of Port-Royal, they must keep silence, reciting the words from Psalm 140 (141): *Pone, Domine, custodiam ori meo, et ostium circumstantiae labiis meis,*[20] and they were to keep this silence until she arrived. So that the sisters at Port-Royal should know who was who, she pinned on each a label bearing her name.

Ostensibly Mère Angélique did this to avoid causing 'dissipation' when they arrived at Port-Royal. But it is an odd proceeding and is perhaps indicative of the rather formal way she sometimes liked to do things. The young nuns obeyed and when the abbess

126

arrived some days later she again formally opened their lips – rather like cardinals in reverse! She did not realise perhaps that the joy with which the community had received them was as damaging as a certain amount of innocent chatter.

Port-Royal remained poor (though now rich in young, vigorous nuns) and Maubuisson was very wealthy. The event had other significance. Saint-Cyran was much moved by this action and, almost certainly for the first time, wrote to Angélique to congratulate her on this 'holy courage'.[21] Among the Cistercians, and although she still had much to suffer from them, she began to be known as the 'Saint Teresa of the Order'.

But there was another visitor who made a greater impression at this time. Francis de Sales, already famous for his *Introduction to the Devout Life*, was in Paris in 1618 on a diplomatic mission. Angélique, now at Maubuisson, ardently wished to meet him and, by what seems to us a pious stratagem, asked him to come and confirm one of the novices. Their meeting was a great success. Not only did the abbess feel that in Francis she had found all she had been looking for for years but he was deeply impressed by her. However, he did not flatter her, except perhaps by taking her seriously and understanding her. She was still a young woman of twenty-seven or so, had had great office thrust on her and had had a life full of tensions and pressures. It is not surprising that she was uncertain of herself and looked for reassurance. Francis gave her this, though he gently but firmly showed her the sources of her self-doubt and lack of tranquillity. She was impulsive, impatient and in a hurry to make saints of her nuns. Francis, in a typical phrase, tried to moderate her eagerness: 'Would it not be better not to go for such big fish but rather to catch a greater number?' Trusting in him implicitly, Angélique felt able to confess her self-satisfaction and the quickness of temper that led her to call people 'fools'. This is a minor revelation of what Angélique was really like and recalls a phrase of her own sister Agnès who remembers Angélique's 'voice of thunder that roused us from our torpor'.[22]

Francis advised her to go forward quietly, step by step, and then, in a charming turn of phrase, he added, 'Let your courage be humble and your humility courageous. Be on your guard about words like 'fool' and 'foolish'. Tame your quickness of temper little by little, by patience, gentleness and kindliness'.[23] He had taken her measure but his personality was so attractive and he was so visibly a saint, that Angélique was ready to take anything from him. They met very few times but a real intimacy grew between them and they confided in each other.[24]

It was through Francis de Sales that Angélique came to know Jeanne Françoise de Chantal, the grandmother of Mme de Sévigné. At first they corresponded and then Jeanne came to Paris and visited Angélique several times, on one occasion staying for two days. The correspondence lapsed for a time and then both letters and visits increased in the last years of Mme de Chantal's life. At first, Angélique felt herself very much the junior partner in the friendship, both spiritually and in years, but in Jeanne she found a spiritual mother and no doubt this did something to make up for the deprivation of her childhood. For Angélique the relationship was deep; she acquired an enormous regard for Jeanne and in these years her one desire was to leave Port-Royal and enter one of her friend's convents. Jeanne put her off gently. This did not affect the friendship and Angélique made her a sort of mother-confessor. In an early letter, written while she was still at Maubuisson, she confesses her faults, her sharp temper, her perpetual busyness, her lack of recollection and so on. Later on in the 1630s, the relationship between the two women is more that of equals, though Jeanne always appears as the more spiritually mature. Even in the toils of self-doubt and apparent dereliction she is visibly the saint.

This is revealed in the last days of her life (she died in 1641) in a letter to Angélique when she reveals her anguish. She felt as if God had abandoned her. Perhaps it was the condition that is called aridity and she actually used the word '*sécherais*'(God has sent me a trial and a pain under which I would become *arid* if his goodness

Antoine Arnauld, engraving by d'Edelinck © Collection Viollet

Mère Angélique Arnauld, portrait by Philippe de Champaigne © ND-Viollet

Jansen, National Library, Paris © Collection Viollet

Pierre Nicole, National Library, Paris
© Collection Viollet

Pierre de Bérulle, engraving by Michel Lasne, National Library, Paris
© Harlingue-Viollet

Robert Arnauld, engraving by Moriseul after Philippe de Champaigne
© Collection Viollet

Antoine Singlin, engraving by J.G. Witt
© Collection Viollet

Angélique Arnauld, Port-Royal-des-Champs Museum
© Collection Viollet

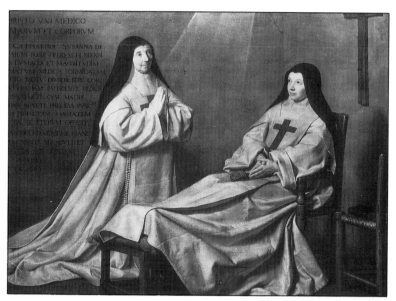

Mère Catherine Agnès & Sainte Catherine de Sainte Suzanne, by Philippe de Champaigne, The Louvre, Paris © Collection Viollet

Charles Sainte-Beuve, engraving by Bornemann © Collection Viollet

Jean Duvergier de Hauranne © CAP-Viollet

Richelieu, by Philippe de Champaigne, The Louvre, Paris © Collection Viollet

did not support me). It was a cry for help. Angélique's reply is a little disconcerting. Though, as she says, she prayed for her friend, she took a month to reply and when she did she seemed to ignore her suffering: 'Your letter came as a surprise to me but [also] with a great feeling of joy and union of my soul with yours that I cannot say what I feel. I feel it [the union] growing day by day and I regard it as a singular mercy of God towards me of which I am quite unworthy'. Later on, she does refer to the trouble: 'I dare not undertake to say anything to you [about it]; I know that God is speaking in your heart and if he is striking you with one hand, he is healing you and supporting you with the other'. Then she goes on about her own condition, confessing her faults, as she had done seventeen years before.[25] It may well be, however, that Angélique felt out of her depth and she wrote to Saint-Cyran, who was in prison, asking him to write to Jeanne de Chantal. This he did and, it would appear, to her satisfaction.

The Return to Port-Royal

When Angélique returned from Maubuisson she was probably exhausted by her experiences there and, although she was happy to be back at Port-Royal, she felt the need for a spiritual director. Francis de Sales had died in 1622 and she knew of no one to turn to. There was also all the turmoil of adapting the newly acquired buildings in 1625 and of settling the community in its new surroundings. Money matters began to worry her and that was something she did not like and had no experience of handling. But when all had been done that could be done, one Sebastian Zamet appeared. He was a descendant of an Italian family who had come to France in the retinue of Catherine de Medici in the sixteenth century. The Zamets had prospered and had become very wealthy. Sebastian had been provided with the diocese of Langres at an early age, but he was a worldly youth until he underwent a conversion of life. He had considerable charm, he was persuasive and, by virtue of his bishopric, he was a duke and peer, an important person.

Though sincere, he seems to have been superficial and given to sudden enthusiasms. He combined a weakness for dramatic gestures with a genuine piety. He thought it possible to take short-cuts to heaven. It is difficult to be just to him.[26] Angélique came under his influence and he became her spiritual director. He seems to have had a hand in liberating Port-Royal from the Cistercians and putting it under the jurisdiction of the Archbishop of Paris, and he won her heart by listening to her plea to be relieved of her office as abbess. By 1630 he had engineered her resignation and sent her sister Agnès far away to the monastery of Tard, near Dijon, which he had also reformed. From there he brought to Paris the abbess, Jeanne de S. Joseph de Bourlan, whose resignation he had also brought about. She, with some of her nuns and under the guidance of Zamet, proceeded to turn Port-Royal upside down. His ideas about the monastic life were very different from Angélique's and all sorts of extravagant practices were introduced. These imported nuns had no regard for the traditions of the house, they despised the connection with Francis de Sales and used his letters as covers for jam pots. The new abbess imposed a number of painful humiliations on Angélique and the new situation made her very miserable. She felt more desolate than ever.

This was not the end of her troubles. Zamet, who was caught up in post-Tridentine devotional practices (which had no place in the Cistercian life), was determined to establish a different kind of religious community. With support in high places, he set about the establishment of his Institute of the Blessed Sacrament with perpetual adoration. It must be near the court at the Louvre to attract great ladies and everything had to be fine and ostentatious. The chapel was fitted up in the most elaborate manner with the finest vestments and pleated linen. The rough habit of Port-Royal had to go and the nuns were clothed in the best kind of material, a scapular with a scarlet cross replacing the old black one. The religious life they were expected to live was what can be described as 'all lilies and languors', alternating with fierce bouts of mortification. Some imposed on themselves fasting on bread and water, others appeared in the community with their faces deliberately ravaged and at other times they indulged in fooleries and uncharitable talk about each other. It seems to have been a sort of primitive exercise in group dynamics.

By 1630 Zamet had obtained the necessary authorisation from Rome but met with strong resistance from the Archbishop of Paris who objected to the establishment in his diocese of a religious community that would not be under his sole control. It had been arranged behind his back that Zamet and Octave de Bellegarde, Archbishop of Sens, should share with him responsibility for the community. He resisted for three years and even then exerted his authority by rejecting the prioress whom Zamet wanted, insisting that Angélique should be the superior. But Zamet, who was evidently a subtle operator, intruded Anne de Jésus de Foissy de Chamesson, who came from a great family but who had never been professed as a religious. She was to be his instrument in creating the sort of community that Zamet wanted. She reported everything to him, she was a spy within the community and countered everything Angélique tried to do. Angélique had no real authority and she looked on all the strange proceedings with dismay.

Help came unexpectedly. It was at this time that the *Chapelet Secret,* which had been circulating in manuscript, had been condemned, and Zamet turned to Saint-Cyran. The story has been told about how he dealt with it and how he became confessor and spiritual director to the nuns. He initiated them into the '*renouvellements*' and, by the time Zamet returned from his diocese, the community had been transformed. Saint-Cyran resigned and his contacts with Port-Royal were henceforth intermittent.

Meanwhile Angélique had realised that the situation was becoming impossible for her. Zamet wanted to get rid of her and tried to engineer the election of the Abbess of Tard whom he had intruded into Port-Royal. At this point the Archbishop of Paris intervened. His authority was being called in question and he probably wanted to get rid of Zamet. He insisted that the prioress and the nuns who had come from Tard should return there and when they objected that they were too poor to pay the travel expenses he said he would do so himself. Mère Le Tardif was re-elected Abbess of Port-Royal and thus became superior of the Institute of the Blessed Sacrament. Angelique had kept in touch with her and now decided that it was time for her to leave the Institute. She invoked the authority of the archbishop and it was agreed that Mère Le Tardif should take her place. With her usual command of difficult situations, she arranged that she would depart in the same instant as Mère Le Tardif arrived. This is what happened. The new superior found Anne de Chamesson as difficult and dangerous as had Angélique and, amid a certain amount of unpleasantness from the Duchess of Longueville (a co-founder of the Institute) and others, she dismissed her. Zamet ceased to take interest in the Institute. It languished until 1638 when the Port-Royal nuns returned to their monastery and then it simply died. The archbishop had ordered that Agnès and the nuns who had accompanied her should return from Tard to Port-Royal and so the community was once more complete. Agnès was the next abbess.

III
Conflict and Controversy

The restored calm of the monastery was shattered in May 1638 by the news of the arrest and imprisonment of Saint-Cyran. His removal was a great blow to Angélique; she owed her definitive conversion to him. However, he continued to write to her from time to time and the blow was softened as Saint-Cyran had already pressed a reluctant Antoine Singlin to take up duties as spiritual director to the community. Although no theologian, he was a gifted and level-headed director, and he served the community well for the next twenty years. On her return Angélique had been appointed Mistress of Novices by her sister Agnès who had been elected abbess. The monastery flourished and the regular life of former years was restored.

Trouble began to come from outside. There were the civil wars of the Fronde in 1649 and 1652 and these had considerable impact on Port-Royal. The solitaries had made their way to the old Port-Royal-des-Champs and had begun to restore some of the buildings. This prepared the way for a number of the Paris community to return there, of necessity, as the house in Paris was proving too small for the ever-increasing number of recruits. Angélique, re-elected abbess in 1642, decided that Port-Royal-des-Champs should once again be occupied. In 1647 she sent part of the community there (some were reluctant to go) and in the next year she herself took up residence. It was not perhaps the most convenient arrangement, but Angélique loved the old Port-Royal. It had been the scene of her conversion, she liked the solitude, and the Paris house had begun to be fashionable. Mme de Guéménée and Mme de Sablé had had apartments attached to the monastic buildings and they, of course, attracted visitors, among them Queen Henrietta Maria, now in exile. After her visit Angélique breathed a sigh of relief: 'I am glad the visit of the Queen of England passed off well enough. But I would to God that by his grace he will preserve us from her return'.[27]

When Angélique arrived with her companions the solitaries received her according to liturgical form, the church bells were rung and there was a Te Deum. The people of the surrounding countryside received her with joy. *Their* mother had come back. Then came the first Fronde and the community in the Faubourg S. Jacques had to move into a private house in Paris and Port-Royal-des-Champs had to be put in a state of siege. It was then that the whole district brought its livestock and belongings into the abbey precincts and the young women of the area were housed in the monastery itself. In spite of ill-health Angélique was unstinting in her care of the people and saved many from hunger and distress. In the next phase of the civil war, which was more serious, the whole

community had to return to Paris where the house became a place
of refuge. Many nuns of other orders had to seek safety in or near
the city and it was estimated that some five hundred religious
passed through the monastery, some staying for shorter periods,
some for longer. Many, said the Port-Royalist historians, were edified by the life of the community and this served to break down
prejudice. In all this, Angélique was tireless, receiving all comers
and working wonders in finding accommodation in an already
overcrowded house. It must have been very exhausting.

There was, however, one great advantage in the upheaval. At
Port-Royal-des-Champs the solitaries, supported by the Duc de
Luynes' generosity, had the outer walls strengthened and provided
watch-towers, and the solitaries, some of whom were old soldiers,
kept constant guard. More important still, they had the valley
drained and the floor of the church was raised several feet to prevent flooding. When Angélique returned after the Fronde with her
flock, Port-Royal-des-Champs was a much healthier place than it
had ever been before. This was just as well as the two communities
had by this time increased to well over a hundred.

These interruptions from the secular world were only part of the
troubles Angélique had to face. There now began all the controversy over the *Augustinus* in which her youngest brother played a leading and very active part. The first condemnation from Rome came
in 1643 but made little impact. Then the Five Propositions were
delated to Rome and were condemned and attributed to Jansen by
the Bull *Cum Occasione* (1653). It was after this that Antoine
Arnauld thought up the lawyer-like distinction between the '*droit*'
and the '*fait*'. A further Bull from the new pope Alexander VII,
alleged to be pro-Jesuit, was issued in 1656. This imposed a
Formulary, requiring an oath that the propositions were the teaching of Jansen and were contained in the *Augustinus*.

At first Angélique saw no reason why Port-Royal should be disturbed. The signing of formularies concerned theologians, the clergy and clerical office-holders, not religious. The community was

quiet and had nothing to do with these matters. She herself had to see visitors in the parlour who insisted on discussing the question, but no one else in the community knew anything about the Five Propositions and all the polemics they had occasioned. She herself understood nothing of the propositions, had not read her brother's notorious *Lettre à un Duc et Pair* and refused to receive a copy at Port-Royal. As for the Bull, Singlin urged submission without reservations in a public sermon and Angélique was very much of his opinion. She had a horror of even a suggestion of schism, 'the greatest of all crimes', and she saw it as a distinct possibility. Her sister Agnès was equally firm: 'We are in no way disquieted by the Bull', she wrote. 'We condemn what it condemns without knowing what it is. It is enough to know that the pope sent it and, as daughters of the Church, we are obliged to reverence all the decrees of the Holy See'.[28] Would that Port-Royal had stuck to that view!

We have further indications of Angélique's mind at this time. Arnauld's *De La Fréquente Communion* had aroused fierce controversy; it was denounced from pulpits and efforts were made to have it condemned at Rome. Angélique commiserated with Arnauld and, recalling their mother's deathbed utterances, wrote: 'Our good mother, when she was dying, gave you a command to suffer and die for the Truth and she asked me to be a mother to you. She bequeathed the love she had for you to me. I hope she will obtain for me the power [to support you] as I see you are suffering with such a good heart and [ready?] to die for the Truth if God makes you worthy of it, as she desired.' It was deeply felt and testifies to her strong love for her brother. But, as usual, she exaggerates. No one was asking Antoine to die for the truth and his sufferings were not exactly severe. As a measure of prudence, he went into hiding for a time. Later, in June 1644, while he was still in hiding, she wrote that she had read *La Tradition de l'Église* (the sequel to *De La Fréquente*) and remarked that she had never read anything that so enlightened her 'on the grandeur and holiness of Christianity'. But in May 1644 she sent copies of her brother's *Apologie pour Jansénius* and *De La Fréquente* to one Macquet with a covering letter. Referring to the *Apologie* she wrote, 'no doubt you will find [in it] a little too much bitterness; that is the opinion of several people. But many think that it is necessary to repel with force and vigour what some are saying insolently against the Truth and those who adore it with love like God, from whom it comes, must defend it vigorously'. She goes on to say that 'the force that throws into confusion the enemies of God is not contrary to charity'.[29] Angélique was evidently in a somewhat untypical battling mood. She realised that what she was saying was dangerous and asked Macquet to burn her letter, which he evidently did not do. Likewise, in another letter she said that she tried to keep the discussions in the world and the literature that was appearing from her community, 'who are happy in their ignorance and only protest to God that they believe all that the Church believes'.[30] In this she was not entirely successful.

She herself was torn between her compassion for her brother and the need to defend the 'Truth', though it may be doubted whether she had any clear idea of what that meant. However, she always tried to maintain charity. As she wrote to the chaplain of the Queen of Poland, 'The more I think of that poor Company [the Jesuits], the more pained I am by their condition. Most people are taken in by them though they fear them more than they love them. There are apparently some who are good, for God has his servants everywhere. In any case, they are our brothers and we are obliged to pray for them even if they say we are very presumptuous to do so. May God have mercy on us all and make us humble and charitable'. There she speaks from the heart; humility and charity had been watchwords with her all her life, even if she sometimes failed to live up to them. When, however, a Père Brisacier published a book entitled *Le Jansénisme confondu* (Jansenism overthrown) full of calumnies of the nuns, accusing them of not believing in the real presence of Christ in the Eucharist and of not going to holy communion, she vigorously protested to the archbishop. He reacted sharply and insisted that the book be withdrawn and its author disciplined.

At the same time, all sorts of rumours and accusations were flying about which were intended to discredit Antoine Arnauld and the community. It was put about, for instance, that Angélique, on one of her regular journeys to the monastery at Paris, had been arrested as a heretic and sent to the Bastille! She took this calmly enough and repeated her horror of schism in a letter to the Queen of Poland: 'If all the efforts of the malign should drive us out of the Church, they may chase out our bodies but will never separate our souls from it'. She ends on her theme of charity: 'The short way to Paradise is to do good to all, especially to those who do us harm'.[31]

Another indication of her attitude to the controversy which raged after Arnauld had been condemned by the Sorbonne and, in particular, to the *Lettres Provinciales*, is her reaction to that sort of polemic. She stated that the *Lettres* had a worldly tone and were incompatible with Christian charity. In this she was supported by Singlin; they were not popular with the hard-liners who believed in answering blow with blow. Whatever Angélique's knowledge of theological Jansenism may have been, and it seems to have been very small indeed, she certainly did not like all the controversy that had been stirred up. When the matter of the Formulary came up she, like Singlin, seems to have been in favour of submission without reservation, but as she was not put to the test we cannot be sure if she really would have submitted. If she had signed, her considerable influence, especially with the older members of the community, makes it probable that the community would have followed her. One thing is clear: it was her deep conviction that the whole matter had nothing to do with the community and she wished to keep them out of it. In this she failed.

IV
The Last Years

After four successive terms as abbess Angélique was able to lay down the burden of office for the last time in 1654. In her place the community elected Agnès de Suireau, who had been formed by Angélique and who had held the arduous office of Abbess of Maubuisson. Though she was in precarious health, she was a firm character and would lead the community through the difficult period that lay ahead. Angélique returned to Port-Royal-des-Champs. At first all was quiet but though Pascal's *Lettres Provinciales* had turned public opinion in favour of Port-Royal, the civil authority (and not the Church) decided to act. Convinced that the author of the *Lettres* was one of the solitaries, in 1656 the government set about dispersing them and with them the *Petites Écoles* (where Racine was a pupil). Angélique records the grief of the solitaries and the boys at having to go but typically she remarked, 'However, we must obey God in all things and, as for them, they are submissive to his holy will.'

This was the first sign of what the Port-Royalists called the persecution. But the history of Port-Royal follows a curious zigzag course. Just at the time when tension was mounting there came a 'miracle of the Holy Thorn'. A priest friend had lent the monastery a reliquary containing what was regarded as a thorn from the Crown of Thorns. In the Lent of 1656, as the nuns and children approached to venerate the relic, Sister Flavie told Margaret Périer (a niece of Sister Euphémie Pascal), who had long been suffering from an unsightly and painful lachrymal fistula, to touch her eye with the relic. The little girl was cured but the matter was at first kept quiet: only the abbess, one or two nuns and Sister Euphémie were told of it. After a few days the abbess thought she had better summon the doctor, Dalencé, who had been attending the child since her arrival at Port-Royal. He examined her and was astonished: the cure seemed complete, there were no scars, no signs of disorder. On returning to Paris he discussed the healing with two of his doctor friends and it was through them that the news got abroad. People flooded to the monastery seeking cures, among them Henrietta Maria of England who made a novena. The Queen Regent, Anne of Austria, heard of the matter and sent one of her own doctors to investigate. Later still, six physicians and surgeons examined the case and all declared that there had been a cure which was beyond the powers of nature and their own healing arts. All Paris was buzzing with the affair, the Queen Regent was impressed and the 'persecution' was called off for the time being.

However, two other factors caused confusion and delay. Alexander VII had published his Bull with a Formulary which was received by the Assembly of the Clergy. The parlement of Paris put up some resistance which was, however, quashed. Mazarin was pre-occupied with another matter. Cardinal de Retz, now lurking in exile in Holland, was still officially Archbishop of Paris, and Mazarin wanted to force his resignation. In an effort to make himself *persona grata* with the pope, he decided, with the support of the Assembly, to do something about implementing the papal orders. In the absence of the cardinal, the *grand vicaires* (vicars-general) in charge of the diocese were instructed to draw up a document containing the papal directives. They did this in a very subtle document drawn up, it was said, with the assistance of Blaise Pascal himself. The distinction of the *droit* and the *fait* was heavily disguised. When Mazarin rejected the document, a second was drawn up, but it was only under pressure from Louis XIV, who assumed power in 1661, that it was imposed. But the see of Paris was not yet vacant; de Retz's resignation was not secured until later that year after which negotiations for the appointment of a successor began. The successful candidate died before being able to take up the post and the process had to begin all over again. It was not until 1664 that Hardouin de Péréfixe received the necessary papal bulls and was able to begin his rule of the diocese.

Meanwhile Port-Royal had not been left unmolested. In 1660

the Petites Ecoles were dispersed, never to assemble again. Singlin was dismissed and threatened with exile to the provinces. Port-Royal was then attacked. A king's officer brought the order that all the children of the school, and the eight postulants, should be sent away within three days. Although Angélique was weak and ill, she came to the Paris house as soon as she got the news to witness the distress the order had caused. As she arrived she met her brother, Robert d'Andilly. In a brief conversation she exhorted him to have courage, to which he replied, 'My courage is unshaken'. 'Brother', she said to him, 'let us be humble. Let us remember that humility without firmness is cowardice but courage without humility is presumption.' Then she entered the house and found all the children in tears. In her rough way, she tried to cheer them up: 'What do I see? Tears? Haven't you any faith? It's [only] men who are doing all this. They are nothing but flies. Are you frightened? You hope in God and yet you are afraid of something? I say to you, if you fear God alone, all will be well. My God, have pity on your children, but your will be done.'[32]

After this painful event it was the turn of the religious. By royal order M. Bail, curé of Montmartre, a known Molinist, was appointed in Singlin's place to extract from the nuns acceptance of the Formulary under oath. He harangued the community in a violent address in which he implied all kinds of activities which made some of the nuns blush. He talked much of the devil, hell and damnation. Having thus alienated the whole community he proceeded to examine them one by one. Although Arnauld and Nicole had previously tried to persuade them to sign, almost all refused. They insisted on adding a clause expressing their reservations. Even then, Angélique's niece, Angélique de Saint-Jean, signed with the greatest reluctance and Euphémie, Pascal's sister, who was opposed to signing at all, went through an anguish of conscience and signed with death in her heart. A few weeks later she died, and it was said to have been because she felt she had ravaged her conscience.

It is not difficult to imagine the turmoil in the community; their sufferings were increased by the knowledge that Angélique, their dear mother, was very ill, too ill to be required to sign the Formulary. She herself knew she was dying. To the Duchess of Chevreuse, who had come to fetch her daughter and who had congratulated her on her steadfastness, she replied, 'If God no longer existed I would lose courage but as long as God is God I will hope in him'. To the child she added, 'We shall see each other elsewhere and there men will have no power to separate us.'[33] Her thoughts were henceforth on that 'elsewhere'.

Angélique's dying months were carefully recorded by her nuns and written down by Angélique de Saint-Jean. Her whole system was collapsing; she is recorded to have been suffering from dropsy which, presumably, means that her heart was ceasing to function adequately. She dragged herself about and insisted on going to choir until her last Easter Day when she had to be carried to the church from her cell. She still managed to write letters and wrote to the prioress of Port-Royal-des-Champs that she saw the hand of God in the distress they were all undergoing. It was a favour and they must try and see it that way: 'We needed all that has come upon us to make us humble. It would have been dangerous for us to enjoy any longer the graces that have been given to us in such abundance'. Then, with a typical touch of exaggeration, she added, 'No house in France was ever more filled with spiritual goods, so enriched with instruction and so regular in observance.' But, 'people were talking about us everywhere', and she had never liked that. She had long thought that the attention the house had attracted would be spiritually dangerous and some suffering would be a corrective: 'Believe me, we need to be humiliated; if we had not been taken down a bit, we should perhaps have fallen.' Again, she said to the community that she was not excessively concerned whether 'they' would give them back the children and the novices: 'My concern is whether the spirit of recollection, simplicity and poverty will be maintained among us. As long as those things exist, let us not bother about the rest. For all "they" do and may intend to do I care as little as for that fly.'[34]

M. Singlin had gone and it was no longer safe for Angélique's nephew Le Maître de Saci to come and minister to her. Some of the nuns came to sympathise with her over the loss of her confessor and spiritual director. To this she replied, 'No, it does not pain me, it is God's will and that is enough for me. I believe that M. Singlin is as present to me by his charity as if I saw him with my eyes.... Let us go straight to the source which is God.... My nephew without God could do nothing for me and without him God will be everything for me...'. Referring again to Singlin, 'I know he is praying for me; I greatly revere him but I do not put a man in the place of God'.[35] If these remarks had been known at the time they might have been regarded as heterodox. The close attendance of one's spiritual director or confessor was regarded as almost a *sine qua non* of a good death. She would, of course, have been ministered to by other chaplains who would have given her holy communion and anointed her. What Angélique was indicating to the community was that they must not rely on particular persons of their own kind – as was the habit of Port-Royal then and long afterwards.

By the end of May Angélique was totally bedridden but her spirit remained undimmed and she managed to write a long letter to Monsieur de Sévigné, an early solitary, exhorting him to recollection and silence: 'Don't talk to anyone about what is happening and if anyone speaks to you, listen and say very little. Remember that excellent remark of M. de Saint-Cyran that the whole gospel and the Passion of our saviour is written with great simplicity and without exaggeration. Pride, vanity and self-regard are everywhere. Since God has united us by his charity, we must always be humble. The best thing about persecution is that it humbles us and humility is best preserved in silence. Hold yourself then at the feet of Jesus Christ and look to his goodness for your support'.[36] It is as if she was talking to herself, reflecting on what was going on around her, and perhaps on her brother Antoine and Pascal who had been engaging in bitter controversy. In view of all that was to happen in the next ten years in Port-Royal, what with the *Relations* of examinations, of legal protests and accounts of 'martyrdoms', which Sainte-Beuve referred to as a real mania, Angélique's words were almost prophetic. But what she wrote to M. de Sévigné she did her best to carry out herself. She soon realised that her nuns were watching her closely, waiting for the last words of one revered by some as a saint. She would have none of that: 'They will make up all sorts of stories about me and they will say 'Our late Mother said this to me' or 'To me she said this'…. That sort of thing is not done…the true preparation for death is to renounce oneself entirely and to sink into God'. 'Bury me', she concluded, 'in the courtyard and let no one indulge in silly talk after my death.'[37] It all sounds a bit rough and unfortunately we cannot now catch the tone of her voice or imagine the expression on her face.

After a last letter to the Queen of Poland, which was more or less dictated to her by the unfeeling Antoine Arnauld and Pierre Nicole, she turned away from this world's affairs altogether. Unhappily she was not destined to make a trouble-free passage from this world to the next. In spite of her long life of dedication and spiritual strivings she now began to experience a terrible fear, a fear of God whom she had tried to serve so faithfully. She thought of herself before God 'as a criminal at the foot of the gallows, awaiting the execution of the judge's sentence'. This dark night of the soul lasted a long time, and even her own affectionate and God-centred sister Agnès could not reassure her. But she understood: 'There are those who are so penetrated by the thought of God's infinite holiness that they find it difficult to understand how a human being, who is nothing but uncleanness, can appear before a Judge who is so holy. They are seized by a religious fear which seems to reduce them to nothing and leaves them no sentiment of joy and consolation…. It seems to be the lot of strong souls and of those who are the most firmly established in piety'.[38] She may have been right. Every pastor knows that even very good Christians who have led irreproachable lives are sometimes seized with the same fear. In Angélique's case we ask if it had anything to do with the

Deus terribilis of the Jansenists. It seems unlikely. She had been spiritually formed before the *Augustinus* appeared and she was an extrovert, at times even bossy, but in prayer she struggled to keep close to God and to do his will.

Peace came before the end. When the nuns came to see her, she told one of them that it was time to cease the struggle and to enter into the eternal Sabbath rest. This she did on 6 August 1661, the Feast of the Transfiguration. She was in her seventieth year.

These last weeks of Angélique's life reveal much of the true woman. Although she had her share of the Arnauld pride she was determined to humble herself. She had striven and worked all her life for Port-Royal, for a community that would be as perfectly observant as she could make it, but she now surrendered everything to God and put everything in his hands. Ambition had gone or, rather, was dismissed, chased away as if it were no more than a fly. The house had prospered and had become famous, but all her thought was of poverty and prayerful recollection. As she lay on her bed in pain and mental distress, that is what came to her at the end. Forthright in her utterances, she had no time for nunnish flutterings and dismissed the sisters, even from round her death-bed. Yet at the same time she had a deep motherly love for her nuns and it was on her breast that the proud Jacqueline Pascal had wept when her brother refused to give her a dowry. All of them returned her love and her sometimes sharp rebukes did not alter their feelings. If she was not a saint – as some of the community wanted to make her – she was a woman with a great heart whose image has been obscured by the bitter polemic with which she had nothing to do. It had been her aim to make of Port-Royal an observant Cistercian monastery. That is what she created, it was there that her heart was, and she worked and prayed and hoped that it would endure.

Note A: Archange de Pembroke

Archange de Pembroke has for many years been described as a scion of the family of the Earls of Pembroke. But as Elfriede Dubois has shown in a well documented article, he was not of that family at all. Originally of Essex, his forebears bought monastic land in Wales. The family name was Barlow. William, son of Roger, who bought the land, became successively Bishop of St David's, Bath and Wells, and Chichester. He had five daughters who all married bishops! Roger Barlow was bestowed with the Commander of Slebech on the coast of Pembrokeshire in 1546 and married Julyan Dawes of Bristol who was a Catholic. Among their sons was one Lewis who was an alumnus of the English College, Douai, and a priest in England. He was eventually imprisoned at Wisbech and was released thanks to the intervention of his episcopal sisters! Roger's brother John, though apparently a recusant, was sheriff of the county and a Justice of Peace in 1561 and 1574. He married Elizabeth Fisher and it was their second son William who became 'Archange de Pembroke'.

In spite of his father's position, William must have been brought up a Catholic but as an adult (he was born in 1568) he evidently found that it was either difficult or impossible to practise his religion. In due course he went to France and joined the Capuchins, then at the height of their fame. In the novitiate he met another Englishman, Benet (Fitch) of Canfield, who became a promoter of 'abstract mysticism', and the famous Frenchman, Anne de Joyeuse. After his profession Archange began to move in the world of the great and became the spiritual director of the Duchess of Guise, among others. With Anne de Joyeuse he went to Rome in 1608 and was in England in 1625 which, with his companion, he had to leave in haste. In Paris he cared for English refugees, and when there were discussions about sending a bishop to England his name was one of those considered. He was guardian more than once, and a definitor, and highly regarded in his order. His last mission seems to have been to the famous Hugo Grotius, then living in Brussels, to convert him to the Catholic faith. He did not succeed.[1]

---

1. For all the above, see E.T. Dubois, 'Le Père Archange de Pembroke: une mise-au-point', *XVIIe Siécle*, Jan/Mar 1981, no. 130, 33e année, no. 1, pp.83-85.

Note B: The 'Miracle' of the Holy Thorn

The authenticity of this miracle has been much discussed. Sainte-Beuve, for instance, spends much time discussing it and, in accordance with his rationalist preconceptions, denied that there had been any miracle. There was no fistula, it was a tumour that with a little pressure from the relic would have emptied itself and everyone thought it was a cure. At the same time he takes care to quote from a long account of the incident by Angélique but he omits some material details on the score that they were distasteful: *'Je supprime de vilains details'*. But those *'vilains details'* reveal that the girl's condition was serious, that its effects were very visible and that both doctor and nuns knew about them very well.[1]

Many years later, although evidently relying on Angélique's account, Racine gives the details in his *Abrégé de l'histoire de Port-Royal*. The fistula could be seen to be very big from the outside and had caused great damage inside. It had eaten into the nose-bone and had pierced the palate. Matter came out through the girl's nose and ran down her face and its smell was so bad as to be insupportable. Margaret had to sleep in a private room with only one other companion. Her eye was partially closed, all the surrounding parts were inflamed and were very painful when touched.

According to the same account, Sister Flavie said to the child as she approached the relic, 'Commend yourself to God and touch [not press] your bad eye with the Holy Thorn'. This she did and when she had gone back to her room she said to her companion, 'There is nothing wrong with me any more; the Holy Thorn has made me better' *(Je n'ai plus de mal, la sainte épine m'a guérie)*. Margaret was only about ten years old and the language is very much that of a girl of her age. Incidentally, she lived to be eighty-four and was alive when Racine was writing.

At first the nuns kept quiet about the matter but soon thought that Dr Dalencé should be informed. A few days later (Sainte-Beuve says seven, Racine three or four) he came and could hardly

---

1. See PR, II, pp. 176-184.

believe his eyes. He examined the child, all the unpleasant manifestations had gone, she felt no pain and there was no scar left. A
day or two later he told two of his surgeon friends and it was
through them that the news of the cure became public.

What are we to make of it all? It seems to me that the external
signs of the disorder are very important. They indicate a very grave
condition indeed and whether its cause is called a fistula or a
tumour does not very much matter. It is a little more doubtful that
the nose was *'carié'*, and that the palate was pierced, though per-
sumably Dalencé could have discerned that, even though he had
not at his disposal modern means of investigation.

The time-lag between the 'miracle' and the cure seems to be
unimportant. Sainte-Beuve insisted that the doctor had not seen
her for two weeks but he had been attending her for two-and-a-
half years and must have known her condition very well. Sainte-
Beuve also thought that the whole case depended on Dalencé's evidence. But the royal doctor was also sent to examine the girl and
one of the six other doctors who considered the evidence was a Dr
Hamon, who was not only highly respected by the faculty for his
medical skill but was a scrupulous man of complete integrity.
Devout though he was, he would never have endorsed evidence
that was suspect.

That briefly is the case in favour of the miracle. But it must be
asked: was Dalencé's diagnosis correct? Could he have discerned
that the nosebone was affected? Again, it might be thought that
there would have been external signs of healing, for example a scar,
however slight. But the account says that there was no such sign.
We have also to trust the account that Margaret shortly after the
alleged cure *did* say that she was healed. That something happened
seems clear, but exactly what? From this distance of time it is probably impossible to say.

A rather different matter is the authenticity of the relic. How
and where did the priest de la Potterie get it? He was apparently an
enthusiastic collector of relics and such people are not too particu-

lar about matters of authenticity. In the thirteenth century St Louis IX had acquired relics of the Passion from Constantinople and had the Sainte Chapelle built to house them. But how authentic were they?

If the relic was not authentic, as seems most likely, we have a nice theological question of whether a fake relic can work a miracle. Sister Flavie told the child to commend herself to God. Could the miracle have taken place in response to the prayer of the child rather than through the application of the relic? The account says that the abbess, Mère Marie Agnès de Suireau, had spent three days in constant prayer but this could not have been for a miracle as no one was expecting it. As it took place during a solemn exposition and veneration of the relic, no doubt the community was praying – but for a miracle?

The whole matter remains a puzzle. It relieved the pressure on Port-Royal for the time being but it had the unfortunate result that the nuns after this looked for miracles (and others were alleged) as acts of God to rescue them from 'persecution'.

Racine adds one or two details that I have not included in the account. He informs us that the 'miracle' took place on 24 March which in 1656 fell on the Friday of the Third Week of Lent when the introit for the Mass was from Psalm 85 (Vulgate): *'Fac mecum signum in bonum…'* (Lord, show forth a wonder that my enemies may see it and be put to shame…). Secondly, the 'miracle' took place after Vespers of the same day when the 'hymns' and prayers were appropriate to the crown of thorns and the mystery of the sorrowful Passion. It was immediately after the office that the veneration of the relic took place. So the whole event took place in an atmosphere of prayer. If, then, a cure did take place it may well have been through the prayers of the community. Racine also records that when one of the religious came next day to comb Margaret's hair but was afraid to comb the left side of her hair as she did not want to hurt her, the child said, 'Sister, the holy thorn has cured me'. 'What do you mean?' replied the sister, and

Margaret said, 'Look and see'. The nun did so and saw that she was completely healed. It was only then that the abbess was informed and she kept the matter quiet for a few days as she did not want the solemn Lenten silence to be broken.

It is a very circumstantial account and Racine seems to have had good sources.[2]

2. See *Abrégé*, ed. de la Pléiade, II, pp. 82-84 (1966).

5

ANTOINE ARNAULD

In his own time he was called 'the great Arnauld' and has often been referred to as such by historians, perhaps to distinguish him from the many Arnaulds of the seventeenth century. It is, however, difficult to understand why. The epithet 'great' usually implies some great work in the world of action or literature or the arts. It is tempting to say that he achieved nothing. Although he spent fifty years of his long life writing, his many books are only read by experts. An inveterate dialectician, he dealt with many subjects but illuminated few. He made himself the leader of French Jansenism but the effect of his work was almost wholly destructive. He had the ability and learning to be a great theologian but he dissipated his talents in polemic. As he himself admitted, he could only write *against* people; his targets included the Jesuits, philosophers like Malebranche, scripture scholars like Richard Simon and many others. In his favour it can be said that he was an honourable man, eschewing intrigue, generous to his friends and, in his last difficult years, loyal to his country. Yet his activity would destroy his own career, inflict considerable suffering on his many relatives at Port-Royal and hand on to the Church in France a *damnosa hereditas* that weakened it for a hundred and fifty years. However, he impressed the people of his own time and remains a historic figure who requires examination if an understanding of the course of events from 1643 to the end of the century is to be acquired.

Antoine Arnauld was born in 1612, the twentieth and youngest child of his parents Antoine and Catherine (née Marion).[1] He was some twenty-four years younger than his eldest brother Robert and twenty-one years younger than his sister Angélique, the abbess of Port-Royal. One wonders whether this fact contributed to his combativeness. Perhaps he decided at an early age not to be overshadowed by his distinguished eldest brother or by Angélique who, as we have seen, was a very strong character.

Little enough is known of his early childhood and education. He studied the humanities with two of his nephews, Antoine le Maître and Le Maître de Saci, who were about his own age, and acquired what seems to have been a certain facility in Greek and a very good knowledge of Latin, as witness his ability to write the flowing Latin of the theologians of the Sorbonne. After the usual course in philosophy, which seems to have been neither very demanding nor exciting, he decided to study law with Antoine le Maître. For a time he led what seems to have been a mildly worldly life; he had his own carriage and horses and he went about town. As he had been tonsured he could hold benefices; he had two, and the income from them no doubt enabled him to live in style. His mother, by now a religious of Port-Royal, perhaps looking upon her son's way of life with a little anxiety, persuaded him to turn from the law to theology. So he began the arduous course of study of the time, first proceeding as bachelor and then to the licentiate, which consisted of a series of public disputations in the mode of the medieval scholastics. But the statutes required that he should first be ordained subdeacon and deacon and this was carried out somewhat hastily. For the licentiate, which carried with it the doctorate, he had to be ordained priest and this gave him pause. He wrote to Saint-Cyran, now in prison, who replied with a characteristic letter indicating that Arnauld should give up the glory of the doctorate: 'The dignity of doctor has led you astray as [human] beauty led the two old men astray.' With typical and not very relevant exaggeration, Saint-Cyran was referring to the two old men in the Book of Daniel who lusted after Susanna! Arnauld pointed out in his reply that if he gave up the doctorate it would cause sensation and that there would be other difficulties. Saint-Cyran gave way but imposed on him the obligation of prayer and fasting twice a week: 'Prayer and fasting will serve as sparks to light up your desire to be united to God.' In addition, Saint-Cyran required him to give alms to three poor persons whom he named. Arnauld was duly ordained priest at the end of his course and took the usual oath 'to defend the truth unto the shedding of blood'.[2] No one ever asked him to shed his blood but he took the matter very seriously.

An earlier incident affected his resolution in this matter. In 1641, when his mother lay on her death-bed, Singlin came to administer the Last Anointing (Extreme Unction). Arnauld asked to assist as a server but Singlin refused: 'It would give too much to nature' – a very Jansenist sentiment. So Arnauld asked that a last message from his mother might be conveyed to him. According to the contemporary account, she said that since God had commited him to the defence of the truth, 'I exhort and conjure you never to let go of it. You must uphold it without fear even if it were to cost a thousand lives. But do it with humility and do not get inflated by the knowledge of the truth which belongs to God alone.' What Mme Arnauld meant by 'the truth' *(la vérité)* is not known, but Antoine took it as a mandate to defend the truth, as he came to see it, of Grace; if he attended to the first part of the injunction he forgot the second. As Saint-Beuve commented, Arnauld went beyond anything his mother or Saint-Cyran were thinking of and led Port-Royal away from its original aims.[3]

Communication between Saint-Cyran and Arnauld continued and after the *Augustinus* appeared in Paris in 1641 it was fiercely attacked by a Dr Habert (later Bishop of Vabres). Saint-Cyran urged Arnauld to defend it. His eyesight was failing and he could have done little more than turn over a few pages and look at the Table of Contents, but it was about Grace and that was enough for him. In a vehement letter to Arnauld he begged him not to take any account of his, Saint-Cyran's, condition as the prisoner of Richelieu; he must speak out: 'Now is the time for speaking, it would be a crime to remain silent and I do not doubt that God will punish us in our own persons in some very visible and palpable way.... If I had been guilty of all the crimes in the world I would still have complete confidence in my salvation if God had given me the grace to defend Grace, not only against heretics but against even those Catholics who decry it and do so all the more danger-ously as they have the right to speak in the Church and who strive by their words to pervert all the ordinary members of the Church.'[4] All this in spite of the fact that he found the book disappointing; it lacked 'unction', he said.

Arnauld, however, set to work. He read the vast tome and pro-duced an *Apologie pour Jansénius* which he soon followed with another, in response to what had been written against his defence. It gained him a certain notoriety but cannot have done him any good with Richelieu, who had already prevented him from becom-ing a fellow of the Sorbonne after graduation. No doubt the cardi-nal, or his spies, had been watching the Arnaulds for some time and he did not like what he learned. Probably he and others began to associate Port-Royal with Jansenism. The relationships between Saint-Cyran, Port-Royal and the Arnaulds were, of course, well known, but here was another of them defending a man whom Richelieu regarded as an enemy of France and who was the object of his hatred.

The *Apologies* were something of a distraction. Arnauld was already working on another and very large work. He had noted Saint-Cyran's spiritual methods at Port-Royal, absorbing his teach-ing on the sacrament of penance and the 'remedy' he had adopted to prevent imperfectly converted 'sinners' from receiving holy com-munion immediately after confession. It was all to do with the business of the *renouvellements* (spiritual renewals). After consult-ing Saint-Cyran, who lent him his extensive dossier of patristic teaching, he set out to write his enormously long book, the full title of which was *De la Fréquente Communion où les sentiments des Pères et des Papes et des Conciles touchant l'usage des Sacrements de Pénitence et de l'Eucharistie sont fidèlement exposés; pour servir d'adresse aux personnes qui pensent à se convertir sérieusement à Dieu, et aux Pasteurs et confesseurs zélés pour le bien des âmes.* It is perhaps the longest title ever attached to a bestseller, as it turned out to be. However, as Richelieu was still alive and Saint-Cyran still in prison, it was thought prudent to delay publication, and it did not appear until 1643, after the cardinal's death. It was an enormous success, two editions came out in the same year and it was read widely for the next two hundred years, as witness a copy of the second edition, once owned by an English recusant priest towards the end of the eighteenth century. He wrote on the title page, 'Whoever thou art, be not alarmed at the size of this book – but read it. Alas! Who can read it without feeling his own sinfulness'.[5] Which is just what Arnauld wanted his readers to feel.

Nor was its size off-putting to the French. Not only did the clergy seize upon it but, because it was in French, it appealed to the laity who were, of course, personally involved in its subject-matter, and it was read and discussed everywhere the *beau monde* gathered. It was unusual for a theological treatise to be written in French and Sainte-Beuve, a good judge, pronounced its style firm and clear and the whole book methodical and well-documented, a tissue of quotations from the scriptures and the Fathers of the Church. To us, who wade wearily through its more than seven hundred pages and the two hundred, more or less, of its 'introduction', its popularity is almost inexplicable. Its injunctions are rigorous, the author browbeats his opponent (a Jesuit of course), and if he quotes a patristic or conciliar text he has misunderstood it or taken it out of context. If Arnauld was master of his material he gives the impression that no one else was. His learning cannot be denied; he quotes long passages from both Greek and Latin Fathers. He also takes care to quote modern authors, St Francis de Sales, Bérulle and the austere St Charles Borromeo, the champion of the Council of Trent who, in a sense, was his trump card, though he does not choose to show that St Charles had hardened sinners in mind. He would crush his opponent with erudition and show that there was a better, a more authentic way to use the sacraments of penance and holy communion than the laxist procedures of the Jesuits. It was sheer polemic from beginning to end. Arnauld never shows any disposition to discuss matters with his opponent and there is no suggestion that the operation of his *modus agendi* might be problematic. It is one of the bitter ironies of the book that Arnauld, recently ordained and without a pastoral charge, had probably never heard a single confession.

Who, then, was the 'opponent' and what was the occasion of this massive piece of apologetics? It all arose out of conflicting advice given by the respective confessors of two ladies of the *haut monde*. A Père Sesmaisons had told Mme de Sablé that she might receive communion the day she went to a ball and he wrote a little treatise for her to that effect. The Princesse de Guéménée, a recent (half-) convert of Saint-Cyran's, showed this treatise to her confessor, Singlin, appointed by Saint-Cyran as the spiritual director of Port-Royal. One can almost hear the conversation: 'My confessor says that I may go to communion', and the other replies, 'But *my* spiritual director says that that is not permissible'. Mme de Sablé showed Sesmaisons' pamplet around and it got to Arnauld. Then Arnauld began to write his book which took about two years. He dealt at length with the conditions for a serious use of penance which must involve a genuine and even prolonged conversion of life which would require abstention for some time from holy communion. For that sacrament there must be a *felt* devotion and even lukewarmness of spirit is a reason for not receiving communion. Indeed, his book is as much about the sacrament of penance and the conditions required to justify absolution as about the devout reception of holy communion. That is why St Vincent de Paul could say that if the book could do some good it would also do great harm, and he calculated that the number of communions at S. Sulpice had dropped by three thousand after its appearance. How he arrived at this figure is not known, but it is undeniable that the long-term effect of the book was to deter generations of people from frequent communion. Thus, rigorous confessions and infrequent communion came to be known simply as 'Jansenism'.

Yet Arnauld had a case. French Catholicism at the time was very conformist and thousands whose lives were not at all devout rushed to confession and communion at Easter-time with little apparent thought for the implications of what they were doing. There was considerable social pressure and in rural areas – and France was still largely rural – not to receive communion put a question mark against the abstainer. If Arnauld had written a different sort of book in which he had pointed out the serious implications of penance and the sacredness of holy communion he could have done much good. His prestige as a theologian was high, he wrote well and, polemics apart, he would have had a large audience. Most people (for there were already those who took a sceptical view of the Christian faith) were unthinking. What they did had always been done and it took the efforts of many others, home missionaries like St John Eudes and spiritual directors of every hue, to deepen understanding of the normal practices of the Christian life. Even Bremond's 'mystical invasion' percolated down to the humbler levels of the population.

Some good things can, of course, be found in the book. Arnauld has a high ideal of the ministerial priesthood. In the sacrament of penance the priest is the instrument of the Holy Spirit: 'The word of the priest is a word of grace which God uses...' (Introduction). The sacraments are sacred mysteries which should be used by both priests and people with respect. Holy Communion should be preceded by a suitable preparation (all the more necessary as communion was often given outside Mass). The times were corrupt and abuse of the sacraments was common, though how Arnauld knew this is not explained. Addressing Sesmaisons he wrote, 'You advise all kinds of people to communicate every week without prescribing in any way what should be their purity of heart and the holiness of their life if they are to approach an altar that is awesome to the saints and even to angels'.[6] Fear is stressed, perhaps a holy fear, but fear nonetheless. And we note that communicants must already have achieved 'holiness of life' if they are to approach the altar. For

156

Arnauld, holy communion was the reward of virtue rather than the means by which we become virtuous.

As for the preparation – some of the conditions he lays down for a devout reception are impracticable. Of course the communicant must avoid occasions of sin – everyone would agree with that – but he or she 'must seek solitude and withdrawal from the world'. How a busy housewife or a farm labourer could do that is not explained. The elitism of the Arnaldists is already apparent. Arnauld relentlessly pursues his theme. Not only must communicants be detached even from venial sin but they must detest all imperfections and *purify themselves from them* and be 'in the fervour of the Holy Spirit who gives the desire to receive communion'.[7] This last reflects Saint-Cyran's emphasis on the indwelling of the Holy Spirit in the soul which, however, would seem to require a felt experience of that presence. All told, the impression given is that communicants should be so busy preparing themselves that they could be ready only rarely to receive communion.

Arnauld also adopted Saint-Cyran's occasional practice of delaying absolution, but whereas Saint-Cyran was more interested in the psychological condition of his penitent, Arnauld turns the whole matter into a kind of theological system. It dominates much of the book even where it is not explicitly stated, and gives a distorted account of the evidence, which he reviews from the Fathers of the Church to St Charles Borromeo. Attempting to blind his opponent with erudition he seeks to apply the rules of the early discipline of penance to the current situation. He naturally says that it is not his intention to restore the old discipline (which had been obsolete for centuries!) but from it he takes his teaching that absolution may and often should be delayed, that it was spiritually profitable to do so and that the time of penance should be spent in prayer, fasting, alms-giving and withdrawal from the world. Here, too, he was following Saint-Cyran who, however, had the sense to see that such conditions could not be applied to everyone.

With the appearance of the *De la Fréquente* Arnauld became a public figure and a battle of books ensued. The learned Jesuit, Denis Pétau, gave a balanced assessment of Arnauld's book and granted, among other things and without censure, that there were holy people who abstained from communion out of humility but, perhaps egged on by his more fiery confrères, he accused Arnauld of being the leader of 'a new sect of penitentaries'! This evoked the enormously long *Tradition de l'Église* which was prefaced by a 'Letter' of some two hundred pages addressed to the Queen Regent, in which Arnauld defended himself against Pétau's attack. No, he was not trying to restore the ancient order of penance. Rather, he wanted to stimulate bishops (Arnauld was always ready to correct his superiors) to insist on the observance of the Council of Trent, presumably as understood by St Charles Borromeo.

In the midst of all this Arnauld had the defence of the *Augustinus* on his hands. After the first papal condemnation of Jansen in 1653 he entered the fray again over another matter which was to have fateful consequences for him.

In 1655 the Duke of Liancourt, a friend of Port-Royal where his daughter was at school and favourable to certain alleged Jansenists, went to make his confession at his parish church of S. Sulpice at the beginning of Lent. The confessor refused him absolution until he had taken his daughter away from Port-Royal and dismissed from his household a Père Bourgeys who was regarded as favourable to the Jansenists. The duke went away unabsolved, his wife complained to the famous Jean-Jacques Olier, the superior, who endorsed the confessor's decision in somewhat rough terms. News of the incident reached Arnauld and he was furious. He immediately sat down and wrote his *Lettre à une personne de condition*. He had some justification, for the *Cum Occasione* had said nothing of what should be done to people who disagreed with it, there was no question of signature and Port-Royal, the monastery, was not involved in the disputes it had occasioned. It was an implied accusation of heresy by association. The confessor's decision amounted to an excommunication which it was not in his competence to pro-

nounce. It implied that the duke was a heretic or that he was breaking a major rule of the Church. None of this was true. Arnauld's
letter provoked a little storm of pamphlets and he decided that he
must make his mind clear once and for all and justify the distinction of the *droit* and the *fait* which thus became public for the first
time.

So it was that Arnauld began his very long letter, this time
addressed to the Duke of Luynes, another friend of Port-Royal:
*Seconde lettre de M. Arnauld à un Duc et Pair de France pour servir
de réponse à plusieurs écrits qui ont été publiés contre la première lettre sur ce qui est arrivé à un Seigneur de la Cour dans une Paroisse de
Paris*. The Jansenist historian Besoigne, though admitting that it is
very long, is in raptures about it. It is eminently fine, marked by the
strength of its reasoning, its eloquence and the profundity of its
researches. A modern authority is inclined to agree: 'It is probably
the best book to come from Arnauld's pen.'[8] In addition to venti-
lating the matter of the *droit* and the *fait*, however, Arnauld made
a serious tactical and psychological blunder. In an attempt to inter-
pret and justify the first of the Five Propositions he brought up the
question of St Peter's fall at the time of the Passion. This is how he
expressed himself: 'This great truth (that even the just can fall without grace) which is established by the Gospel and attested by the
Fathers, reveals to us in the person of Peter a just man in whom
grace (without which we can do nothing) was wanting on an occasion when we cannot say that he did not sin'. First, this brought
Peter into the argument, sending shudders down certain spines and
raising the spectre of an equivocal statement in the preface of *De la
Fréquente* that Peter and Paul were two heads in one (!) of the
Roman Church, a phrase that had been inserted by Barcos, the
nephew of Saint-Cyran. Although it had been condemned in
Rome, this time there was no reaction. But the anti-Jansenists
immediately leaped on it and said that it was nothing more than
another way of expressing the First Proposition to the effect that
without grace (even) the just find God's commandments impossi-

ble to obey. Grace of course is the equivocal term. In the Five Propositions it always means efficacious, coercive grace, and if that is assumed it is difficult to see how Arnauld's statement differs from Jansen's.

It was this letter which sparked off the action of the Sorbonne. Meanwhile, Arnauld had sent a copy to Pope Alexander VII, apologising for its length, as well he might, and it cannot have been very welcome. Then he wrote to the Dean of the faculty, pleading that the commission should be impartial (which it was not) and asking that the accusations against him should be made known to him. Unhappily, and perhaps inevitably, he rushed into publication again and issued a pamphlet on what was happening in the assembly of the Sorbonne. The one point of interest that emerges is that the reason given for the assembly was to make clear to everyone that the Bull of 1656 was authoritative. Arnauld replied that he had already accepted the condemnation of the doctrine contained in the Five Propositions but his own *Lettre* must have thrown doubt on that.

These moves were without effect and the assembly got under way amid protests from Arnauld and his supporters and counter-protests from their opponents. The former raised the question of the legality of the admission of the *moines,* religious who were doctors of the Sorbonne. Traditionally only two from each order had been allowed to attend but now all were admitted. Hence Pascal's jibe that it was easier to find *moines* than reasons. So noisy did the assembly become that towards the end of December Mazarin ordered the Chancellor (Séguier) to attend with all his officers, ostensibly to keep order. The Jansenists of course alleged that they were there to intimidate. However, the assembly invited Arnauld to come and state his case *candide et simpliciter* but without the disputation which Arnauld wanted. He always thought he could refute anyone. He refused the invitation and wrote a letter which was read by a supporter of his, the towering Dr Gorin de Saint-Amor, who read it out in his stentorian voice. All to no avail.

The line of Arnauld's defence was not without its importance for the future. He wrote, he said, on the question of the *fait* in the *Lettre* only because he had been accused of heresy for not acknowledging that the Five Propositions *were* in the *Augustinus*. He had read the work, had not been able to find them there and it was against his conscience to say that they were. Indeed, it would be a sin for him to say so. From the beginning he had decided to keep silent on the matter; he could not be accused of disrespect for the pope and the bishops since it was not against the Catholic faith to doubt a fact contained in a papal document. There was something to be said for his point of view as there was as yet no definitive statement of council or pope that had pronounced on the connection of what came to be called a dogmatic fact with the prerogative of infallibility. This was exactly the defence of Angélique de Saint-Jean and those who followed her, and it is clear where she got her information.

The assembly, however, would have none of it. They had already said that the question before them was not whether the Five Propositions were in the *Augustinus* or not, and here they showed a certain wisdom, for they knew that such a discussion would be endless. What was at issue was the importance of the papal decision: after the pope had spoken no one could doubt that Jansen had taught the doctrine in the Five Propositions.

Arnauld also attempted to defend his interpretation of the First Proposition which, of course, he backed up with quotations from the Fathers. When he said that Peter lacked grace he had not meant that all interior grace was wanting, but only efficacious grace, which gives the immediate and proximate power to act. But his 'interior grace' looks suspiciously like 'sufficient grace', of which he and Jansen had denied the existence. If that were the case, Arnauld was coming very close to the current Thomist view – this was so is clear from a book he wrote after the condemnation. In his *Dissertatio Theologica in qua Augustiniana propositio... cum variis Thomisticae sententiis conciliatur* (a theological dissertation in which a proposition from the *Augustinus* is reconciled with

Thomistic opinions). he wrote that 'interior grace' is sufficient grace, understood in a Thomist and not a Molinist sense. This view has been endorsed by subsequent writers and in the end we must come to the conclusion that Arnauld caused all the rumpus for very little. It is ironical that the Sorbonne, Gallican in ecclesiology, should have used the pope as a stick with which to beat its enemy.

As the debate went on during the last part of January Arnauld saw that it was going against him and he made one last desperate attempt to exonerate himself. In a humiliating statement, the like of which he never again made in his long lifetime, he said he would not have written the *Lettre* if he had foreseen that it would be held against him as a crime. He wished he had not written it. He condemned the Five Propositions in whatever book they were to be found without exception, including that of Jansen. Finally, he asked pardon of the pope and the bishops. It was a complete disavowal and more. It was a complete collapse and quite out of character. It was no doubt a sign that the long and weary contention had worn him down; the humiliation he experienced affected his whole life. Henceforth and doggedly he would not move from his position on the *droit* and the *fait* and dragged others with him in the interminable and bitter dispute.

Nonetheless his views were condemned by the Sorbonne as impious, blasphemous (!) and heretical and he was given fifteen days to repent. But before this a flash of lightning appeared out of the sky, the First Provincial Letter. Later still came the alleged miracle of the Holy Thorn and the situation eased a little. Arnauld, however, had already gone into hiding in a safe house in Paris.[9] After a consultation his friends urged him to issue another defence of his views. He wearily consented and produced a draft, full of theology and unlikely to be read by the public. From the reaction of his friends he realised that it would not do and he turned to Blaise Pascal saying, 'You are young. You ought to do something'. Pascal agreed but all he would promise was a draft which others could revise and prepare for publication. It duly appeared and was a great success. The rest followed at intervals during the next twelve months and Arnauld (and almost certainly Nicole, who read everything) provided him with the material he used to such advantage.

In the years that followed Arnauld shot off one tract after another but as time went by it was clear that things were going badly for Arnauld and Port-Royal. By 1662, however, the Bishop of Comminges, Gilbert du Plessis-Praslin Choiseul, saw that as things were there could be no meeting of minds and he decided to attempt a reconciliation. Carefully preparing the way by obtaining the consent of the king, he sought to bring together representatives of the two sides. It was his sensible conviction that only face-to-face conversations were likely to resolve the differences; only in that way could the two parties begin to understand each other. His representative for the anti-Jansenists was an accommodating Jesuit, Père Ferrier, professor of theology at Toulouse and a neighbour of the bishop. For the Jansenists there were Arnauld, Singlin (who was no theologian), a theologian called Girard, Barcos and others who were all allowed to come out of hiding. Of these Singlin and Barcos were against the distinction and the former wanted to keep the nuns out of the whole affair of a signature involving the distinction. Girard played the most important part and Arnauld refused to attend at all! He who, as Sainte-Beuve said, was so ready with his pen made a poor showing in face-to-face discussions and he had such a horror and mistrust of Jesuits that he could not bring himself to sit down with one.[10] In the event two Jansenists, one of whom was Girard, acted in person for the Jansenist party.

Arnauld, however, was a necessary partner; without him no agreement could be reached and his absence meant that sheaves of paper had to pass between the parties, leading to intolerable delays. He replied to every proposal with a memorandum and he also insisted on consulting his friends, including the Bishop of Beauvais, causing more delays and more paperwork. From all this we must conclude that Arnauld did not want a reconciliation. He and his niece Angélique de Saint-Jean (who privately was egging him on) were afraid of being compromised. 'The idea of humiliating himself in cowardly fashion, to seem to betray the truth and to be giving way was something he could not tolerate; it seemed to him that on the slippery way that lay before him, everyone was pushing him towards the precipice wanting only his fall.' What proved to be the sticking point was a sentence of a draft statement which began, 'We submit to all the constitutions of the sovereign Pontiff...'. He and his supporters were invited to sign this but for Arnauld it was too inclusive and the word 'submit' was probably too much for him. It was in vain that Choiseul and some other bishops he called to his aid explained that it was a formula that did not commit Arnauld to an absolute interior assent of faith to all that the document contained; all it implied was a mark of respect for authority. He rejected this interpretation as well as the offer of a signed statement by the bishops that this was the sense in which he would have given his assent. Their suggestion that it should be kept secret, if only for a few days, outraged Arnauld. It went against his sense of honesty and would compromise his integrity before the world. As Sainte-Beuve remarks, he remained 'inflexible, irreducible, coming back always to his point and his mathematical line of truth'.[11] It was the end and the whole project failed.

His intransigence threw even some of Arnauld's own family and his supporters into disarray. His elder brother Robert wrote to him that ever since the negotiations had started he had noticed that he, Antoine, had been sad when they seemed to be succeeding and happy when it seemed likely they would be broken off. His nephew, M. de Pomponne, Robert's son, attacked him, saying that he would cause his father to die of sadness and vexation. From another quarter came what amounted to a rebuke. M. le Nain de Tillemont, the father of the historian, a supporter of the party and a highly respected member of the lawyer class, wrote a strong letter of disapproval on behalf of several others: 'I have learned with sorrow of the breakdown of an affair which is so important for the glory of God and the good of the Church. What would the world

say if they knew that this worthy prelate [Choiseul] who, while
accusing others of harshness, had accused you of an "excess of firmness on your part and a too great delicacy of conscience"? And what
would they say if they knew that M. l'Abbé de Saint-Cyran [i.e.
Barcos], a man who was so enlightened and judicious, had welcomed the approach and the proposals of M. de Comminges for
the signing of the two Constitutions [those of Innocent X and
Alexander VII] with the word *Subjicimus*, believing as he does that
this can be done with a good conscience?' He was setting himself
against not only his closest intimates, including Singlin, but against
the Church. The long letter ends with a sentiment that Arnauld
might well have taken to heart. If his reputation ran the risk of
being damaged by signing the documents presented to him 'in
these circumstances he must suffer the humiliations God permits,
especially when they are advantageous to the Church'.[12] But this
was precisely what Arnauld did not take sufficiently into account.
It was *his* honour, *his* integrity and *his* reputation as defender of the
truth that was at stake and any even apparent surrender on his part
seemed dishonourable to him.

Yet another rift appeared between M. Girard and Angélique de
Saint-Jean. She was constantly trying to stiffen the resolve of her
uncle to whom she wrote that 'the least equivocal word' would be
a shock to delicate consciences. Indeed, an unfriendly Oratorian
alleged that 'she was so obstinate that she thought no one should
sign anything'. She was at this time more extreme than Barcos
whose mind was that the Formulary should not be signed but that
the condemnation of the *Augustinus* should be accepted. He was
one of the intransigents at one end of the spectrum while she was
equally intransigent at the other and, into the bargain, she quite
inconsistently and inaccurately blamed Barcos for initiating the
whole negotiation. She intrigued, she reproached Arnauld, Barcos
and Nicole, whom she thought soft, and in the months that followed had discussions with Girard in which she took a very high
tone: 'Her decrees expressed in a haughty manner are sufficient to

prove that if there was a tyranny at Port-Royal it was not Arnauld who was responsible.'[13] The proposed 'submission' was dangerous 'because it is a commitment which could serve as a temptation in a year, ten years if there is any further talk of an agreement'. Girard, who had been the chief representative for the Jansenists, pleaded that he had gone no further than the University of Louvain and Arnauld had always been in agreement with what he had done. To this she replied that he could only repudiate his representatives; it was they who had drawn down upon *him* all the reproaches and odium of the enemy with all its terrible consequences. In a later interview at which Girard had shown himself to be even more accommodating, 'with fewer and fewer scruples' about what had been done, she replied, 'So that is how conscience accustoms itself' to what is wrong. He was ready to abandon not only Jansen but his own conscience 'which she did not think was permissible'. When Girard ventured to say it was only at this price that they could be 'the protectors of efficacious grace' since the pope had approved it in their Articles (which they had drawn up), she was understood to reply that 'in that case it would be the same as condemning it in their books'. Writing to her uncle, she shows her fury: 'You find no fault in the affair, for you it is no more than hazardous'; and M. de Choiseul had gone so far as to claim that Arnauld had approved what had been done, once he had been better informed. Now there was no longer any question of getting out of it: 'What was the rumour based on? I don't like it'. The bishop and Girard have come to an agreement and have written it up to trap him: 'You will consider whether there is not something to be done to remove that impression and every pretext for saying so.'[14] She was now giving orders and it is after this outburst that Orcibal makes his remark about 'tyranny'.

The decline of Port-Royal would mainly be due to Arnauld's intransigence but Angélique de Saint-Jean was also to blame. The days were not far distant when the religious would be exiled, Port-Royal would become a prison and its life sterilised.

What prompted Arnauld's stance in this matter? For something like ten years he had been propagating the distinction of the *droit* and the *fait* and like many another controversialist he had become hung up on his own viewpoint. He had ceased to *think* and entertained the pathetic belief that by the continual iteration of his theory he would eventually win over the opposition, including Rome. He seems to have forgotten St Ambrose's saying, *'Non in dialectica voluit Deus hominem salvum fieri'.*[15] It was a hardening of the mental arteries. He was now about fifty, an age when new ideas often find it difficult to enter certain minds and though Arnauld's was keen it was never flexible. We remember Sainte-Beuve's 'mathematical line'. It was Arnauld's habit to impose on the subject-matter before him a rigid, logical pattern and then find an infinity of reasons to support it. There was also his humiliation when he was ejected from the Sorbonne. Compromise had achieved nothing and he would not take that way again for a long time to come.

Now he felt that his personal integrity was in question and if he gave way he would cease to be a credible witness of the truth as he perceived it. If he was mistaken in thinking so, as so many of his friends believed, it was because he had too narrow a notion of the truth and, in addition, he was unfortunately blind to the wider issues. For all his loyalty to the Church he did not see that his action would lead to a division in the Church which could have been avoided if he had been willing to submit to its authority, a submission which involved not only the pope but almost the entire episcopate of France. He appealed to his conscience and in doing so set his conscience against a considered decision of the Church. Infallibility as such was not in question as it had not yet been defined and the doctrine was not held widely in France at the time. There were some who held that Arnauld was justified in resisting a non-infallible pronouncement of the Church, and nowadays he would be seen, at least by some, as a pioneer of a more reasonable relationship between the individual and authority. But it is a delicate matter and in this case one person's resistance led to a great evil. It also raises the question of whether he had done all that was possible to inform his conscience. He associated constantly with like-minded people whom, indeed, he largely dominated. He does not seem to have been willing to *listen* to others of a different opinion; he always had a compulsion to take up his pen and refute them. But hanging over the whole affair was a confusion of respectful silence, interior assent and what Angélique de Saint-Jean called *blind obedience.* It does seem possible that on more than one occasion a respectful silence would have been acceptable and sufficient, but all the time there was pressure from the king and others who were concerned to annihilate Jansenism by whatever means. Arnauld was the leader and he must be crushed.

In the events of the next few years it was Port-Royal itself that was at the centre of the storm. There were the visits of Péréfixe, Archbishop of Paris, the interrogations, the imprisonment of a group of the religious and the deprivation of the sacraments. Arnauld could only play a secret role. Communication became very difficult and for a time ceased altogether. When the whole community was gathered at Port-Royal-des-Champs contact between Arnauld and his supporters and the monastery was precarious. When reconciliation was put in train in 1668 Arnauld had the difficult and invidious task of persuading his niece and the hard core of the resistance to accept the terms of the agreement.

By 1668 a stalemate had been reached and the impact of the affair had gone beyond Port-Royal. The bishops of France were becoming concerned and four of them, the venerated Pavillon, Bishop of Aleth, Henry Arnauld, Bishop of Angers, and two others had come out publicly in favour of Port-Royal and against the continued harassment of the community. With the election of a new pope, Clement IX, who was less rigid than his predecessors, it seemed that reconciliation might be possible. Negotiations began and although Arnauld suffered much anguish of soul and heartsearching he was willing to participate, all the more so as the Jesuits (as well as Péréfixe) were excluded from the negotiations. He was also under the illusion that the pope was willing to grant all that he and his party wanted. This misunderstanding was never cleared up though the pope must have been aware that his view of the matter was different from that of the Jansenists. In this sense it was a flawed agreement and Angélique de Saint-Jean was percipient enough to see (and say) that the whole question would be raised again at some future date.

However, by the end of 1668 all seemed to be well although Arnauld (among others) would have to sign the necessary document. To avoid doing so in the diocese of Paris (where the hated Péréfixe reigned) he took care to get his brother Henry to provide him with a nominal and possibly non-existent benefice in his diocese of Angers. He signed the document there, releasing a wave of emotion and bringing about his own rehabilitation.

Formal visits must now be paid, first to the nuncio, Bargellini, who had been helpful in negotiating the 'peace' with Rome. Archbishop de Gondrin, who was inclined to the Jansenist cause, took Arnauld with Nicole and a Dr Lalane to the nunciature. Arnauld paid his compliments to the nuncio who, in his reply, described Arnauld's pen as a *plume d'or*, a typical piece of Italian courtesy. Then the king heard of the visit and expressed his desire to see the famous Dr Arnauld; an audience was duly arranged for 24 October. Arnauld was greatly disturbed by the prospect of seeing the king and having to make a speech. For days he turned over in his mind what he should say to the king and how to say what would be appropriate. A friend who visited him found him in a state of considerable distress. After a good deal of talk the friend urged him to write down there and then what came into his mind, which he did, though no doubt he would have looked over it anxiously in the next few days.[16]

When the great day arrived M. de Pomponne (Arnauld's nephew), recently appointed ambassador in Holland, came to fetch him early in the morning and took him to the court at St Germain. They were met by an official, M. de Lyonne, who took them to the

royal apartment for the *lever du roi* – apparently, the *roi* did not rise
very early. Since there was something of a crowd there, as there usually was, they were taken to a private room where they met M. Le
Tellier, Coadjutor of Reims, who gave the visitor a copy of his
approbation of Arnauld's own book against the Huguenot minister,
Claude. There Arnauld was introduced to M. le Prince, who
received him warmly. But, as the king was approaching, Arnauld
had to be hidden in a wardrobe so that he could be produced with
all due ceremony. All the rest of the courtiers having been dismissed, Arnauld, accompanied by de Lyonne, de Pomponne and Le
Tellier, was duly presented to the king. He made his very polished
speech in proper courtly style, speaking of the honour done him by
being received by the king, who was so good as to forget the alleged
offence against his Majesty that some had purveyed to him, for
whom he had never had any other than sentiments of respect, veneration and admiration, 'since in my solitude I have learned the
great feats of your Majesty' (a reference to the war against Holland).
Among the king's bounties he counts his own grant of freedom and
ends by saying that there is nothing he is not ready to sacrifice for
him, even the freedom he had regained. It was all a touch hyper-
bolic, indeed adulatory, but it was in the style of the time. What
the cold-eyed king thought of it all cannot be known but he listened to him without interruption. His reply was brief but gracious. He was very happy to see a man of Arnauld's worth about
whom he had heard much from those who held him in high esteem
and it was his desire that he should use the gifts God had given him
for the defence of the Church. Although the interview was clearly
at an end Arnauld wanted to express the sorrow he had felt in being
involved in the 'contestations' of the past. But the king cut him
short: 'What is past is past and it is not to be talked about.' He
added that he would be happy if Arnauld never wrote anything
again that would embitter people's minds. Then turning to the
nephew he said, 'M. de Pomponne, I am sure that what you have
witnessed has given you much joy.' Arnauld, profoundly moved by

the royal condescension, was led away to meet other members of the royal family and those who had made the interview possible.[17]

One more interview remained. Péréfixe, who had been excluded from the peace negotiations, was not very pleased about the turn events had taken. He was inclined to resist the meeting with Arnauld, but the king put an end to that: he was not to be more difficult than the pope. So, a few days later, the Bishop of Meaux, M. de Ligny, conducted Arnauld and Dr Lalane to the archbishop and the encounter passed off in apparently friendly fashion. The 'Peace of the Church' seemed assured but there were too many ambiguities in the agreement for it to last. It held for ten years and then the persecution began all over again.

Meanwhile, Arnauld had to turn his mind to other things. He had had a hand in the translation of the New Testament which was mainly the work of M. de Saci who, before the 'peace', had been thrust into prison where he finished his translation of the whole of the Old Testament. But the king had spoken of the defence of the Church and, as Sainte-Beuve said with some wit, the Huguenots always had to pay for peace of the Jansenists. Arnauld had already put in hand a book on the Eucharist in refutation of the minister Claude, to which Le Tellier referred when he met Arnauld. It was a massive work of which Nicole was the principal author; Arnauld contributed to the first volume only. It naturally led to another and very long controversy which kept Arnauld busy for some time to come.[18]

The peace was only apparent. Arnauld and his party thought they had won everything they had asked for, principally a recognition that the Five Propositions were not in the *Augustinus* and that they could go on as before. They had, however, agreed that they would cease writing on the matter. In the new atmosphere they felt that they could undertake the publication of books it had been imprudent to publish earlier. The first edition of Pascal's *Pensées* appeared in 1670, a further edition of the Letters of Saint-Cyran a little later and the New Testament of 'Mons' about the same time. Port-Royal flourished and became a fashionable resort.

Then came the affair of the *Régale*. Louis wanted to extend the royal rights over sees and other benefices which had hitherto been exempt. Four bishops resisted him, including Henry Arnauld of Angers. Antoine kept quiet about this but his views were either known or suspected. When his nephew Pomponne invited him to declare publicly that he had had nothing to do with the resistance he indignantly rejected the proposal. All his sympathies were, in fact, with the bishops but he did not see why he should be asked to say what his views were. That anyone should ask him to declare that he was neutral on the subject, he wrote to Pomponne, 'is indeed so shameful a thing that I cannot understand how anyone could have proposed it to me…. For of those who thought such a declaration sincere some would take us for cowards, others for deceivers and the king would laugh at us…'.[19] There were those, he continued (meaning no doubt his nephew), who thought that the holy house (Port-Royal) would be brought to ruin, but even that would not deter him from saying what he thought to be the truth. Since he was in constant contact with Angélique de Saint-Jean he probably thought he had the community with him. The letter goes on, Arnauld twists and turns and is evidently unhappy about the whole matter. He shows all his old intransigence. If he were formally asked to express his mind he would do so and his answer would not please the king. As usual, he was in the mood to disregard the consequences of such a statement, and in a Paris that was full of gossip, the general sense of his letter to Pomponne may have reached the king's ears. Arnauld, now as earlier, seems to have been willing to take on the role of a latter-day Samson, but he did not take into account that he might bring the temple down on the heads of others.

In fact, and although Arnauld did not realise it, the situation was precarious. It needed only slight and trivial incidents to revive opposition to Arnauld and Port-Royal. In the ten years from the 'peace' to Arnauld's exile two matters caused trouble. Choiseul, now Bishop of Tournai, drew up a list of laxist propositions which he intended to send to Rome for condemnation. It would be another nail in the Jesuit coffin! He asked Nicole, an excellent Latinist, to translate the document. At first Nicole refused, perhaps sensing the danger, but then, obliging as he was by nature, he gave way. News got about that *he* had drawn up the list and, indeed, that Arnauld had had a hand in it. Neither allegation was true, but when the king heard of the matter he was not pleased. In 1679 Arnauld received a message from the archbishop that the 'assemblies' he held in the Faubourg S. Jacques (near Port-Royal) were causing people to talk, the king did not like them and they must cease. Louis had a fixed idea that Arnauld was at the centre of a cabal, though in view of the king's enormous power, one wonders what exactly he feared. Other disturbing rumours reached Arnauld's ears, and he decided that he must go into exile. He would never be free to express his mind in a France where the régime was becoming ever more oppressive. After making his arrangements, gathering his papers and necessary books and sending a warning only to Angélique de Saint-Jean, he set off on the morning of 17 June in disguise, travelling towards Mons in a coach and six horses. This small territory was independent of France and there he could be safe, at least for a while.

For the next fourteen years Arnauld's life was that of an exile. Over the years he moved from place to place, sometimes when he or his friends got wind of dangers from the French king's spies, sometimes on account of the war between France and Holland, and sometimes at the urging of his friends, notably Neercassel, the Vicar-Apostolic of the United Provinces. For a long period he lived safely at Utrecht or nearby with Dutch Catholics whose sobriety of morals and very liturgical worship he came to admire. Other journeys took him to Ghent, Courtrai, Tournai and Antwerp. Arnauld was now in his seventies and he had to travel by the uncomfortable transport of the day, great lumbering coaches, private chaises and, in Holland, the more comfortable public boats along the canals. He seems to have withstood all this remarkably well although he was afflicted with bronchial asthma which the climate of the Low Countries did nothing to improve. Everywhere he went he settled to writing after a day or two, attacking anything and everything that seemed to him to be contrary to *la vérité*. He wrote to both the Archbishop of Paris and Chancellor Le Tellier that all he wanted was to live quietly and in solitude. As Sainte-Beuve remarks drily, he was promising more than he could deliver.[20]

Thanks to devoted Flemish friends Arnauld was finally able to settle in Brussels. His house backed on to the gardens of the residence of the Oratorians, who had always been friendly. He went out very little and, at one time, when he took the air in his own little garden an awning was spread over part of it to protect him from spying eyes. One would have thought that this was likely to draw attention to the fact that an important person was living as an unidentified occupier of what, in effect, was someone else's house. But perhaps only the Oratorians could see the awning.

His way of life, which hardly varied through the years, is described by Guelfe, his constant companion and amanuensis.

He usually rose at 5.00 a.m. when he prayed and recited the Matins and Lauds of the Breviary of Paris, edited under the auspices of his enemy, Archbishop Harlay. He said Mass almost daily between 7.00 and 8.00, before which it was his habit to read the Instructions of M. de Saci or those of M. de Fossé on the scriptures. With the New Testament he read P. Quesnel's *Réflexions morales*. In addition, he always had a spiritual book to hand, either M. Le Tourneux's commentaries on the epistles and gospels of the liturgical year, or some other book which he read after Mass. He then said Terce, after which he worked until the midday meal which was preceded by Sext. During the meal there was more reading of the scriptures, followed by edifying conversation. Afterwards, the little company took a turn in the garden until about 2.00 when, after saying None together, they retired to work until 7.00 p.m. or so. Before that there was private prayer and at 7.00 all said Vespers. After this there was supper when the order was the same as for dinner. Compline was said at 9.00 and for the servants there were prayers in French. Then all retired.[21]

This edifying and quiet life was the *obbligato*, as it were, to a ceaseless polemic that continued until Arnauld died. Opposition was by now an ingrained habit; he could never bring himself to write a calm exposition of some point of Christian doctrine which would have edified the many people he thought were in need of such teaching. As Bossuet observed on one occasion, and Arnauld agreed with him, he could only write *against* some view which he regarded as heterodox or misleading. With a different cast of mind he could have written something of permanent worth. His erudition was recognised by all, even by some of his enemies. He had great competence as a theologian and knew the whole range of writers from the Fathers of the Church to the Scholastics to those of his own time. Like so many of his contemporaries he knew the Vulgate very well, and he was well acquainted with the Greek New Testament, though it is not clear that he knew Hebrew. He kept abreast of current affairs in the Low Countries, in Rome (through his agent Du Vaucel) and in France. In spite of the secrecy of his lodging there was a constant coming and going of visitors – Edward Ruth d'Ans, Pontchâteau and others – as well as occasional residents like Duguet and Quesnel. All of them brought new information and a certain amount of rumour, some of which stimulated Arnauld to further polemical efforts, notably his controversy with the gentle Malebranche. One or two other events and controversies require some mention as they throw some light on Arnauld's character and activities.

Once in comparative safety, Arnauld wished to have his various publications distributed in France and, as early as 1680, with the help of friends and certain contacts in France, he set up a whole network. Packages of books, one consignment hidden in a barrel of biscuits, were sent via Soissons and Rouen to intermediaries who would pass them on to booksellers for sale. The king's police got wind of the traffic between 1680 and 1682 and, in the latter year, they uncovered the smuggled books at both distribution points. At the same time they discovered the names of the assignees, an Abbé Dubois (*vere* Gilles) and a Père Du Breuil, an Oratorian of Rouen. Abbé Dubois, though seriously ill, was imprisoned in the Bastille, condemned to the galleys and died on his way to Marseilles. Père Du Breuil was also imprisoned, treated most brutally, and for years until his death was sent from one prison to another all over France.[22] Le Tourneux, the preacher and liturgical scholar, was also involved and it was only thanks to friends in high places that he escaped the fate of the rest.[23]

Arnauld's reaction to these events was at first somewhat surprising. He seemed more concerned with the loss of his books than with the arrest of the two priests. But when he heard what had been done to them he grieved deeply. In the years that lay ahead he never forgot Père Du Breuil and, through Quesnel, managed to keep in touch with him and console him as best he could. In a way Arnauld never grew up. Anyone else would have realised that unlawful trafficking in forbidden books would have placed people in jeopardy; one would have thought that there were other ways of getting his books into France. For years the Jansenists had had books published under false imprints, usually those of firms in the Low Countries although printed in France, and it would not have been impossible for him to do the same. Packets of papers can be smuggled more easily than hardbound books. Nor did these transactions do him any good with the king who only wanted him to keep quiet: Arnauld really had only himself to blame for his death in exile.

Louis XIV's regime was undoubtedly repressive and Arnauld knew it. The king persecuted people either through his own officers or through those of Harlay, Archbishop of Paris. Communities such as the Institut de l'Enfance near Bordeaux were brutally suppressed on the ground that they harboured or were in contact with undesirable persons, which was untrue, and a number of people on a list were proceeded against under civil law for an offence that would now be regarded as purely ecclesiastical. But political questions did crop up, though one, at least, did not concern Louis.

Arnauld's defence of English Catholics at the time of the alleged Oates Plot was perhaps excusable, especially as Jesuits were accused of involvement, but his broadside against William of Orange after the abdication of James II was both stupid and dangerous. Arnauld had enjoyed the hospitality of the United Provinces and at one time it looked as if it would be the only safe refuge for him. Yet in a tract that he issued he called William a 'new Absalom, new Herod, new Cromwell, new Nero'! When, once again, he had to seek refuge in the United Provinces it was only thanks to the skill and devoted care of Dutch Catholics that he was able to escape detection.

Then, unexpectedly, a certain turn of events gave Arnauld hope that he might be allowed to return to France. The king had appointed Pomponne a Minister of State; when Arnauld heard of this he sent Guelfe to a battle camp near the Netherlands (which Louis was invading) to see what the possibilities were. But Pomponne, always timid and always in awe of his master, was horrified, and he bundled Guelfe back as quickly as he could. On another, later occasion, when the king asked after his uncle's health, Pomponne failed to take the opportunity to put in a good word for Arnauld, to suggest for instance that now he was getting old and might safely be readmitted to France. But if Pomponne was timid he was also a statesman with ambassadorial experience and he was probably well aware that his uncle would cause trouble in some way or another.

However, to Arnauld the atmosphere seemed favourable, for rumours had circulated that there was a possibility of his returning to France. But he would do so only on his own terms, which are revealed in letters addressed to friends in France and which were meant to be shown to people in high places. They read rather like a treaty drawn up by one sovereign power to another! He would deal only with the king. He absolutely refused to have anything to do with Harlay, who was not to be an intermediary, and he, Arnauld, would not even pay him a formal visit if he returned to

France. His return must not be construed as a sort of reprieve for some crime which he had never committed. The king must be enlightened on the doctrinal points at issue and, especially, that Arnauld was not a heretic. True, he differed from the Jesuits on the matter of grace but the difference was no more than a matter of dispute in the schools. On Church matters the king should trust to the judgement of the bishops and not simply to that of Archbishop Harlay and Père de la Chaise (the king's confessor). He was not the leader of a sect and his book, the *Fantôme de Jansénisme,* should be properly examined by an episcopal commission to show that Jansenism did not exist! He agreed that he would not write against the Jesuits provided they did not write against him. Finally, he requested that the case against Père Du Breuil should be re-examined and that some satisfactory arrangement should be made about Port-Royal which by now was visibly declining, all recruitment having been forbidden for a long time. He would be responsible to the king alone, through Pomponne, for, as he concluded, 'I have nothing to fear except false reports.... I will keep myself quiet and hidden in my little household. I will see only very few people and I shall feel tranquil because I shall be assured that I have the approval of my Prince and I shall have nothing to fear from spies and malicious gossip.'[24]

It is all utterly incredible and whether or not it ever got to the king's ears is not known. In any case, it is more interesting as providing an insight to Arnauld's mind at this time. He was nearly eighty and his unshakeable conviction that he was right remained unchanged. The wrongs that he had suffered burned deeply in his soul. He was an honourable man, he had done nothing but seek the truth and that was not a crime. He had apparently forgotten that his rigidity at the time of Choiseul's attempt at reconciliation had brought nothing but suffering to Port-Royal and had destroyed its reputation in the eyes of the king. He could not see that for the king he was a disturbing and potentially rebellious subject. In fact, and for all his devotion to the monarchy, he totally failed to see the king's viewpoint at all. There was nothing of the diplomat in him, nothing of the psychologist, and here he was still arguing his case like a lawyer. He was almost obsessed by Harlay's iniquity – and here we can have some sympathy with him – but he misread Père de la Chaise, the king's confessor, who was honest and a man of peace. Hope of a return to France began to fade, and Arnauld began to realise with great sadness that he would never again see the country he loved so much.

It was not, however, until the last two years of his life that he gave up all hope of returning to France. Writing to Nicole in 1692 he expresses his resignation to exile: 'Thanks be to God, I am as content to be here in this little house as if I were at liberty in Paris. True, I have hardly left it for the four months, more or less, since I came here…. As for the time that remains for me to live, it is not of great importance to me whether I spend it in retirement or enjoying greater freedom [elsewhere].' In any case he was not alone and was visited by his Jansenist friends. To the list we can add M. de Sainte-Marthe, a former confessor at Port-Royal, Du Vaucel from Rome, the historian, Tillemont, and Mme de Fontpertuis, a loyal supporter. Arnauld must have realised that such visits from his friends would have been impossible in Paris.

In the light of his own situation his attitude to the Revocation of the Edict of Nantes (1685) is of considerable interest. Although he always saw himself as a faithful and loyal Catholic his position was not entirely dissimilar to that of the Huguenots. *He* had a conscientious objection to the ruling of Rome and indeed of the majority view in France about the *fait*. The Huguenots also conscientiously believed that their faith was the faith of the gospel and they were persecuted for it far more severely than Arnauld ever had been. Whether he ever held the thesis that 'error has no rights' is not clear, but he certainly acted as if he did. The Huguenots were heretics, their doctrine was a false one, they had torn the seamless robe of the Church and must be shown the errors of their ways, and he had spent a good deal of his time trying to do that. Continual efforts had been made by others throughout the century but the Huguenots had remained steadfast. They had been given every chance to renounce their errors but they had repudiated all advances, and had refused to see the light. Neither the king nor Arnauld could believe that such people could hold to their faith in good conscience. To use the conventional phrase, they were *culpably* ignorant. Hence measures to 'compel them to come in' were justifiable. Arnauld invoked the Roman Emperor's measures against the Donatists to justify the royal repression! At the same time he remained troubled and he is not always consistent. Writing to Mme de Fontpertuis he says, 'The Declaration took us by surprise here but since we are good Catholics there has been much joy'. One suspects irony though that was not Arnauld's style. But, he goes on, 'Apparently those in Holland (he meant the Catholics) will be considerably alarmed'.[25] And with reason! But this statement shows that he was well aware of the adverse effects the declaration might have in countries outside France. In fact, the authorities of the United Provinces took no action.

When writing to his agent in Rome, however, his embarrassment is a little more obvious: 'I think that they have not done too badly in Rome in refusing to have any public rejoicing over the Revocation of the Edict of Nantes and the conversion (!) of so many heretics, for in France they have used somewhat violent methods which, however, I do not think are unjust. But it is better not to be triumphant about it'. 'The methods were not unjust' – that phrase reveals a good deal of Arnauld's thinking. Before this he had written another letter to the same correspondent which sounded an equally unpleasant note: 'No doubt you have received the great news of the king's Declaration by which he has annulled the Edict of Nantes and has repressed all worship, public or private, other than that of the Roman Catholic religion. He has given the ministers nine months to make up their minds either to be converted or to be banished for ever from the kingdom. But they have been assured that those who become converts will receive a stipend one third bigger than the one they have received as ministers and [on their death] this will pass to their widows.[26] This attempt to buy off ministers appears too often in this affair and evidently Arnauld did not rise above the morality of his times in giving apparent approval to it. It is an unhappy episode in Arnauld's life and shows that his famous logic was wanting. He was not in France of course and he may not have known that the methods were rather more than somewhat violent, but like so many at the time, he failed to see that conversions under pressure of any kind were a contradiction in terms.

Another cause that attracted his attention in these last years was the permissibility of the reading of the scriptures by the laity in the vernacular. Precipiano, Archbishop of Malines, had imposed severe restrictions on the circulation and use of French versions of the Bible. Arnauld was incensed and he wrote yet another tract, this time to defend the practice of the reading of the Bible. His mind is revealed in a letter to Du Vaucel in 1689. He argues very reasonably that since Pius IV (died 1565) times had changed. Then people wanted to read the scriptures to make up a religion of their own fashioning. Now the position was quite the contrary and, in fact, there was an extraordinary neglect in instructing the people in the gospels and the epistles and in what Jesus Christ requires of them: 'I am convinced that these prohibitions cannot be justified without great sin. It takes away from Christians what is theirs by divine right. For the Gospel was written for those who know nothing but their mother tongue as well as for those who understand Latin. To this I would add that they [the authors of the restrictions] will have to answer before God for the obstacles they put in the way of the conversion of heretics.'[27] Arnauld was thinking of those inclined to be Catholics, who wanted to go on reading the Bible and would be deterred by such prohibitions. At least in this matter he showed a great deal of common sense.

On the other hand his view of the Bible was, with most of his contemporaries, uncritical. It is not surprising then that, with

Bossuet, who egged him on, he vehemently opposed the embryonic higher criticism of Richard Simon, author of the *Critical History of the Old Testament*. Simon had previously criticised the New Testament of Mons and Arnauld had already been in conflict but, like Bossuet, he underrated Simon's work, or rather, totally misunderstood it. He made his own the sentiments of Nicole on the man and his works: 'He is a man of tremendous memory, of much reading but of little judgement. He comes to conclusions on the most important matters for the slightest of reasons and he has an incredible audacity in putting forward his "imaginations" without troubling to take into account the damage they will do to religion.'[28]

Arnauld worked up to the last but the end came quickly. On 1 August he contracted a heavy cold which turned to pleurisy and congestion of the lungs. He lingered for a week and died a little after midnight on 18 August 1694. His heart was taken to Port-Royal and, thanks to the willing co-operation of a Jansenising priest, his body was buried in the church of St Catherine in Brussels. 'For fear of enemies', the place of burial was long kept secret.

This portrait of Antoine Arnauld may seem unduly harsh. It doesn't record the affection of his friends and the esteem in which he was held by men like Bossuet. Some regarded him as a valiant defender of the Church and that is how he saw himself. But it was the Huguenots who had to pay the price. Unlike Bossuet who, when he was a young priest at Metz, tried to understand his opponents and acquired some affection for them, Arnauld never sought reconciliation. The 'enemy' must be vanquished by force of argument and then the only thing for him to do was to submit. Arnauld never really moved beyond the procedures of the theological schools of the time. For him a dialectical victory was a complete victory. Bossuet's later discussions with Leibniz and his attempts at reunion with the Anglicans were beyond Arnauld's thought and feeling. Victory over the Jesuits and the anti-Jansenists, who ranged from bishops to theologians, was all that he sought. Given this

mentality, it was inevitable that Arnauld's whole life should be
spent in controversy, and controversialists do not win the affections
of posterity. Most of his vast output, enclosed in more than forty
volumes, is now of interest only to the research scholar. But one
book, the *Logic of Port-Royal,* in which he had a large hand, had a
future. It was used in France even in this century. Otherwise there
are only his letters which, if republished, would throw light on his
own life and that of his niece Angélique de Saint-Jean, with whom
he kept up a correspondence until she died. They were kindred
spirits, though she proved to be even more intransigent than he
was.

Of his personal piety there can be no doubt. As we have seen,
his day was framed by prayer and his work alternated with it.
However, there seems to be one element missing; it is not clear that
he had a personal devotion to Jesus Christ, nothing, it would seem,
of the ardent feeling for Christ and his Gospel that comes through
the often gloomy commentaries of Le Tourneux on the liturgical
year (though Arnauld read these). In this Arnauld does not measure
up to his sister Angélique who, for all her bossiness and self-doubt,
showed that Christ was a living person to her and the mainstay of
her life. It may be that his untutored sister had much to teach her
learned brother, but it is not apparent that he ever sat at her feet.
He was the youngest son, twenty years lay between them, and he
may have felt that he had to assert himself. Certainly his relationship with Henry, Bishop of Angers, who was only six years younger
than Angélique, was difficult, and Henry showed no interest either
in the literary fame of his brother after the publication of the *De la
Fréquente* or in his defence of Jansenism.

Another factor in his make-up was of course the legal tradition
of his family. As R. A. Knox has said, 'A theologian by trade,
Arnauld was a barrister by instinct, like his father and his grandfather before him. Like his fellow-Jansenists he must always be talking about 'the Truth', but what really mattered to him was his
brief'.[29] The same 'disease' afflicted the nuns of Port-Royal who

met every measure of 'persecution' with appeals (drawn up in correct legal form) to the parliament, to the Primate of All the Gauls (the Archbishop of Lyon) and to the pope. This legalism might be called the 'Arnaldist vice' and was the fruitful source of so much of the trouble that Arnauld and Port-Royal brought upon themselves. It was this same urge to prove his case and to justify himself that prevented Arnauld from becoming the theologian he might have been. Two now obscure theologians, Henry Holden, Doctor of the Sorbonne and Edward Hawarden, Doctor of the University of Douai, members of the persecuted English Catholic community who were teaching at Paris and Douai, showed how it was possible to teach a sound Augustinian-Thomistic theology in the midst of all the Jansenist turmoil.[30]

Arnauld had great intellectual gifts and a very considerable erudition but the first were directed to polemic and the second dissipated in controversial tracts that no one now wishes to read. It seems harsh to say it, but the sum total of Arnauld's work was negative and the heritage he left was damaging to the Church in France.

6

ANGÉLIQUE DE SAINT-JEAN ARNAULD D'ANDILLY

Angélique de Saint-Jean, daughter of Robert Arnauld d'Andilly and niece of the two abbesses Angélique and Agnès, was very different from either of them. A child of the monastery from the age of six, an excellent religious who combined strict observance with personal devotion, she was, fatally, an intellectual. Her aunt Angélique had the strong intellect of the Arnaulds but she turned it to practical matters. Agnès, more subtle than her sister, saw the life of the spirit as all-important. The swirling and bitter controversies of the time forced themselves on her attention but, apart from her official role as abbess, she took little part in them. Angélique de Saint-Jean, on the other hand, saw the dispute about grace as a matter of life and death. To sign the Formulary without reservations was to betray all that Port-Royal (and the Arnauld family?) stood for. Whether she ever read the formidable *Augustinus* is doubtful but Père Rapin SJ (a hostile witness) said that she knew Greek and Latin and read the Fathers of the Church in the original. In spite of her protestations to the contrary she was well-informed on all the theological issues concerning grace and, unhappily, Antoine Arnauld was always at her elbow to keep her up to date. Like him she could not resist an argument and, more from him than from her grandfather, she seems to have inherited the Arnauld itch for legal forms, appeals against the abuse of the law and what is called due process.

Yet she has attracted the admiration of some writers, notably Sainte-Beuve, who speaks of her 'masculine' intellect and more than once uses the term 'noble'. Others have described her as haughty; she certainly knew how to keep people at a distance when she wanted to. Her first confrontation with Archbishop Péréfixe showed him that she was a superior spirit and he rapidly realised that she was the leader of the resistance. Unfortunately for her and the community her intellectualism was doctrinaire and rigid; she was totally convinced that she and the Arnaldists possessed *la vérité* which they proclaimed ceaselessly. Jacqueline Pascal (Sr Euphémie) was of a similar mentality and she and Angélique were close friends, though the latter seems to have taken little from the broader culture that Jacqueline brought to the monastery. She knew the scriptures (in the Vulgate version) and constantly quoted from them but it is difficult to discern in anything she wrote or said any echoes of secular literature. Her great mentor, however, was her uncle Antoine Arnauld (who was not much older than herself), who constantly instructed and counselled her. She could be said to have been his theological other self. She was enormously tenacious and became even more unbending than he was. She seems to have suffered from a theological tunnel-vision of her uncle's form of Jansenism which was not that of Jansen. The influence of Blaise Pascal must be added to this in some measure. Though they do not seem to have been intimate she admired his brilliance, and his final intransigence must have been greatly to her liking. Indeed, she must be grouped with the intransigents of Jansenism whose motto could have been *Fiat iustitia, ruat caelum.* It was better that Port-Royal should go to ruin rather than that there should be compromise about the sacred *vérité.* As she wrote to Antoine at the time of Archbishop's Péréfixe's visitation: 'We must live dangerously. Perhaps we shall be the foot-soldiers of Ahab's army who must go first into battle', a battle that she and the community were bound to lose. She agreed completely with the sentiment of Jacqueline Pascal: 'Since the bishops have no more courage than girls, it is for us to have the courage of bishops. But if we alone are left to defend *la vérité* we must also die for it.'[1] Angélique and the party she led in the community became almost obsessed with the thought of martyrdom, though no one asked them to lay down their lives for what they believed. Unhappily, this unbalanced and unhealthy mentality was a distortion of certain sayings of Saint-Cyran which they applied to their own situation.

There is another side to Angélique's character. Although her bearing was austere, especially to those she wanted to keep at a distance, including certain members of the community, she could also show great charm. Generally, she repressed her feelings and this caused her great suffering, as she revealed in her *Relation de Capitivité*, when she was separated from her community. For she could also be very affectionate, sometimes excessively so. She seems to have been a successful Mistress of the Children, a post she held for twenty years, but she became too attached to some of them. When a favourite pupil, Mlle de Bagnols, chose the 'world' rather than the religious life, she took it very hard. As Mistress of the Novices, an office she held for many years, she had a decisive influence on the second Port-Royal (after the death of her aunt, Mère Angélique) and rather spoilt two young religious, Sr Christine Briquet and Sr Eustoquie de Brégy, who were her ardent disciples and showed themselves to be both sharp and very pert in their interviews with the archbishop. Angélique also had a strong affection for her cousin Antoine le Maître, Saint-Cyran's famous convert, and for another cousin, Le Maître de Saci, who became the spiritual director of Port-Royal and who for years was her friend and counsellor.

In the 'persecution' that lasted from 1664 to 1669 Angélique is the dominant figure in the community, the core of resistance, and it was she who imprinted a certain view of Port-Royal on posterity.

Born in 1624, Angélique Lefèvre de S. Jean was the daughter of Robert Arnauld d'Andilly and Catherine Lefèvre de La Boderie, whose father was for a time ambassador to England. Both her father and her mother moved in court circles and were well-to-do. At the early age of six she was sent to Port-Royal (at Paris) which already housed five of her aunts. Although she spent short holidays at home in what are described as *les beaux domaines* of Andilly, she preferred the monastery, and at the early age of seventeen she entered the novitiate. Unfortunately we know nothing of the education she was given in the 'school'. As for her spiritual formation she can hardly have known Saint-Cyran personally as she was only fourteen when he was imprisoned. Perhaps she heard some of his sermons and since he had a very great influence on her aunt Angélique (but less so on Agnès) she must have received a good deal of information from her. He wrote to her, however, from prison and he made a deep impression which lasted for the rest of her life. In the addresses to the community, referred to as *Misericordes,* years later when she was abbess, his name occurs several times. His first letter to her on entering the religious life in 1641 emphasises the need for a deep interior life if she was to be a true religious. It was a lesson she took to heart. Almost immediately after her profession in 1644 she was made Mistress of the Children and a little later Mistress of the Novices. Both Angélique and Agnès saw in her a future successor to themselves.

In the years from 1648 to 1659 she moved between the reconstituted community at Port-Royal-des-Champs and the house in Paris. In the first she was appointed sub-prioress, an office she continued to hold in Paris. While at Port-Royal-des-Champs she fell gravely ill, the third of her considerable illnesses. Although tuberculosis had earlier been suspected, this last illness is not specified. If it was tuberculosis it may account for the rather feverish way in which she participated in the disputes that had already begun. There was, however, another event, far less dramatic, but of far greater consequence. She became the historiographer of Port-Royal, first collecting materials for the hoped-for canonisation of her aunt Angélique! Although Angélique de Saint-Jean was a woman of complete integrity, as future events would show, she created the enduring image of Port-Royal. It is difficult even now to reconstruct the history and spirit of the community as it was actually lived. One thing is certain, she suppressed facts that did not suit her view of things, notably her stormy relationship with Flavie Passart who abounded in visions, dreams, locutions and miracles of healing. Angélique was also anti-mystical and, unforgivably, she destroyed some writings of Mère Geneviève Le Tardif which had a mystical element. Angélique's practice and theory of prayer was discursive and intellectual, rather like a certain tradition, used in her time, of the Exercises of St Ignatius!

However, her accounts of Port-Royal were persuasive if only because she generally wrote well. But, like so many writers of Port-Royal, inside the community and outside it, she had a weakness for saying too much, to the detriment of her style. In her *Relation de Captivité*, for instance, there are long, winding sentences, one of them running to twenty-five printed lines (pp.44-45). In mitigation it must be said that she was writing under emotional stress and, as she said, *currente calamo,* and she never corrected it. At the same time, she had a gift for phraseology and may well have sharpened up some of the sayings of her aunt Angélique.[2]

After 1656, of the Formularies issued, one was withdrawn and another not implemented until Louis XIV took power and Péréfixe was able to take up his office as Archbishop of Paris in 1664. The community knew they were under threat and, to prepare for eventualities the abbess, Agnès Arnauld, 'assisted by Angélique de Saint-Jean', drew up a document to advise the nuns what should be done if the abbess was removed, if strangers were appointed in her place and if they were deprived of the sacraments and/or exiled. Cécile Gazier, who was pro Port-Royal, remarks that the 'Avis' seems to have been more the work of Angélique de Saint-Jean than of Agnès: 'There is in the little work a decisiveness, a deep faith, and absolute submission to the decrees of Providence, and in some places a certain grandeur, as in her entreaty to the religious "never to agree to traffic with their souls", but there is also something of the legalist spirit and a welcoming, almost a desire, for combat which would have been unknown in the time of Angélique'.[3]

The observation of 'a desire for combat' seems very just and reveals a good deal about Angélique de Saint-Jean. Although he admired her, Sainte-Beuve agreed: she had a penchant for *le démon de contestation,* a sentiment echoed by Nicole who did not get on with her; she was 'far too scientific' – by which he seems to have meant too much of an intellectual, much given to dialectics. This is revealed in her encounters with Mme de Rantzau during her captivity.

On 9 June 1664 the archbishop came to Port-Royal de Paris for an official visitation and he interrogated members of the community one by one, even including the lay-sisters. It was on this occasion that Christine Briquet and Eustoquie de Brégy 'performed'. They turned their interview into near comedy – at the expense of the archbishop – and immediately afterwards they wrote down their account of it which was distributed all over Paris. The encounter of Marguerite de S.Gertrude with the archbishop was stormy. She had formerly belonged to the Congregation of Notre Dame in Flanders and had been initiated into Jansenism by the theologians of that place. At one point she flounced out and then came back to apologise. Later she recanted her Jansenism and then retracted her recantation.

Angélique de Saint-Jean was the next to be interrogated but the interview was very different: 'Grave and serious, there was much politeness in word but some hard-hitting in substance. Angélique was a person who inspired respect for her great intelligence, her profound Christian faith, too much imbued however with the controversies in which her friends and the whole house (?) were involved'. Nor, says Sainte-Beuve, did she disguise the fact that she had read all that had been written about these matters.[4]

The Archbishop began by saying that she should not waste her time on all that: 'As far as you [the nuns] are concerned you should try to put aside those vexatious affairs. Now an easy opportunity is offered you to do so'. Angélique rather threw him off his stroke by unpredictably bringing up past attacks on Port-Royal, a matter that had evidently been rankling for years. 'Monseigneur', she replied,

'I do not think it is so easy to escape from the persecution to which we have been exposed for twenty-five years.' She was referring to the imprisonment of Saint-Cyran in 1638 when she was only fourteen! She continued: 'Our trouble did not begin with the matter of the signature and I doubt whether it will be the end. I confess that if we had nothing but our experience to persuade us that all that is asked of us is but a sign of obedience, it would be very difficult for us to believe that there may not be some other undeclared reason for the way we are being treated today.' This may have been a guess but it was very near the truth. She recalls that the day before, in his address to the community, he praised them for the edification they had always given, for their piety and their regular observance – all to their great confusion. There was then only one point on which they were suspect, obedience to their ecclesiastical superiors: 'Allow me to say, Monseigneur, that if we are accused of that fault it is only two years since that we are guilty of it but it is for twenty-five years that we have been ceaselessly harassed, as today, by continual threats based on calumnies which have been invented about this house.' [5]

As an argument it is not of great consequence. No one accused Port-Royal of disobedience in 1638 or for years afterwards and obedience was the crucial point. Quite apart from the pressure from the king and Péréfixe's personal inclinations (and at this time he wished to be benevolent), he was their official superior. However, as Angélique knew, there were greater issues at stake, namely obedience to Church authority as represented by the pope. Ultimately it was the wretched question of the *droit* and the *fait* foisted into the controversy by Arnauld and Nicole, and whatever Angélique did not know, she knew all about that. Her mention of 'attacks' over the years and of the calumnies that were spread about the community was a pretty clear reference to the Jesuits, some of whom, like Père Brisacier, had 'invented' them and had called forth an indignant reply from both Arnauld and Pascal. That, however, had nothing to do with Péréfixe, though he would have been aware

191

of it. In reply he took up the case of Saint-Cyran (about which he knew a good deal as he had been in the household of Richelieu) and he launched into a justification of the cardinal. That did not cut any ice with Angélique who had a profound veneration for Saint-Cyran. Péréfixe did not realise, she wrote later, with what horror she listened to such accusations against the holiest man she had ever known who was so attached to the Church that one could say it was his unique passion. However, she said nothing, though she suspected that the expression on her face revealed her feelings. There the matter rested.

Other interrogations followed until 14 June when the archbishop addressed the whole community. All had been in vain; the measured responses of Angélique and the pert ripostes of Christine Briquet and Eustoquie de Brégy had done nothing to turn the archbishop from his purpose. In fact, the result had been pre-ordained and, perhaps unwittingly, he allowed the nuns to see what the whole visitation and interrogations were really about. The community had been contaminated by the Jansenists: 'You prefer the private opinions of a little handful of people to those of the pope and your archbishop. Those people have prejudiced you and drawn you into supporting their party. I do not wish to pass judgment on their intentions but perhaps they will prefer to see you ruined than that you should submit what is desired of you. They are quite happy to have such a community on their side. You are a great body, you are virtuous religious and that makes a great impression. So they do everything they can to hold you to their opinions. You will not convince me that you have not read their writings, or at least several of them, as I see from your answers. Some of you say the same things as are in their sheets and in the rubbishy things [*paperasses*] they publish'.[6]

It was not exactly conciliatory but it was near the mark and some of it seems to have been addressed to Angélique in particular. His was the official view, or at least that of the court, and probably of others too. The community had been seduced and the real

enemy was Arnauld and those who supported him. The archbishop was striking at the Arnaldian Jansenists under orders. Port-Royal
had been cleared of the solitaries and Arnauld, Nicole and others
were in hiding. It was a policy that looked like succeeding.

There were, however, other defenders of the community. Great
ladies like the Duchess de Longueville and Mme de Guéménée
were among their supporters and the latter made her feelings
known in very public fashion at court. But to no avail. For his part
the archbishop took little account of the agony of conscience which
the nuns were suffering. Moreover, most of the community, which
was very large (about one hundred and fifty), and of very varying
attainments, knew little of the theological implications of the
whole affair. There can be little doubt that Angélique de Saint-Jean,
whom the archbishop rightly saw was the spearhead of the resistance, had indoctrinated a few of the community and *they* knew
more than was good for them.[7] In the event only a dozen (and then
seven more) were imprisoned. The prevalent view of the community was that Saint-Cyran, for whom they had a great regard, was
the friend of Jansen, Antoine Arnauld had defended him in print,
and they could not believe that the saintly bishop (as they called
him) could be a heretic. In other words, their resistance was based
on personal considerations and could not be described as theological. It is not at all clear that the abbess, Mère Agnès, endorsed her
niece's views, and her sister, Mère Angélique, while appreciating her
niece's distinguished qualities, once expressed the view that they
could either be for the good or could lead her into trouble.

The archbishop's other observation that 'the party' was willing
to sacrifice the community for the sake of their views was also
uncomfortably close to the truth. Whether or not he knew it, it was
a fact that Angélique de Saint-Jean was in constant correspondence
with Arnauld and, it seems, he egged her on. No doubt unwittingly, he did not realise that what he was doing would lead to disaster
for, as Bremond remarked, he was the least reflective of men. He
was utterly convinced of the rightness of the distinction of the *droit*

and the *fait* and he was concerned to gain a victory over the enemy through his niece.

The question of the *droit* and the *fait* was the heart of the matter, and in view of the very severe treatment that was meted out to the community it is appropriate that something more should be said about it. Bremond, who had no very high regard for the community, except Mère Agnès, is both generous and just on this subject. Using an article written by a Jesuit, Père Gazeau, he sums up the position along the following lines[8]. In view of the uncertainty of several Gallican theologians, including Péréfixe and Bossuet, about extending infallibility (whether of the Church or the pope) to a dogmatic fact, they had no right to demand an oath from the nuns. Gazeau wrote that the reasons Bossuet presented to them 'were such that *they ought to have refused the signature pure and simple*',which they were willing to do, as they declared solemnly many times. Gazeau continues, 'The poor sisters were confirmed by Bossuet in their fear that [in signing] they would be committing a sin [perjury] in testifying to something as true that could have been false'. That was in fact the very source of their conscientious agony. Furthermore, Bremond points out, Gazeau took over the argument which Fénelon, who had suffered on account of inaccurate statements in his *Maximes des Saints*, used later on. Bossuet could have distinguished between Jansen's *meaning* and what he wrote. Fénelon, perhaps wise after the event, was able to do this: 'The internal meaning of an author which *the Church cannot judge* is different from the external meaning of a text which the Church can judge'. What, said Gazeau, the nuns were asked to accept was that Jansen held ideas that were frightful (*affreuses*). What the Church was asking for was the condemnation of a *text* about which, as Agnès said, they knew nothing. As Bremond concludes, 'She would not have let all the doctors indoctrinate the nuns at their leisure and prepare them for war. In short, the house of prayer would not have become the citadel of a party. At least it is possible to think so.'

In any case Péréfixe was acting *ultra vires*. The papal bull had not mentioned communities of women but the royal ordinance did. It is not clear what went on unofficially or whether the king gave verbal instructions to the archbishop.[9] But between April and June Angélique may have got wind of something; hence her remark to the archbishop that there was some undeclared purpose to the inquisition. Arnauld, however, decided to intervene with a tract, stuffed with patristic quotations, pleading with the archbishop to spare the community. He may have begun to see the effects of his actions. At this stage, at least, he showed that he did not want the nuns to suffer.

But suffer they did and in a way that neither he nor they could have expected. The archbishop returned on 21 August to pronounce his sentence. He seems to have arrived in a bad mood. These women were infuriating, he was fed up with them, and feeling pressed between the upper millstone of the king and the lower one of the nuns, he gives the impression that he had been driven to extreme measures. First he declared that they were rebellious, stubborn and disobedient and forthwith prohibited them from receiving the sacraments. After a short interval, which he spent avoiding Mme du Fossé and the Princesse de Guéménée, he went back to the nuns, some of whom he found weeping and lamenting and others protesting that the excommunication (for such it was) was legally dubious. At this he lost his temper and his dignity. As the Abbess de Ligny, a sister of the Bishop of Meaux and a calm and holy woman, approached to speak to him he abused her in the most unepiscopal language. 'Shut up', he said. 'You are nothing but a stubborn and proud little woman. You've got no mind and you get yourself mixed up in matters of which you understand nothing'. And, his anger mounting, he added 'You are nothing but a pretentious silly, a little ignorant fool. You don't even know what you want to say. Your very look shows it. It is written all over your face.'[10] All this and a good deal more was written up almost immediately and sent to Mlle de Vertus and circulated by her all over Paris, as were all the other

Relations of the previous interviews. The archbishop became the laughing-stock of the town. But it is all a sad reflection on the spiritual state of Port-Royal. How could the nuns have prayed with any tranquillity of soul when they were caught up in all this, discussing it with each other and, in anything but a spirit of charity, making a very mockery of their lawful superior? The first Port-Royal was dead. Agnès, no longer abbess, and thinking of the *'chers defunts'* (the 'dear dead') Angélique and M. Singlin, wrote in a letter to an old friend: 'When I think of those two and how they are looking on all that is happening I don't know what to say except to express my approval of what they approved and with them to adore the will of God whose ways are incomprehensibly wise and hidden in impenetrable mysteries. If he has chosen this way to save us what matters all the rest...'. [11] *They* had not approved contestation and involvement in worldly disputes that had nothing to do with the community. Hers was a voice from the past.

Five days later the archbishop came to complete the sentence he had begun. He arrived with the Civil Lieutenant, the Knight of the Watch, the Provost, four commissaries, twenty police officers and about a hundred archers. He could not have made his plan more public or more offensive. It was as if he was saying that there was a new Fronde which must be ruthlessly suppressed. Apparently he feared some resistance though from whom is not clear. If the people around the monastery, which they loved for its kindness to them, had had their way, he might well have learned what it was like to be booed and threatened by a Paris mob. No doubt the police and the soldiers kept them back.

He arrived about 2.00 p.m. He got out of his coach and, as if to indicate that he was about to perform a solemn liturgical act, he was wearing purple cassock, rochet and mozetta and was preceded by his secretaries and his cross-bearer carrying the archiepiscopal cross. Eight other coaches also drew up in the outer court of the monastery. The archbishop proceeded to the chapter house and at first he seemed calm, but when the abbess, supported by all the nuns, protested and appealed against the sentence he broke out again: 'I don't care a fig for your protests. Protest, appeal, do what you want, you will obey me'; and to the abbess and Agnès he said, 'If all the world is damned and there are only you who go to Paradise, there will be plenty of room for the rest'. He was becoming incoherent.

Then he proceeded to business. Twelve nuns were to be sent away to be confined in various religious houses – for the most part in Paris. The abbess was to got to Meaux, a kindly thought as her brother the bishop would be able to visit her. With Agnès, now old and infirm, would go her niece, Angélique de Sainte-Thérèse Arnauld, who would do her best to look after her. And so the roll-call continued and the coaches were gradually filled up. Robert Arnauld d'Andilly, in the phrase of Sainte-Beuve, the ceremonialist of these occasions, was on hand and, with great difficulty, helped his sister into her coach. None knew where the others were going, those regarded as the ring-leaders were deliberately dispersed with the intention of weakening their resolve and getting them to sign the Formulary. Few did so.

Angélique de Saint-Jean was among the last to leave and while waiting she thought of the Last Judgment as described in Matthew 25.

> The sheep will be separated from the goats without regard for their condition or dignity and each will be placed according to what they had merited by their deeds to the right or the left in a last judgment from which there will be no appeal. *Then* a kind of fear will banish the empty fear of the unjust judgments of men who one day will themselves be judged.

Her view of Jansenism, then, admitted the taking into account of 'merits'! But while waiting she had time to warn the nuns of the perfidy of Sister Flavie Passart, who had signed. Angélique regarded her as a traitor who had informed on the community to the archbishop. She was certainly a dubious character, unstable and filled with ambition to become abbess herself.

197

After seeking the blessing of the archbishop Angélique went to the door where she found her father waiting for her. She fell at his feet and begged his blessing 'for it was but right that he should bless the victim which he was going to offer to God for the third time'.[12] As she made her way from the chapel she met the Civil Lieutenant there who asked her her name; 'I was surprised to hear his voice…because I did not know that he was to take part in the festival. I gave him my name in religion but he asked for my family name. Someone among the people standing round whispered to him, 'Look, here is M. d'Andilly who is accompanying her'. The Lieutenant indicated with a gesture that he knew that and he repeated, 'Your name.' 'Without a blush I pronounced it in a loud voice, *for in such circumstances it is to confess the name of God to confess ours* when there are those who want to dishonour it on account of him.'[13] This 'profession of faith' sounds very bad to our ears and understandably it has been the subject of much criticism. It is, it seems, an expression of inordinate pride in the family name, and also of Angélique's own pride, all the more so as the non-italicised words have often been omitted. Whatever has been said by some authors in justification there still remains too strong a suggestion of family pride. But her mind was concentrated on the idea of martyrdom. She and her fellow sisters were being led like lambs to the slaughter – although in fact they were being sent away to cool their heels (or their heads) in convents where most of them were received kindly if reluctantly. At the least Angélique's language was somewhat inflated and she continued in this vein as her father led her to the altar rail of the chapel: 'I do not doubt that he was sacrificing me to God in his heart like Isaac, although I was not his only child unless I had become so in that moment because he had already *immolated* my two sisters who had left before me. for my part I offered myself and I believe that I could say, "I will offer you a rich sacrifice". For nothing could be wanting in a sacrifice from which I held back nothing and I abandoned myself entirely to God, except for the hope I had in his mercy…'. Angélique was impassioned, excited, a mood that lasted for some days.[14]

Her ageing father kept his courage to the end and led her to the coach through all the people and the soldiers who filled the court.

Angélique was sent to the convent of the Annonciades, also known as the Blue Sisters. Founded at the beginning of the century by Victoria Fornari with the help of her Jesuit confessor at Genoa in 1602, the Paris house had been established as recently as 1622. It was a post-Tridentine community, with a tradition of post-Tridentine piety and, what was unusual in France at the time, of an ultramontane tendency. Angélique realised this almost at once. She passed by a statue of the Immaculate Conception, 'a devotion unknown to us', and when later she heard that Père Nouet SJ was coming to preach a week's retreat, she shuddered and asked to be excused chapel while he was in the house. He had previously preached a strong denunciation of the *De la Fréquente Communion*. She was, however, received kindly and, while some sisters were preparing her room, the superior and others walked up and down with her, evidently trying to size her up. She hid her feelings as well as she could, all the more easily perhaps because the full impact of all that had happened had not sunk in. Her first shock was the room allocated to her. It was right at the top of the house, almost an attic, cut off from the rest of the house by three locked doors which were only opened when a lay sister came to give her her meals or take her to chapel. Angélique now realised that she really was a prisoner. She was however still in her 'excited' mood and was not unduly perturbed. What she felt most keenly was her separation from her beloved community and she worried about what was happening at Port-Royal and how the other eleven exiles were faring. Neither she nor they nor any of the other nuns knew where they were. That was the archbishop's deliberate policy. Once they were separated he thought he could break them down and get them to sign the Formulary. He had some success but not a great deal and it was his form of torture to let Angélique know that one or other had given way. This became particularly painful when she was told that her own sister, who was with Agnès, had signed. In spite of all, however, she never gave way herself. She was treated more rigorously than the others though, as she came to realise, the dear nuns were acting under orders. They were as kind to her as they were allowed to be and Angélique was eventually grateful to them.

Péréfixe had, however, determinedly imposed severe restrictions and had sent her to this sort of convent precisely because he thought the nuns could break her resolve. There was in the community a sister called Mme de Rantzau, the widow of the Maréchal de Rantzau, both Danes who had converted from Lutheranism. Péréfixe regarded her as a very learned woman. She had had some success in converting Protestants; why should she not be able to do the same with Angélique? Were not the Jansenists a kind of Protestant? He did not make much distinction between Lutheranism and Calvinism; they were dissidents who had to be brought back to the fold. Mme de Rantzau should be able to do the trick.

After a week Angélique's mood changed. She was left entirely alone to think her own thoughts. Sleep was sometimes difficult and through the long hours of the day and night she could only consider her own condition and the meaning of all that had happened. From time to time she wept, she felt abandoned, she had no one to consult. She wondered what the archbishop's intentions were. Was she just to stay where she was, doing and saying nothing? Since she was now being punished, was she still to be deprived of holy communion? Hearing that M. de Contes, the Dean of the Chapter, who had shown some friendliness towards Port-Royal, visited the convent from time to time she decided to send a letter through him to the archbishop. This she did, asking that she might be re-admitted to communion. Three days later the archbishop came and interviewed her in the presence of the Mother Superior and Mme de Rantzau. There ensued a long conversation in which he talked some good sense. First and rather boringly he repeated at length all he had previously said to the community at Port-Royal. To this she could do nothing but listen. But he touched the crucial point when he impressed on her the need to separate herself from the quarrel her uncle (Antoine) had with the Jesuits. To sugar the pill he praised *De la Fréquente Communion* and said he had read it many times with profit. Angélique remarked that this did not please the *bonnes Mères*. Then he went on to Jansen. He had submitted his *Augustinus* to the judgement of the pope, as she could read at the front of his book. Angélique replied that she had never read it; she had only come to know of it from the ordinance of the archbishop himself. He allowed himself a little joke: 'At least I hope no one will accuse me of quoting him wrongly.' Angélique then went on to say that all Catholic writers did the same and she did not believe that Jansen suspected that his doctrine was erroneous. What M. d'Ypres had done was in no way singular and one could not draw prejudicial conclusions about the orthodoxy of his teaching from all that. Péréfixe then pointed out the distinction to be made between his reputation as a man and a bishop and what he had written. No one was accusing Jansen of being a heretic. To be a heretic one had to be contumacious and resist correction. Angélique rejected that view. If he was to be praised for showing he was ready to submit to the judgment of the Church and if it had been shown that he had departed from the truth, for her it did not follow that there was an obligation to be ready to condemn him as the author of a heresy. She continued to press the rightness of the distinction of the *droit* and the *fait*. She and Port-Royal were willing to condemn the doctrine but refused to believe that Jansen had taught it. In other words, she rejected the archbishop's suggestion that she should abandon Arnauld's position.

Turning to Mme de Rantzau the archbishop asked what she thought of the matter. She was astonished that anyone should dare to make such distinctions about a papal pronouncement, as 'every judgement of a pope ought to be regarded as an article of faith'. To this Angélique replied that the archbishop himself had distinguished divine faith from human and ecclesiastical faith in the formulary, the latter referring only to the *fait*. 'That is mere quibbling',

remarked Mme de Rantzau contemptuously. This time the archbishop was not pleased with *her* and was visibly embarrassed. At this
point Mme de Rantzau took charge of the conversation. She repeated even more strongly what she had said about the impropriety of
making distinctions. Equal respect was due to everything popes
decided, they were guided by the Holy Spirit and that was true of
the matter in hand. Angélique was irritated. The woman did not
know what she was talking about, and she countered that it was difficult to make a right judgement on a matter of which she had not
even a basic knowledge. (It was the old trouble – only Angélique
and her advisers understood what was at issue.) Mme de Rantzau
replied with some heat, 'I know everything that I can say. I know all
about Moulina [*sic*] and all the rest'. Like many French people then
and now Angélique mocked the lady in her *Relation* for her 'foreign'
pronunciation of Molina. All this was rather petty and the archbishop intervened again and gave vent to his sense of injury regarding all the accounts put about Paris of his behaviour and improper
language at Port-Royal. The writers (the nuns) had accused him
among other things of calling the abbess a *mijaurée*, (a simpering
fool), and he didn't even know the word. All Angélique could say
was that she had not heard it. His complaint went on and on; evidently the mocking descriptions had gone straight to his heart.
Angélique repeated her request – which was the point of the whole
interview – that she might be allowed to receive communion. Since
the nuns at Port-Royal were now in the good hands of the
Visitandines and were in a better disposition (which in fact was
doubtful) he had allowed them to go to communion, but as long as
Angélique still held to her views he would not and could not allow
her the same permission. He would pray for her and would remember her at Mass. Angélique kept a profound silence and she withdrew 'more confirmed by the grace of God in my beliefs than I was
when I entered the room'.

   Perhaps there is little need to comment on this half-serious and
semi-comic discussion which was so much like the various *Relations*

the nuns of Port-Royal had written up and got distributed. As so often in the story of the monastery there was a peculiar mixture of tragedy and comedy. There were great issues at stake but the behaviour of the archbishop and the accounts of the nuns had at times turned the whole affair into near farce.

The whole session must have taken a long time but the debate was not yet over. Mme de Rantzau followed Angélique to her room where they had to wait outside as the lay-sister with the key had not accompanied them. There was a certain amount of repetition. Mme de Rantzau went on about the impropriety of making distinctions regarding papal pronouncements and alleged that the defenders of Jansen had had a fair hearing in Rome. She mentioned the *Journal de Saint-Amour*, attributed to Gorin de Saint-Amour, the Doctor of the Sorbonne, though it had been largely written up by Antoine Arnauld, a fact which Mme de Rantzau could not have known. Angélique said she had not read the book, but she disputed Mme de Rantzau's account. Then ensued a wrangle about the facts, but Mme de Rantzau returned to the charge. Angélique had been misled and that is why she had separated herself from the faith of the Church (which was plainly untrue). The Church had always regarded as heretics those who refused to condemn heresies and their authors. With a display of erudition she then brought up the remote question of the Origenists who had been forced to anathematise Origen. Angélique was equal to her. She cited the reply of St Jerome to John of Jerusalem: he could either condemn Origen along with his errors or he could deny that the errors were Origen's. Defeated on that point, Mme de Rantzau turned to the Council of Chalcedon. Theodoret had been forced to condemn Nestorius. Not to be outdone, Angélique came back with observations about the Fifth and Sixth General Councils, the first of which concerned the Three Chapters (Origenism) and the second Pope Honorius. Reference to him put Mme de Rantzau on the defensive. Honorius had *not* been condemned, the Acts of the Council had been falsified. Angélique replied that according to what she had *heard* all scholars rejected the falsification theory as no more substantial than a dream.

Angélique, understandably, was tiring, and she wanted to break off the conversation as she realised that Mme de Rantzau was not concerned 'to seek the truth'. She replied briefly that the whole dispute about councils was irrelevant as it was accepted that popes and councils could err in matters of fact (which all theologians admit). But Mme de Rantzau, perhaps feeling that she was not winning the battle, then said, 'I know the whole history of the Church. I know. I've got an answer for everything.'[15] With some heat Angélique replied, 'And I, Mother, know nothing. I beg you, leave me and let me pray to God.' At this she turned towards a window, sank to her knees and prayed. After a few moments she had mastered her rising temper and got up to say that if Mme de Rantzau were under orders from the archbishop to say what she had said she would listen 'with all the respect and patience she could muster'. Mme de Rantzau rejected the suggestion; she had said what she had for Angélique's good and out of compassion for her condition. At this point the lay-sister appeared with the key.[16]

It seems worth while to give these somewhat lengthy summaries of Angélique's dialogues with the archbishop and Mme de Rantzau. Although during this second encounter she was somewhat weary, she retained her combative spirit. Now, one feels, she was being the foot-soldier in the army of Ahab, of which she had spoken before. But in her conversation with the archbishop she is very guarded about admitting what she had *read*. Yes, she had *heard* about these matters and perhaps her interlocutors drew the conclusion, which they hinted at, that she had been all too well instructed by Arnauld. Where did she acquire all that information about the Fathers of the Church and the General Councils? It is improbable that the great tomes of the day were in the Port-Royal library. At the same time she reveals the rigidity of her mind. By now she was over forty years old and was completely convinced of the Arnaldian case, though there was always the lurking suspicion, not without foundation, that she did not regard Jansen's doctrine as heretical. Combined with this is the evidence that she was strongly emotional and that it was this which gave power and urgency to her reasoning. She was passionately attached to the cause and she would argue for it with all the strength of her being. Indeed, and for all her undoubted intelligence, she was a little obsessive and was no longer open to arguments from the other side. Like her uncle, harking back to the long legal tradition of her family, she would build up an impregnable case and refute all comers. Although all witnesses, both friendly and hostile, admitted that she was an exemplary religious, all the contention must have been seriously damaging to her spiritual life. And, as her proud statement equating the cause of the Arnauld family with the cause of God shows, she had a large share, too large a share, of the family pride. It was all a great pity.[17]

These encounters disturbed Angélique more deeply than perhaps she first realised. Two days before the visit of the archbishop she had entered upon a time of affliction of spirit. At first her chief anxiety was for the other sisters who had been confined. She and they were involved in the same battle, perhaps because God wanted ed to demonstrate in them 'the powers of victorious grace'. Then the loneliness, the feeling of complete abandonment and the dearth of counsellors who would not harass her and try to convert her bore down on her. She could not sleep and the thought came to her that God was showing her the importance of certain faults she had thought nothing of. One wonders whether these included pride. She suffered a profound sense of humiliation. Perhaps, she mused, God had raised her and her fellow religious too high in giving them a share in the persecution for *la vérité* and she was afraid to lift her eyes to God. Yet at the same time she saw that all her sufferings were very much less than what she deserved if it was his will to treat her according to his justice. 'That first night' her interior sufferings were so great that she ran a high fever and the next day she was so weak that she thought she was really ill. The nuns noticed it with sympathy but, as she said, they did not know the reason.

Her time of desolation, however, was only beginning. First she sought comfort in prayer and in the scriptures, especially in the words of the prophets which she thought would support her in exile. This succeeded in raising her spirits for a time but as she reflected she became more and more convinced that her condition was the just punishment that God was imposing on her. She affirmed to herself that she was submissive to God's will 'even though he should condemn me', but she saw in this a temptation and began to be filled with an 'excessive fear'. So she turned to God and repeated again and again the prayer of Esther: 'God, stronger than all, hear the voice of those who have no hope but in you, and rescue me from my fear' (Esther 14:29, Vulgate). She found some consolation in thus expressing her hope in God and went on to ask for forgiveness: 'In time of trial you take away the sins of those who call upon you' (Tobias 3:13), and 'the words of the wicked have prevailed against us and you look upon our sins with a favourable countenance' (Psalm 64, Vulgate).

How long these thoughts gave her comfort is not clear as she does not date all the phases of her distress. One day, she wrote, her anguish returned with double force and the thought came to her that some time in the distant past she had been wanting in charity. Was she thinking of the animus she had felt towards the enemies of Port-Royal or of the encouragement she gave to some of the younger nuns to write down their interviews with the archbishop, making a mockery of him and smuggling them out so that all Paris could read them? So much in her *Relation* is obscure and it now becomes even more so. Her emotions become more and more conflicting. At the thought of her complete helplessness she prostrated herself before God who was her only hope. She must no longer think of herself and her needs, she must not look for human help; God was giving her the grace to offer all she had suffered and she must hope in his mercy. This gave her some tranquillity of soul but this examination was apparently accompanied by such frightful thoughts that she realised that she had been close to despair. She

206

saw in all this a 'strange temptation', she had come near 'the gates
of darkness which God spoke of to Job', and it was only by the
grace of God that she was able to glimpse them without entering
them as she would have done if he had not given her the necessary
light: 'In that condition I found that prayer and the avowal of my
wretchedness before God, whose justice I adored, were all the
means of help I had. But if the temptation had lasted for a long
time I realised later that I was in danger of extinguishing my lamp
because I had not had sufficient trust to maintain my charity and
the light of my faith.' It seems that she felt herself losing not only
hope in God but her very faith, and this becomes a little clearer in
the next passage.

The agony lasted for some six weeks and it was towards the end
of the period, on 3 October, the Feast of the Holy Angels, that God
revealed to her what the temptation had been. She was meditating
on the words of the psalm, 'Lest you dash your foot against a stone'.
'It came to me that Jesus Christ is himself that stone as well as the
way along which we walk, and although there are those who are
scandalised by the severity of his law and tire of suffering for *la
vérité*, when they are called to do so, and it is they who fall and
break themselves on the stone, there are however others who are
willing to suffer and yet take occasion of their sufferings to fear that
God's rigorous treatment of them is a mark of his wrath which they
have well deserved and, as a consequence of this disposition of
mind which appears to be humble, have less confidence in
approaching Jesus Christ since they feel rejected by him on account
of their unworthiness. It is they too who dash their foot against the
stone, their affection and their love becomes languid and are no
longer inspired by the love God has for them and this temptation
attacks faith as well as hope and charity.'[18]

As has been said above the account is obscure. Angélique's mood
fluctuated during those six weeks but when she is describing what
others go through we have to ask whether she was writing about
herself. There seems little doubt that she experienced a crisis of

faith. Its very foundations were endangered, all her previous formation, both intellectual and spiritual, seems to have been in question and, although it is speculative, it seems that she may have
begun to doubt the validity of what she had fought so long to
maintain. Such a view, moreover, seems to be supported by a letter
to Antoine Arnauld which she wrote in 1666 or 1667 when she was
no longer with the Blue Sisters:

> I remember that I purposely omitted in that Relation a diffi-
> culty that tormented my mind not only in the beginning. It
> came back to me from time to time that I spoke of 'the gates
> of darkness' without saying what I meant. It was in fact a
> mental image that did not trouble me interiorly but its very
> presence was horribly painful…. It was a kind *of doubt about
> all matters of faith* and of Providence. But I did not dwell on
> it for long for fear that by reasoning about it I would let the
> temptation take hold of me. My mind seemed to reject it as a
> certain thought came to me that it [the temptation] would be
> contrary to faith because it included a sort of doubt as if I was
> saying that there would be something uncertain in what
> seemed to me to be *la vérité* and that all I believe about the
> immortality of the soul etc. could be doubtful….[19]

It must be confessed that all is not clear; it is as if after two years'
reflection she could not have admitted that any doubt had ever
entered her mind. And what exactly did she mean by *la vérité* here?
It was a slogan of the Jansenists. *They* had the 'truth' about grace
and they thought it was the whole truth. Why did she again throw
in that phrase about 'the immortality of the soul' which is not at all
on a par with the theology of grace? It seems fair to say that, as
many others have done in times of great spiritual desolation, she
felt the very bases of the whole Christian faith were in question,
including the doctrine of grace. It seems that she looked into the
abyss but drew back, her implicit faith was too strong for her to

give way to any radical doubt, and her trust in God, though shaken for a time, held her back from entering the abyss. The pity of it is that the experience, however painful, could have been creative. If she had let her mind seriously consider the validity of the Jansenism she held to, she might have come to take a different view of it to her own benefit and that of the community.

That Angélique suffered greatly cannot be doubted and, whatever her faults, we cannot but feel compassion for her. In her distress she reveals her strengths and her weaknesses of which one sign was the copious tears she shed very frequently. Although at one time she seems so independent, at others she feels intensely the loss of the companionship of the community and displays very evidently the need for counsellors. Unfortunately she was too dependent on Antoine Arnauld and it might have been better for her if she had been separated from him for even longer than she was. As will appear later on, she did everything in her power to stiffen his resolve.

The Mother Superior of the Blue Sisters, accompanied by Mme de Rantzau, made repeated efforts to break Angélique's determination. One example of this occurred when the two nuns came to her cell and the Superior said that she had some good news for her. Ten of the sisters had signed the Formulary. Naturally Angélique was shocked and answered somewhat sharply, 'So that is what you call good news, Mother.' In her mind she blamed Sr Flavie, the 'traitor', towards whom she had an enormous animus. Mme de Rantzau then took over. Arguing along the usual lines about *droit* and *fait* she said that what was at stake was Angélique's eternal salvation, there was no salvation outside the Church and she was putting herself outside it by daring to question the pope's decision. Then, mixing up Matthew 16:18 with John 14:26 (or possibly John 16:13), she averred that the promise to *Peter* included everything, both faith and fact, *everything*. Angélique asked sarcastically, 'Can you believe that the pope knows everything? That indeed is a universal knowledge.' She disposed of the confusion of texts and invited

Mme de Rantzau to search in the Bible which she handed to her; somewhat to her confusion as she could not find them at once. But of course she replied that she meant those things that concerned the government of the Church. The discussion went on and Angélique brought up the case of Pope Liberius who had condemned Athanasius. Mme de Rantzau replied that one must not make too much of what had happened about *Anastasius,* a reply that gave Angélique a certain amount of self-satisfaction as she realised that Mme de Rantzau's famous knowledge was somewhat patchy.[20] Angélique of course seized upon the point and triumphantly replied that a pope *had* erred, with the implication that another could do the same. All that Mme de Rantzau could come back with at this point was to say that nonetheless one must obey one's superiors when in doubt. 'When one has doubts', replied Angélique, 'one cannot believe because doubt is nothing other than a failure to believe and since one has no belief in a fact one cannot testify to it with a signature as that would be to lie to the Church'! The argument seems circular. Seeing the drift of Angélique's remarks Mme de Rantzau brought up the name of Augustine. Very sensibly she said it was not just one Father of the Church who must be believed; it was the general consensus of all of them and Augustine had retracted some of his opinions. Angélique came back quickly; he had retracted but not in matters of faith, and his doctrine had been approved by Fathers and councils. Mme de Rantzau *also* had her reply ready. *Three* popes had condemned Jansen. That was not all of the argument or the end of it but it is enough to illustrate the battle of wits between these two women.

As her two visitors were leaving the Superior remarked that Mère Agnès was ill. Although she and Angélique were of very different temperaments Angélique loved Agnès dearly and when they had gone she broke down and wept and prayed earnestly for her aunt, her sisters in religion and herself.

Although Angélique's seclusion in the convent only lasted for ten months she thought she was there for life and that she would never see her community again. This was a source of great grief and depression to her which was not at all eased when the Mother Superior came from time to time to tell her that another nun had signed. First, there was her own sister Angélique de Sainte-Thérèse who was with Mère Agnès. This was a devastating blow and it was not until she was released that she learned the whole truth. Her sister had seen various priests, had listened to them and had eventually made up her mind that she could sign. What was scandalous to the more rigid sect of the Jansenists outside was that Agnès had not prevented her from doing so. But she said that she would not dominate anyone's conscience, a sentiment that was not at all to the liking of the Jansenists, and the poor old lady was penalised when she got back to Port-Royal. Then she was told that another nun at Port-Royal had 'fallen', a Sr Candide, in whom Angélique had had complete trust. She blamed it all on Sr Flavie who, according to Angélique, had given Candide a very bad time. These events reduced Angélique to tears and almost desperate prayers, but by reflecting on their situation and her own she arrived at a more tranquil state of mind. In an eloquent passage she wrote: 'Neither the thought of my sins nor the sufferings of my sisters nor the danger to which our community and our friends (i.e. Antoine Arnauld, le Maître de Saci and others in hiding) were exposed, nor the troubles that were afflicting the Church nor my own painful condition [took] away' her feelings of trust that God was with them as well as herself. She even felt some joy.

Visitors, including the famous Mme de Sévigné, came to the convent from time to time and wanted to see Angélique, if only by catching a glimpse of her. This was not allowed. In the month of November Mlle Houdin, a benefactress of the convent and also the sister of a nun at Port-Royal, was refused permission to see Angélique. However, she quite contentedly heard Mass in the chapel which was a poor enough place, without decoration, of which Angélique approved. There was enough there to arouse devotion 'for there is no need of things that attract the senses for one to be carried away and enter the wounds of Christ'. Moreover, Angélique liked attending Mass there as she could hear every word, whereas when she was in choir she hardly knew whether the Mass had begun until the Gospel because it was said by priests 'who spoke in a very low voice'. The 'blessed mutter of the Mass' was not a nineteenth-century invention![21]

From time to time her solitude was interrupted by little events. In the autumn she was given a brief note from her father which gave her great joy and she was allowed to send an equally brief reply though her greetings to Henry Arnauld, Bishop of Angers, and her brother Luzancy were struck out. Then, before Advent the Superior came to tell her that Père Nouet SJ would be preaching during that season and Angélique begged to be excused as it would be too painful to her. Afterwards she wrote that she didn't have faith in her own strength, and feared that her resolution might be weakened. So she was not so sure of herself after all! She went to Mass in the little chapel of the infirmary but otherwise she spent the whole of Advent in her cell. She 'made her prison a church'. She then gives a moving description of her liturgical and devotional practices.

She sang as well as she could almost the whole of the Office every day and on Sundays those parts of the Mass usually sung, The Kyrie, the Gloria, etc. and followed it in spirit as the nuns had given her a missal. She says that when she was praying the Office in her alcove she was more recollected than she had sometimes been in choir at Port-Royal. In addition, she made processions round her room, which she says was fairly large, and sprinkled her bed, her work-table and the alcove with holy water. As she was unable to take any exercise, in the evenings she walked up and down her room reciting all the names of her religious sisters, praying after each one *Miserere eius*. She added certain psalms and all the time she was praying she was knitting girdles for albs, as was the custom at Port-Royal. She commemorated the 26th of every month as the day of her imprisonment and prayed to the saints in heaven, since she was deprived of the help of people on earth. In her reflections and meditations she came to terms with her condition and tried to turn it to her spiritual profit. As she wrote, her 'affliction was a great mercy of God'. The anguish of the first weeks and her rebelliousness were passing and, whatever may be said about Angélique's stubbornness, her imprisonment was evidently a time of growth in her interior life.

Another day Angélique was surprised to have a visit from Mme de Rantzau who, however, did not want to discuss theology. She brought a relic of St Victor, a martyr, which she had received from Cardinal Albizzi, who was largely responsible for the condemnation of the Five Propositions and Jansen, though Angélique cannot have known that. Mme de Rantzau asked her to decorate a reliquary for the relic and Angélique undertook this task with good grace. The nun also brought another relic of one of the martyrs of Montmartre and Angélique ruefully remarked that it was appropriate to her condition. Mme de Rantzau took it in good part. The two women were learning to respect each other and before Angélique left the convent a certain affection grew between them.[22]

Before Christmas she wrote another letter to the archbishop asking for permission to receive Holy Communion but to no avail. In Lent she tried again and in a long letter she reveals her mind very clearly. Is she being deprived of communion, she asked, because she was weak in a matter that does not concern the faith on which one's salvation depends? 'For you know, Monseigneur, that is the reason that prevents me from giving a testimony of belief which you ask of me and which you want to be sincere and from the heart. Without that you would think it very wrong of me to testify with my hand to what my mind rejects. That would not be to obey you but to do what you forbid.' Of course the archbishop wanted both. Then she turned the tables on him. He had said that belief in the *fact* was not a matter of divine faith and that was not what he had demanded of her, and she continued, 'If anyone wants to say that it is a sin to have mental doubts, which one cannot overcome, in a matter not of faith, at least that is no more than a sin of weakness and ignorance'.[23]

In reply she received a dossier from Mme de Rantzau who could not come because she was unwell. It listed all the 'authorities' from the scriptures and the Fathers of the Church about obedience to superiors. Nothing daunted, Angélique replied with a small treatise of seven (printed) pages. Mme de Rantzau came again after a few days and the controversy continued, though politely. No new points emerged except that Angélique quoted at length from the works of St Bernard (which she had been lent). At the end of it all she decided not to write to the archbishop again. It is not improbable that he was much relieved. He was no theologian, he was short-tempered, and Angélique's long argumentative letters probably bored him.

In these months after Christmas there was a little compromise on either side. The lay-sister who had looked after Angélique was allocated to other duties and she was replaced by another whom Angélique noticed was tired. She learned that she was overburdened with work and to save her coming up all the stairs several times a day she suggested that the three doors might be left unlocked. She promised that she would not try to see anyone or talk to anyone. The Superior agreed to this without difficulty and Angélique had a little more freedom of movement in her quarters. On her side when she was invited to hear a sermon from a Jesuit (*not* Père Nouet) she agreed to go. The preacher was an old Jesuit whose discourse pleased her. In his old-fashioned French he spoke of grace and Angélique had the satisfaction of hearing about '*la grâce victorieuse en la bouche*'[24] of her enemies. She seems to have thought that Jesuits did not believe in grace at all! The good father only put her off a little when at the end of his sermon he suggested that it was necessary to make efforts to cooperate with grace!

The nuns, however, did not give up their efforts to change her mind and they continued their attempts to wear down her resistance by telling her of those of her religious sisters who had signed. Then the superior asked her what she would think if Mère Agnès had signed. Angèlique felt stunned. She made no reply but rushed up to her room: 'I thought I would die. I could hardly breathe. My pulse was extremely agitated and it would not quieten down for several hours'. She spent a long time prostrate before God. Thoughts that overwhelmed her came into her mind as she considered the mysterious ways of God. How could he allow such a thing? She was afraid that her faith would founder on the rocks. Eventually calm came. God so moved her that she felt able to 'accept the truth of his promises in blind faith'. Finally, she realised that what she had been told was only conjecture, as she ought to have realised before.

In the pages of the *Relation* that follow there is much repetition and Angélique sometimes gives the impression that she is trying to convince herself. In the days before Lent she felt very ill and lest anyone should think, if she died, that she had weakened, she decided to write an explanation and an apologia. It is very long, covering eight pages. Like so many Jansenists Angélique did not economise on words. She rehearses the arguments so often used. She is not guilty of disobedience because her doubt about the *fact* was partly based on ignorance which made it impossible for her to read the book (the *Augustinus),* and partly on the knowledge she had of certain matters concerning the *fact* which raised suspicions that there were motives in play other than a love of truth and purity of faith.[25]

From time to time she was told of other nuns who had signed but she decided to say nothing, though she realised that the expression on her face revealed her grief. Her feelings did indeed fluctuate a good deal from desolation to a sense of coming closer to God: 'I was lost in wonder at God's graces [to me] and I remember one morning that I shed so many tears in that chapel where I heard Mass and those tears had so many causes, a realisation of my unfaithfulness to God, thankfulness for his goodness, desire to possess him, love of suffering which is the way towards love, that I felt filled with consolation and a holy pleasure in those tears'. This, I think, illustrates her deep devotion and her clinging to God even in her worst

215

moments. We also learn how almost tremulously sensitive she was, a sensitiveness that she tried fiercely to repress. In some ways her *Relation* is a prolonged conversation with God, though it must be remembered that *some* of it was written down after her release. We note too not only her constant quotations from the Bible but also the almost innumerable implicit references that are everywhere in the text. Her spirituality was deeply marked by the liturgy and the Bible but, as we have seen, this could result in a proliferation of devotional practices of various kinds. It is all the more regrettable that so much of this spiritual wealth was dissipated in sterile theological polemic. This was one thing she could never give up. She remained unable to make this one sacrifice to God.

Discussions with Mme de Rantzau continued intermittently and the respect of each for the other grew to such an extent that it was almost affection. Angélique remarks after one such occasion that Mme de Rantzau was 'altogether good and sincere'. During one conversation Angélique reveals some knowledge of the Fathers. She quotes from St Leo and she refers to the *Moralia* of St Gregory. Mme de Rantzau asked where it had come from and what its context was. Unwittingly she left herself open to a rather damaging reply. Angélique immediately gave the reference to the twenty-ninth book of the *Moralia*, chapter 6, and she continued that if people were so reasonable as to require the context for a passage, all they had to do was to extend the principle to other authors and not to constrain others to condemn propositions without examining their context. In the book of the Bishop of Ypres only the first of the Five Propositions is to be found in the text, and lest it should be defined in a wholly Catholic sense, the context was not examined. Taken alone, it was equivocal and susceptible of a wrong sense, which was what had, rightly, been condemned. To this Mme de Rantzau had nothing to say but it shows that Angélique knew a great deal more about the Jansen case than she ever admitted explicitly. It was in fact pure Antoine Arnauld and it was from him that she had got it all. On another occasion when St Peter, St

Gregory and the Holy See were being discussed, Angélique spoke in such a way as to please Mme de Rantzau who said, with good humour, 'Really, Mother, I believe you would like to persuade me of your way of thinking.' Angélique laughed and replied, 'Only in that matter.'

In the first months of 1665 rumours began to circulate of yet another papal bull which some thought would lead to the formal excommunication of those sisters of Port-Royal who had not signed the Formulary. The Superior told Angélique of the rumours; if it did come to excommunication the convent could no longer keep her and she would have to ask the archbishop to send her elsewhere. This naturally disturbed Angélique a great deal but in fact nothing happened. The famous four bishops, led by Nicolas Pavillon and including Henry Arnauld, Bishop of Angers, published the Bull but with the distinction between the *droit* and the *fait*. Père Annat SJ, the king's confessor, pressed for the removal of the bishops but as they were the best known of the reforming bishops and were held in high esteem not only by their own people but throughout France, the king and his more cautious advisers decided they could not risk an open defiance of the people. It was in fact the beginning of the end for the imprisoned nuns and for those under interdict at Port-Royal. Péréfixe began to realise that he had lost the battle. Nineteen nuns had been imprisoned and of these, even the ones who signed eventually recanted, and the great majority at Port-Royal remained solid. The convents were getting tired of the whole business; they did not want to hold the nuns prisoner and, what is more, their pensions from the royal treasury were paid only intermittently or not at all. The statements of the four bishops appeared between June and July and many now began to think that some change would have to be made. Reconciliation, however, was still some way off.

In the convent discussions continued but they reveal nothing new except that Angélique's mood began to change. As she herself confesses she became a little aggressive and tried to convert the

Superior and one or two of the nuns to her way of thinking. She was becoming more sure of herself and, while she constantly asserts that the nuns were 'good', so very good, she thought they were over-simple, and she does not disguise her contempt for their simplicity. Blind obedience was not for the nuns of Port-Royal. Some time in these last weeks more rumours began to fly about and the Superior hinted that the imprisoned nuns might be returning to Port-Royal. Angélique apparently took all this rather calmly but some time previously she had had a curious dream which turned into a nightmare of going back to Port-Royal and seeing Singlin! In the dream she had a premonition that Port-Royal de Paris was gong to be separated from Port-Royal-des-Champs – as indeed happened. Angélique was convinced that she would be imprisoned for life and she realised that if the Blue Sisters would no longer have her she might well be sent somewhere worse.

Then, on 2 July, the Feast of the Visitation, Mme de Rantzau came to wish her a happy feast and to bring her some good news; when she saw that 'good news' had an ominous sound for Angélique she immediately said it was not that sort of news. M. l'Abbé de Lamothe, an emissary from the archbishop, wanted to know if Angélique would like to see Mère Agnès at her convent of Sainte Marie. Angélique was suspicious, at first wondering whether there was some trap in the invitation. Mme de Rantzau, 'who well understood my feelings', tried to reassure her, and since Angélique was still reluctant to give a reply she said that the priest was waiting for one. After all she had gone through at the hands of Péréfixe she was amazed that she should have been *asked* what she would like to do. She was unwilling to accept a favour from the archbishop and she replied that she was ready to obey him in whatever he wished to do with her. When Mme de Rantzau had gone she mulled the whole matter over. She did not want to anticipate the will of God and we might wonder if she had begun to love her chains. In the afternoon three of the 'Mothers' came to see her and said that they wished to take recreation with her. They were overjoyed on Angélique's behalf but, as Angélique confesses – at considerable length – her attitude was ungracious. She had regarded herself, she said, as in purgatory where souls were moved from one part of it to another and their pains were only diminished as they approached their end in that place. The nuns had nothing to say to that and what they thought of the mini-sermon must remain a matter of speculation. Later in the afternoon Mme de Rantzau came again, this time alone. As Angélique suspected, she knew more about the arrangement than she had revealed earlier in the day and now she explained that as far as she knew all the nuns were to be sent to Port-Royal-des-Champs with the agreement of Mère Agnès. Mme de Rantzau was indeed well informed. Agnès had had to write to the nuns persuading them to go to Port-Royal-des-Champs, as some had resisted. At least, she wrote, they would all be together. On hearing Agnès' name Angélique's 'blood ran cold'. The last time she had heard of her Mme de Rantzau had suggested that Agnès had signed. However, better thoughts came with reflection and she decided to abandon herself to God and follow him wherever he should lead her.

What is remarkable is the real kindness of Mme de Rantzau who showed that she was far from being the ogress that Angélique had once thought her. On the other hand, Angélique was suffering from ten months of seclusion. It had made her suspicious of everyone and everything and it was taking some time for her to shake off her psychological shackles.

The afternoon was not yet over. As it was the Feast of the Visitation there was a sermon to which Angélique was invited. The priest (unnamed) was not a great preacher but he moved Angélique. He spoke of the meaning and usefulness of visits among Christians for the purpose of engaging in conversation. Angélique confessed that she was frightened of going back into that world as she was unprepared for it. She tried to tell herself that she was indifferent to the impending change and that she would commit herself absolutely to the pleasure of God.

Now that the day of Angélique's release was near the atmosphere in the house changed completely. The good nuns showed her all the affection they had not dared to give her when they had been under orders as her gaolers. When the Superior spoke to her of her departure there were tears in her eyes. She and her community wanted to keep her for a little longer and she mentioned the little statues that Angélique had cast in wax during her imprisonment. She wished she could stay just to finish another. She was not just self-interested, she and her nuns had come to admire and, it seems, to like Angélique. Mme de Rantzau said jokingly they would like her to join their community and, with similar good humour, Angélique asked if she would have to undergo a year's probation, always of course on the understanding that she had first signed. So it went on for a whole afternoon, and although Angélique made it clear that she still held her opinions, the nuns took it all in good part. One suspects that all this did Angélique much good. When her defences were down and she let go a little she appears to have been very charming. Of course there was no question of her staying, even for a few days more, as the Superior ruefully admitted. M. de Lamothe had told her that Angélique was to be taken away soon, in the next day or two, and the Superior pleaded that Angélique might be left at least until the afternoon of the day she was to go. This display of esteem and affection did not end at this point. The nuns and Angélique continued to correspond for some time.

Two other incidents before she left reveal the nuns' good will towards her. The Superior and two senior nuns came to invite her to come to choir and take part in a clothing of one of their nuns when a famous preacher, the Oratorian, Père Sénault, would deliver a discourse. They pressed her very hard. To avoid discussion they offered to make her inconspicuous by putting their scapular over her habit with its great red cross on the front. They said she could help them with the chant as they knew she loved singing the liturgical music. Angélique felt highly honoured and was much moved but, after what seems to have been a long discussion, she refused. She felt she should seek authority from her own abbess, as it was something that had not been foreseen when they were planning their conduct in the event of exile, and on this point the nuns gave way. It was a touching effort to make Angélique an honorary member, as it were, of their community, even for a short time. It does them great credit and Angélique was very gracious about it.

On the same occasion the Mother Superior explained at some length how the archbishop had forced her to accept Angélique at the convent. He had come two days before the removal of the nuns from Port-Royal and pressed her very hard to have Angélique. She protested that their Rule absolutely forbade them to have any visitors in the house except a postulant trying her vocation. The archbishop said that it was so extraordinary a situation that he would dispense them. The Superior refused to be browbeaten and said that even during the Fronde she had had to turn away refugee nuns although it went against her heart to do so. She went on insisting, the archbishop became very annoyed and went away very angry. He would find somewhere else – if he could. That is why when Angélique arrived nothing had been prepared for her. The Superior had evidently put up a good fight but, as she said, they could not turn her away as they could not risk the displeasure of the archbishop. Angélique was not entirely convinced and it is possible that she indulged in a long speech in which she did not hesitate to repeat that the nuns had been her 'gaolers'. In her *Relation* she went on and on about them not understanding her case, though she did not say all this to the good nun.

Thinking that Angélique would not be collected until the afternoon of the next day, the Superior begged her to cast a statue in wax as a souvenir. Putting aside her own packing she set to work and then, at about 9.00 p.m., the Superior came in some agitation to say that there was a cleric waiting to take her away. The Superior strongly disapproved as it was no time of the night to transport religious through the city, but the cleric had come with an 'obedience' from the archbishop and she and Angélique had to obey. Angélique made no difficulty about that and began getting together the few things she had. She was particularly concerned about some papers she had written (part of the *Relation*) and understandably she did not want the nuns to see them. She had put them in a chest with her linen and in her flurry could not find them. Just as she was telling the waiting nuns what she was looking for, she found them. She said that they contained no more than some pious sentiments she had written down from time to time, which was only half true but no one said anything.

After this little crisis Angélique went downstairs with the two nuns and was told that Mme de Rantzau was getting up to say goodbye to her. She could not refuse such a kindness, 'for I should have been extremely sorry not to have the honour of thanking her yet once more for all the care and kindness she had shown me'. She distinguished her role as *propagatrice* of the Catholic religion' (a curious phrase) from her role as a friend who had overwhelmed her with kindness and charity, 'she was so humble and good' – the direct opposite of what she had said nine months before! Before leaving she threw herself on her knees before her and Mme de Rantzau did likewise. She said she was very sorry to see Angélique being forced to go in such haste and Angélique poured out her heart to her in thanks for her charity towards her. They even ended with a joke. Mme de Rantzau begged her never to break unity with the Church and Angélique replied affectionately that she would do what she requested.

Angélique was led into the courtyard and the Superior continued to show her concern – there were still many people about – suggesting that Angélique should go into the chapel for a few moments while she went to see the waiting cleric. There Angélique made her last prayer from the Compline psalm, 'If I walk in the midst of darkness, no evil shall I fear, because you are with me'. The darkness, she reflected, was not only that of the night but of the future that lay before her but, 'as God is with us we walk with assurance when God's grace is with us'. The nuns came back, embraced her for the last time and led her to the coach. There she found the cleric with a lady and they set off. Angélique noticed the lights still on in the shops (a scene she had not witnessed for many years). After a while they stopped. Angélique knew where she was going but did not know the way and she sensed that the priest was going to pick up someone else. There was a long wait. Péréfixe evidently did not mind inconveniencing a great number of people for his purposes. He did not want to let the people of Paris see what he was up to. While they were waiting the anonymous lady in the coach remarked that it was a very extraordinary business to be transporting religious at that hour of the night but she revealed that Péréfixe had got back late from St Germain (where the court was), evidently after receiving his orders. The lady commiserated with Angélique who replied, 'It is only right that we should be as ready to carry out the orders of God as to execute promptly the orders of the court.'[26] Angélique was nothing if not sententious.

After a long wait the cleric brought a religious from the disturbed convent and sat her down next to Angélique: 'I did not know who she was either by face or by bearing for we could not see each other. But I was not left long in doubt. She threw herself on my neck and asked "Is it my aunt?" I replied, "It is, my child".'[27] It was, in fact, the young Sr Christine Briquet, dear to Angélique and one she had formed, not entirely for her good.

Angélique was much consoled by this meeting. Her indifference to all that was happening to her fell away: 'The joy of seeing this child again whom God had supported in so terrible a trial, especially as she was so young, gave me such hope that I no longer paid any attention to my fears and all my thought was to praise God who was giving us such sweet pledges of his great mercy. He was beginning to close our wounds and to bring us together again'.[28]

They continued on their way in complete silence, watching the candles go out one by one in the shops. They felt almost stifled in the closed coach, for the July night was hot and stuffy. Soon they were in complete darkness; there were no lamps on the coach and the coachmen had no torches. The journey seemed very long and they could see nothing . One wonders if the driver had lost his way in the dark streets of old Paris. As they went along slowly Angélique reflected. Was she afraid, should she be afraid of robbers? But no, 'it was foolish to fear anything when one had no reason to be afraid of death, for to die in such circumstances, obeying God and one's archbishop, could hardly be anything other than a kind of martyrdom'![29]

Eventually they stopped and when she heard the bells of the Carthusians ringing for the night office (it was 11.00 p.m.) she knew that she was in the rue Saint-Jacques close to the Faubourg Saint-Jacques where Port-Royal was. Her spirits rose at the thought that they were near home. They had arrived at the Visitandine convent of Sainte Marie where Mère Agnès and her sister Angélique Thérèse were imprisoned with one other.

The portresses had to be roused, they had not got the key of the outer gate and they had to wake the Superior as well as some of the senior nuns. It is not difficult to imagine their displeasure and the scurrying about in the dim candlelight. Nevertheless the nuns gave them a great reception, the Superior expressed her joy on seeing them and hoped that they too were happy to be released. Angélique responded, 'Alas, Mother we are no more than prisoners who are being transferred from one prison to another'.[30] However she forgot all about that as her two sisters ran to meet her. She had been a little worried about their meeting as they had both signed, but they showed so much humility before her and such affection that she was filled 'with extraordinary tenderness'.[31] Nothing was apparently said about the past. Now she was anxious to see Mère Agnès who was old and infirm and still in bed.

After a visit to the chapel for the adoration of the Blessed Sacrament the nuns led her up to Agnès' room. There she was welcomed 'with the joy with which angels welcome those who have escaped the snares of the devil'. They had much to say to each other but Angélique felt she could not describe what they said. The nuns were fussing round but eventually realised that the three wanted to be alone. Before going they indicated they wanted to prepare beds for them but Angélique and Christine politely refused. It was midnight. The nuns were surprised 'as they already knew that early in the morning they would all be taken to Port-Royal-des-Champs'. Angélique stayed with her aunt a little longer and then left her to rest before the long journey that was before them. She then rejoined her sisters who told her all they had gone through and how it had come about that they had signed. But they had recanted and, with typical exaggeration, Angélique felt that they had been raised from the dead. They told her the latest news of their fellow religious, how three of them had recanted, how the 'holy bishops' were resisting and much more. Angélique felt she had now come out of the tomb where she had lain for ten months. At the end of it all she consented to go to bed for the few remaining hours of night, but she was soon up again writing a note to 'our friends' to tell them of their release.

Angélique was still writing some time before 5.00 a.m. when a nun came to see how she and the other 'guests' were and took them round the house and the gardens as the Superior had invited them to do some hours before. Angélique greatly appreciated their kindness and with her sisters she saw the cloister, a little oratory of St Francis de Sales 'to whom Angélique had much to say'; as time was short her prayers had to be brief. She was shown the chapter room, the community room, the refectory and the kitchen and she thought it all 'very fine, very clean and well appointed in a way that was fitting for religious'. They were taken to the garden which also won their approval. They noted particularly a fine Calvary in stone with its 'figures well carved, almost life-size and very lifelike'.[32] But their sight-seeing was cut short. At about 5.30 the tower bell was rung very vigorously and a nun came hurrying to tell them that a chaplain of the archbishop had arrived. They must make haste, the coach was waiting and they must be on their way. Poor Mère Agnès was still in bed and she had to dress quickly. The Mother Superior had already had breakfast prepared for them and insisted that they should eat something in spite of pressure from the chaplain. Nuns have a way of dealing with clerics! Then came the moment of departure, which is described in moving terms by Angélique: 'We took our leave of each other with every mark of charity and friendliness and as for me who had spent no more than six hours with these good sisters I thanked them more profusely than all the others because I had received nothing but kindness and compliments and those who had been there longer had had to put up with everything'. No doubt she learned about what they had had to put up with later, and how severe Mère Eugénie, of this very house of Sainte Marie, had been with the sisters of Port-Royal.

When she wasn't sermonising it is clear that Angélique could write a vivid narrative, the dramatic elements of which are obvious. It is no wonder that Sainte-Beuve could compare the whole story of Port-Royal to a Greek tragedy and that a modern dramatist, Henri de Montherlant, could find in the exile of Angélique and the others the material for his play called, precisely, *Port-Royal.* There is drama too in the sudden call at 9.00 p.m., the words *'ma tante'*, *'mon enfant'*, the long journey through the dark city and the sudden ringing of the bell at 11.00 p.m. at the Carthusians, the affectionate meeting of Angélique with her aunt and sisters and, if the tragedy had to have a happy ending, the overwhelming kindness of the Visitandines. As the Port-Royal nuns climbed into the coach the tension was all but gone though all was not over yet. They still had a long way to go and they did not know what awaited them.

There were five in the coach – it must have been a crush – and the chaplain led the way on horseback. As they made their way through the outskirts of the city and out onto the road towards Versailles – not yet the great temple of the Sun-King – they first said the office of Prime together. Angélique took out a little bible she had with her and offered it to Mère Agnès to look for a suitable text. The Port-Royal nuns were much given to the *sortes biblicae* (drawing lots from the Bible) and always found a text appropriate to the occasion. Agnès opened the bible at random at Jeremiah 23 and read out in Latin, 'Woe to the shepherds who scatter and lacerate the flock of my pasture,' and the rest. Angélique took great satisfaction from it; after their exile the flock was being gathered together again and she saw in it a sign of God's providence. As was her wont, she spoke about it at length and does not say what the others thought.

After they had gone only four kilometres one horse lost a shoe – as Angélique remarks later they were poor slow beasts – and there was a long delay while someone went to fetch a blacksmith. While they were waiting they saw in the distance six other coaches approaching; as they came nearer they were able to discern the white habits with their red crosses and they were filled with 'a transport of joy'. But they were not allowed to stop; all they could do was 'to greet each other with cries of joy'. The horse was reshod and as they moved on slowly Angélique noticed that there was another coach that always kept behind them. Later, near Jouy, where the road was difficult and the coaches were forced to come near to each other they were able to exchange snatches of conversation but no more.

As they went along Angélique noticed the coach again and she wondered who was in it. She found out from a footman that among those in it were M. de la Brunetière, Vicar General, and M. Chéron, Official or head of the diocesan tribunal. She was filled with foreboding. Were they going to impose Visitandines as superiors as had happened at Paris? Were they going to pronounce some sentence of excommunication? Whatever lay ahead, she realised that they were being moved from one prison to another, their own monastery, where they could live without expense to the king. Her fears, however, proved to be unfounded. The priests in the coach were Dr Chamillard, who had taken part in the interrogations the year before and was distinctly *persona non grata* at Port-Royal, and a M. du Saugey, who was to be their chaplain. Later he was described as a young man who had not even said his first Mass, and who was uneducated and coarse.

The joy of the meeting of the two communities was naturally very great but it was muted; bells might not be rung and the people who had vivid memories of the charity of the great Angélique were not there. After the first greetings eighty-four nuns filed into the church in silence and prayed. Then Mme du Fargis, the prioress, gave an enthusiastic welcome to Abbess Agnès and all those who had been separated from them for nearly ten months. In due course the Vicar General formally announced their fate. They were to be deprived of all sacraments, they were no longer a community, they might not sing the Divine Office in choir and, as events were to show, they were even deprived of Christian burial. Whatever the legal term used, they were to all intents and purposes excommunicated, as Angélique had foreseen. Later in the day the Civil Lieutenant arrived with his officers and announced that all outer doors were to be locked and the keys handed over to him; his officers would patrol the grounds and the nuns would be allowed into the gardens for only an hour or two a day. The community was well and truly cut off from the world. The current chaplain was dismissed and replaced by Saugey, the sacristan was dismissed, all in the interests of cutting off communications, and only a M. Hilaire, the business manager for the monastery, was allowed to remain. That was probably a mistake as he had to go from the house into the world outside. In spite of all the precautions messages were passed from the nuns to friends outside, often with great difficulty, and with considerable ingenuity letters were inserted into cracks between the stones in the walls surrounding the property and collected by friends when the guards were not on the look-out; messages in small writing were put in hollowed-out fruit and similarly collected. Angélique managed to get letters out to her brother Luzancy and to her uncle Antoine Arnauld. Even the *Relations* of some of the nuns were smuggled out, perhaps by Hilaire, and published in Paris.

Inside the house various stratagems were used to circumvent the liturgical injunctions. The lay-sisters were not touched by the prohibition of holy communion and choir nuns, disguised as lay-sisters, received communion from time to time. Consecrated hosts were occasionally sent in and petitions for absolution sent out. The physician Hamon was allowed to return and attend sick and dying nuns and, under the hostile gaze of a portress, even managed to give spiritual consolation. This troubled his tender conscience as he felt he was acting as a priest and although he was strictly confined to his little house in the grounds word came to him (from Arnauld?) that he must go on doing it. More bizarrely, M. de Sainte Marthe, one of the monastery's former chaplains, stole up to the walls and, lying on the branch of an overhanging tree, preached little sermons. And so it went on for three years. In the light of all this and much more, Angélique's professions of obedience to the archbishop sound more than a little hollow.

The situation of Port-Royal was so intertwined with events outside it that it is necessary to go back a little to explain the return of the nuns to Port-Royal-des-Champs. To bring pressure and in response to the Bull *Regiminis apostolici* (which reiterated the obligation to sign the Formulary) the king had decided to separate the two houses. Those who had signed, less than a dozen, were to go to Port-Royal de Paris which was made an independent monastery with its own abbess. The rest were sent to Port-Royal-des-Champs, there to be strictly confined, and deprived of the sacraments, in the hope that these measures would break down their resistance. That move failed but others now came to relieve the pressure on the beleaguered nuns. The famous Four Bishops, led by Nicholas Pavillon, did indeed publish the contents of the Bull but with an instruction maintaining the distinction of the *droit* and the *fait*. They were four of the most respected bishops in France but Père Annat suggested that either they should be deposed by Rome, or that Pavillon should be ordered to Paris to be tried by his fellow bishops. Both suggestions were rejected; the thought of Pavillon making an almost triumphal progress through the length of France (his see was in the Pyrenees) made the authorities blench. These and some other considerations divided opinion among all the French bishops and there grew a feeling in favour of the Four Bishops and against the rigours imposed by the papal pulls. Discussions about these matters took time, Church and state were moving apart and it seems fair to say that no one knew what to do. Right at the end of Alexander VII's reign, in January 1667, the Inquisition condemned the Four Bishops' instructions and the pope set up a commission of nine bishops to begin their trial. This was too much for the French episcopate; nineteen bishops decided to support the Four and twenty others were known to be in sympathy with them. A painful confrontation between the papacy and the French Church was only averted by the death of Alexander.

His successor, Clement IX, elected after a long conclave in June 1667, realised that there was a danger of schism. This was to be avoided, if not at all costs, then through some process of reconciliation. The new pope was conciliatory by nature, and King Louis, for his part, had turned his attentions to the Low Countries where he wanted to weaken Spanish power – he did not want to leave behind a divided France. The pope initiated proceedings and to facilitate matters he appointed a new nuncio, Bargellini. Long and difficult negotiations began, from which Péréfixe and the Jesuits were excluded. As for the Four Bishops, they had to suppress their instructions out of respect for the Holy See, though they were eventually allowed to put their signature at the bottom of a *procès-verbal* distinguishing the *droit* from the *fait*, and Pavillon insisted that Port-Royal must be included in the 'peace'. Pavillon, who held that he was 'a judge of the faith', pope in his own diocese, proved to be the most resistant and since he was so far away progress was necessarily slow. Arnauld, Nicole, and others who thought like them, found the conditions satisfactory and, in the phrase of Louis Cognet, 'were ready to throw Jansen overboard'. Finally, agreement was reached between king and pope and what was called somewhat grandiloquently the 'Peace of the Church' was established. The Four Bishops signed in January 1668 and, after some difficult negotiations with Péréfixe, who was not pleased with the whole arrangement, Port-Royal was released from its restrictions in February 1669.[33]

Péréfixe, however, was not the only one who was not pleased. Angélique, 'whose influence had become predominant in the community', led a veritable campaign against signing even the new document. Once the negotiations had got under way a series of letters passed between her and Arnauld in which she averred that it would be better for Port-Royal to resist to the end even if it meant the destruction of the monastery. She thus grouped herself with the intransigents like Barcos, Saint Cyran's nephew, who held that no one should sign anything whatever the consequences. Long before, in the abortive attempt to bring about reconciliation in 1663, when Bishop Comminges was the go-between, she unwittingly revealed to Sr Flavie[34] during an argument that she did not believe that Jansen's teaching was heretical. Yet she continued to make much of the *droit* and the *fait* and her arguments did not change from those she had wearisomely repeated to Péréfixe, Mme de Rantzau and others. Now she was confronted by the very people who had thought up the distinction in the beginning, Arnauld and Nicole. Both wrote to her, and Arnauld, writing only a few days before the agreement between the community and the archbishop showed that he was weary, sad and finally irritated by her attitude: 'It would seem that we are in labour. The nearer we come to term, our pains are redoubled and if this were to go on much longer I do not know whether I could hold out. I am overwhelmed by the fear of the evils that could come if what is so near to completion should break down because if it does, the whole blame will be attributed to us [himself and Nicole]. If we do not give way to what he desires M. de Paris will be in such a position that everyone will take his part'. If they go their own way, he continued, 'I do not know what we should be able to say to anyone of a community of women who, in a grave matter of conscience involving their spiritual and temporal good, are determined to follow their own opinion without taking counsel of any ecclesiastic, even of those who guided them and of all those in whom they should have confidence who are now opposed to them, or better, of all the bishops and the ecclesiastics of the Church of Jesus Christ'. Thus he turned the tables on 'them', though he had Angélique in mind. As he writes his exasperation grows: 'That is why [I say] if our counsel is suspect to you, go and find others to advise you, but in the name of God do not stay in a path that will lead you astray, for if you do, without consulting priest or bishop, you would take a decision that would be generally disapproved by all the pastors of the Church.'[35]

Pavillon, more rigid than anyone else, wrote to persuade Angélique, and le Maître de Saci also wrote. 'I beg only', he implored, 'that you place yourself before God without the slightest prejudice and consider well what you owe not only to the love of the truth but also to the authority of those who are estimable in the Church because of their dignity, virtue and insight. Consider also the fear of giving scandal, and the good edification which St Paul demands of all the faithful and even more of you than of others.'[36]

In the middle of February there was a formal visit led by the friendly Bishop of Meaux, brother of the Abbess Ligny, accompanied by Arnauld and de Saci. Angélique signed with the rest of the community but, it was said, she was in no way convinced. If, as Orcibal drily remarks, her intellectual difficulties were not entirely overcome, perhaps she had learnt when she was with the Blue Sisters that there is only one recourse against certain psychological catastrophes, namely 'blind faith', which is not so very different from the 'blind obedience' for which she had shown so much scorn.[37]

Angélique's story now becomes largely the story of Port-Royal. Mère du Fargis, strong but not fanatical, was elected abbess in 1669 and appointed Angélique prioress, a position she held until 1678 when she herself was elected abbess.

After the liturgical celebrations, the expressed joy of the humble people of the district and the congratulations of a vast number of friends and letters of thanks to those who had helped, including of course Bishop Nicholas Pavillon, life once again returned to normal. Novices could be admitted and children brought back. It was like a new but rather cold spring. As Angélique wrote to her father, 'The white of the flowers vied with that of the snow but the burgeoning leaves have fought against the cold east wind and have not yielded.' It was the beginning of a new era. Although impoverished by the separation from the Paris house (which by order of the king received the lion's share of the funds) the community gradually became prosperous and all inside and their friends outside were able to enjoy a freedom they had not known for more than ten years.

The valley was peopled again by the solitaries, among them the distinguished historian Le Nain de Tillemont, and great ladies like the Duchesse de Longueville established houses near the monastery which became a resort for considerable numbers of people. Among them were many bishops, including Cardinal de Retz, the Duc and Duchesse de Liancourt, the Princesse de Guéménée and the letter-writer, the Marquise de Sévigné. Indeed, Port-Royal became the vogue; during the season there was a constant coming and going of carriages and the nuns spent more time in the parlours than was probably good for them. There were old friends of the house who, looking back to the former times of simplicity, regretted what they called the increasing worldliness of Port-Royal. In the words of the king, he was always hearing about Port-Royal and he did not like it.

What was Angélique's mood after the restoration of community life? For her it had been only half a victory. The house had regained its freedom but the hated question of the *fait,* though smudged over in the document she had signed, nonetheless remained. She may have felt that she had been defeated. Even the friendly bishops and the close friends of the monastery like Arnauld and de Saci had compromised and compromise went against her whole nature. A well-informed modern writer, F. Ellen Weaver, is of the opinion that a change came over Angélique: 'The vitality, the spirit – even the literary beauty – is almost gone. The letters become the usual sort a prioress, then an abbess, would write to friends outside the monastery: orders for silk for the vestments, condolences for illness and deaths, bits of spiritual advice, etc. The only truly exceptional letters are those to Mme Fonspertius (sometimes spelt Fontpertuis), one of the great patrons of the latter days of Port-Royal, in which she gave firm and enlightened spiritual direction over a number of years.'[38] It was possible, however, to take a different view. When Angélique's distinguished brother M. de Pomponne was demoted by the king from his office as Minister of State, Angélique wrote to Mme de Lesdiguières, one of the 'friends of Port-Royal', rejoicing over his 'disgrace'. There was now a possibility of him saving his soul! Mme de Sévigné was given a copy of the letter and in her turn she wrote about it enthusiastically and, it must be admitted, with tremendous exaggeration, to her daughter in Provence: 'This is the first time I have seen a religious speak and think as a religious. I have seen many of them worked up about the marriage of their relatives who were not married; some were vindictive scandal-mongers, self-interested and prejudiced. It is not difficult to find them. But I have not seen one who was truly and sincerely dead to the world. Share my joy, then, that so rare a sight has been granted me. It was the dear daughter of M. d'Andilly who said of her, 'Make no mistake, compared with Angélique all my brothers (including Antoine!) are stupid!' Mme de Sévigné's remarks about nuns were unpardonably damning. She knew the inside of many convents, especially those of the Visitandines (whom, since she was the grand-daughter of Saint Jeanne Françoise de Chantal, they called their *petite relique)* whose life was strict and fervent. But there is worse to come; she piles exaggeration on exaggeration. Angélique knows every language, all the sciences, by a gift of infused knowledge! She concludes, 'In short she is a prodigy which is all the more remarkable as she entered "religion" at the age of six.'[39] As of course she did not. Her father sent her to Port-Royal at that early age to be educated. Mme de Sévigné was not unlearned herself but she had the sometimes tiresome habit of enthusing about all sorts of people and things. To put the matter in plain language, she evidently had a very high esteem for Angélique de Saint-Jean.

The years from 1669 to 1679 were a time of apparent prosperity for Port-Royal even though they were marked by the deaths of many of the religious, notably Mère Agnès, and friends among the solitaries, including the now very old Robert Arnauld d'Andilly, who finally returned to the 'desert' with four servants! They also lost an old enemy when Péréfixe died in January 1671 but acquired a new one in Françoise de Harlay de Champvallon, of scandalous life, described by Sainte-Beuve as 'cunning and perfidious'. Port-Royal also had powerful friends, the chief of whom was the Duchesse de Longueville, a cousin of the king. Louis was at this time much occupied with war and Port-Royal was left in peace.

As prioress Angélique played a dominant role in the life of the house. In writing obituaries and editing other documents concerning the history of Port-Royal and in drawing up the final version of the Constitutions which were published in 1678, she set her stamp on Port-Royal as it was known to historians until recent times. Even now we see it largely through her eyes. Her accounts of her aunts Angélique and Agnès, among others, were exercises in hagiography, prepared as it were for canonisation. People and events that did not suit her view of things were glossed over or, in at least one case, suppressed. As said above, she burnt the letters of Geneviève de Tardif who had mystical tendencies and her account of the treacherous Flavie Passart comes close to being a veritable indictment. Ellen Weaver goes so far as to say that Angélique created the 'myth' of Port-Royal.[40] What her relations with Antoine Arnauld were after the signature of 1669 it is not possible to discern, but as he was now free to visit Port-Royal and did so, they must have continued their discussions as before. Contemporary evidence shows that she had not changed her mind about the *fait* or any major matter but, meanwhile, she was content to let it lie.

Angélique's main concern was with the internal life of the house. A prioress is second-in-command to the abbess, the executive officer, as it were, and Abbess du Fargis must have had complete confidence in her as she kept her in office for nine years. As novice mistress, prioress and, finally, abbess, she had had a long experience of the spiritual formation of the postulants and novices. Some samples of her instruction give an indication of what she said to them.

The first thing she liked to emphasise was total abnegation of self; without this, poverty, obedience and the rest were no more than an empty shell. Love of self was as dangerous as love of the world. It is useless to detach oneself from things if one does not put Jesus Christ in their place, and she identifies him with love: love – charity – is the virginity of the heart and the throne of love is humility. Angélique was a superior person and as she continues to speak of humility one wonders if her words reflected some of her own struggles to be humble. But by humility she does not mean a denial of whatever gifts one has. Using a paradox she said there is a kind of pride in thinking that one is capable of little because that is just a *human* sentiment, and Angélique, like so many of the people of her time, had a deep distrust of anything human. 'Nature' for her and the Jansenists was suspect, for though redeemed it contained much that was corrupt. Only engraced movements of the heart were acceptable and in more than one place she seems to think that grace should be experienced or even felt. She says there is a false humility in thinking that one is incapable of the greatest perfection since such distrust is displeasing to Christ. As an exhortation to greater spiritual efforts this may pass muster, but she does not seem to have realised that there was a danger in that too, a danger that Sr Flavie (with her aspirations to mysticism which turned out to be false) did not avoid. Then there is a rather peculiar statement on the external duties and obligations of the monastic life.

These have their limits if they are to be spiritually valuable but interior virtues have none. This is not quite true; there can be an excess of justice if it is not tempered by mercy, and St Thomas Aquinas said all the virtues except charity could suffer from excess.

With her mind still focusing on humility, and almost as if speaking of herself, she goes on to say that brilliant qualities are but a matter for (self-) humiliation since they lead to pride which is the most humiliating of all vices. Even, she says, the grace we receive to make good use of our talents is rare (which seems an extraordinary thing to say) and abuse of them is normal. We should think ourselves unfortunate if we are tempted in that direction for we might lose everything and lose him who saves only the humble. Here again there seems to be a dichotomy between nature and grace and one would have thought that religious praying many times a day and striving to serve God in all they did would not be deprived of grace when they used their talents. When Angélique was modelling in wax, was this a purely 'secular' and ungraced activity?

Somewhat surprisingly she is said to have preferred humble young women of 'mediocre talents' as postulants and novices, and this is what she looked for when discerning vocation. It looks as if there were to be no more Christines and Eustoquies who would out-face an archbishop. After the notoriety they earned for themselves they receded into the background and became good and observant religious.

In her conduct of the house Angélique did indeed insist on the small points of observance and was very concerned that there should be no relaxation of discipline or the Rule.[41] To give way on smaller matters was to endanger the spiritual life of the house. Among the things nearest to her heart was the celebration of the liturgy, as can be gathered from the *Relation de Captivité* as well as from the Constitutions. She herself had what is described as a deep voice and no doubt it was she who trained the young novices to sing. They were to put away all worldy affectations, they must submerge their voices in those of the whole community, all singing with one voice, as it were. For some weeks aspirants to the religious life were not allowed to sing and might do so only when they had acquired the right attitude and techniques. At a time when various kinds of flowery music accompanied or even smothered the liturgy (as often enough in the royal chapel), at Port-Royal there was nothing but plainsong unaccompanied by organ or any other instrument. Visitors came from far and wide to hear the sisters. There were also many other devotions, processions, special antiphons and prayers that marked occasions, both grave and joyful, of the life of the monastery. Port-Royal had a great devotion to the Blessed Virgin Mary, as is understandable in a house of Bernardines, to the saints and to relics, which became a bit of a fetish. This and more was revealed in a long letter, almost a small treatise, which Angélique wrote to refute a calumny that the nuns of Port-Royal had no devotion to Mary and the saints. The controlled indignation of her letter reveals something of her own deep devotion.[43]

Under an austere appearance there was that intense sensitivity. It is known that that is how she appeared to the nuns, especially, it would seem, to the young ones. A letter apparently written by a Sr Jeanne de Sainte-Domitille to Antoine Arnauld after the election of Angélique as abbess gives a lifelike picture of Angélique's bearing both before and after her election. Sr Jeanne first apologises for writing at length about the matter (her phrase is 'for spreading herself on it') but she wants 'to dispel the false impressions' that some of the nuns had of Angélique. Everyone knows that she has a fine mind and is very capable 'but there are those who do not believe that she is more humble than she is clever'; or, removing the negative, who believe that she was more clever than she was humble. For 'she gave the appearance of being somewhat haughty, and somewhat brisk in her rule of the community'. She did everything to keep people at a distance and this, says the writer, had been her attitude 'to all of us' for many years. 'She was so successful in this that there were very few who were not prejudiced in her regard and were afraid to see her in the position she now occupies.' After her election things were different: 'However, now that God has resolved to give so great a gift to this community, we have become so united through this election and there was never one so unanimous as hers. More and more as we have experience of the usefulness of her rule, the prejudices of several of us have disappeared. As you know, I was one of them and now I can never give God sufficient thanks'.[44] As abbess, Angélique became more relaxed and sometimes even dared to show her affection more openly.

One of the conditions of the Peace of the Church was that there should be no more writing about the contentious matter of grace, that men like Arnauld and Nicole should keep quiet and that the question of the signature of the Formulary, 'pure and simple', without reservations, should not be raised or imposed. Henry Arnauld was the first to break the peace. To settle a dispute in the university of Angers he said that candidates for the priesthood could sign the Formulary with the distinction of the *droit* and the *fait*. This caused the king grave displeasure and from his camp at Ninove in Flanders he condemned the bishop and his action. Even the Jansenists were dismayed by the bishop's provocative decision. Then followed the business of the condemnation of Nicole for his alleged drawing up of a list of laxist propositions, the rebuke to Antoine Arnauld for holding 'cabals', and in 1679 the death of the Duchess of Longueville, the powerful protector of Port-Royal, which now became very vulnerable. The previous year the king had signed the Treaty of Nijmegen and he was free to turn his mind to matters other than war. With his morganatic marriage to Mme de Maintenon he entered upon his 'pious' period and, as some wit said, he began to expiate his sins on the backs of others.

When Angélique was elected abbess in 1678 she very soon ran into a crisis of the kind she had experienced so many years before. François de Harlay visited Port-Royal for the first time in eight years and with many a sigh and an insidious courtesy he banned the postulants, sent the children away and withdrew the confessors. There were to be no more scenes such as his predecessor had provoked but the rigour was the same. Parents, some very distinguished, protested and pleaded with him in person but to no avail.

The archbishop's interview with Angélique (which she recorded in yet another *Relation*) was on her part grave but firm, though one can detect a note of sadness in her replies. Never, she said, had she and her community expected to be faced again with the situation they had experienced more than a decade earlier. De Harlay's opening gambit was that there were too many religious in the house in view of the meagreness of their resources since the division of the two monasteries. To this Angélique replied that it was a curious solution of their problems that he should send away the children whose fees were an important financial support. Then de Harlay revealed his mind. With a frankness surprising in so subtle a politician he admitted that politics entered into the matter, and he went on to list all the grievances, which were in fact the grievances of the king: the misdeeds of Nicole, the 'cabals' of Antoine Arnauld, the affair of Henry Arnauld, all the noise that the Messieurs of Port-Royal were making in one way or another. The king did not like it. The king's *idée fixe* was that Port-Royal was a nest of dissension and had grown ever stronger and the monastery was to pay the price of the activities, real or imagined, of the Messieurs. But it was an act of naked political power without excuse or justification, as Angélique saw very well. As she wrote to her uncle, the Bishop of Angers, how could a king who had all Europe at his feet think that this community of women could be a danger to the state? Such, however, was the mind of Louis XIV. Once he had suppressed one dissident group he would go on to exterminate another. Soon the persecution of the Huguenots would begin, and they would be dragooned into the Church by force; by the Revocation of the Edict of Nantes (1685) they would

240

cease to exist as a community, their civil rights would be taken away, and thus France lost, through emigration, tens of thousands of its most industrious citizens.

Angélique wrote to the pope, the austere Innocent XI, who had shown a friendly attitude to Arnauld and Port-Royal but, embroiled as he was with the king over the affair of the *Régale* (the appointment of bishops), he could do nothing. He sent back kindly messages but that was all. Then there was the question of confessors. On leaving, the archbishop had said quite casually to M. de Saci that he and all the confessors must leave within two weeks. Unsuitable men were appointed and letter upon letter followed from Angélique. A list of twenty was offered by the archbishop and all were rejected. Of these and others she wrote that 'they do not know us and we do not know them, they have no connection with our friends and their ability is very mediocre, not suitable for us who, as it is said, are very well instructed'. The elitist spirit is very marked. Angélique vainly wanted confessors who, if not 'ours', would be as much like them as possible. De Harlay either got a bit tired of all this or he relaxed his vigilance as he let through one or two sympathisers, notably the Abbé Le Tourneux who was austere and had had a brief fame as a Lenten preacher in Paris. He was very much *persona grata* with the community but as soon as de Harlay realised his mistake he sent him away and forced him into exile to the little priory that he held *in commendam*. Port-Royal was slowly stifled but it took another thirty years to extinguish the community and destroy the very buildings.

The whole situation put a great strain on Angélique. But she continued to hold the community together, probably a little wearily, delivering her *Misericordes*,[45] some of considerable length, and taking over the spiritual direction of the nuns. Aristocratic friends might try to intercede for them but the world outside became increasingly bleak. Antoine Arnauld had gone into exile in 1679 with Nicole (who returned) and one or two others. The Messieurs were dispersed and inaccessible and threat of further action by de

Harlay (i.e. the king) hung over the community. Angélique was re-elected in 1681 but a deadly blow came from an unexpected quarter with the death in January 1681 of M. de Saci, her cousin, her friend, and her director for so many years. His body was brought for burial from Pomponne, his brother's estate, to Port-Royal. During the funeral services, an observer recorded that Angélique's voice, low and solemn, could be heard as she looked down, her eyes fixed on the ground. She was in fact emotionally devastated. Before she was elected abbess she had been seriously ill and now her health was giving way altogether. She was taken ill again three weeks later as she was going to choir to sing Vespers. She had a pain in her side and a temperature but even so she first went to de Saci's grave and prayed there, weeping for a long time. At the end of Vespers, as she was singing the Pater Noster, her voice broke but she insisted on going to the parlour where someone wanted to see her. It was too much for her. Suffering greatly, she immediately took to her bed but her mind was perfectly lucid and when one of the nuns asked her if she would like to take off her veil she said no, she would give it back to the Lord from whom she had received it forty years before. And so, on 29 January, three weeks after the burial of her cousin, she died.[46]

With her, wrote Sainte-Beuve, Port-Royal lost its last greatness. We can agree only in part. In spite of her obsession with the Formulary, the signature and all that went with them, Angélique had a touch of greatness and a certain nobility of character. Although very unlike her aunts Angélique and Agnès she was in some ways their worthy successor. That good man Antoine Arnauld, so opinionated and so argumentative, was her evil genius. Unlike his elder sisters she could not think of him as the *'petit Arnauld'* and distance herself from him as they did. He was her oracle and her guide and but for him she might have been a really great abbess and perhaps have saved Port-Royal.

Note A: Sr Flavie Passart

If this book were a history of Port-Royal it would have been necessary to give a long account of Flavie Passart who became the most
detested enemy of the community and of Angélique de Saint-Jean.
Her supreme crime was that she betrayed Port-Royal, feeding
Archbishop Péréfixe with all sorts of damaging information about
the sentiments and opinions current in the community. She was
the 'traitor' who, after proclaiming loudly and emphatically that
she would never sign the Formulary in any form whatsoever, went
over to the enemy, the archbishop, and signed without any reservations. To say the least she was a very unstable character and Jean
Orcibal gives a long account of her in his *Port-Royal Entre le Miracle
et l'Obéisance* (1957). In chapter V, 'Une Enigme Psycho-
Physiologique', he attempts a lengthy analysis of her psychology. It
is too long and too technical to be summarised here. One example
may be given. Writing of the time of Péréfixe's investigations he
describes her feverish activity; she was meddlesome, mischief-mak-
ing, turbulent, intriguing, concerned to make trouble, and this was
a manifestation of her usual and natural impetuosity and her normal agitation of spirit. The tale of her peculiar goings-on is a long
one and Orcibal gives a list of them. There were numerous 'mirac-
ulous' cures of herself and others suffering from what are described
as *'coliques néphrétyques'* (whatever they may have been). She was
cured by drinking water in which the hand of Saint-Cyran had
been dipped. On another occasion she was subject to a fever and so
swelled up that she could not sleep in her bed or even speak.
Angélique de Saint-Jean (no less) touched her with the office book
(the Diurnale of Antoine le Maître, recently dead) and Flavie was
cured. At other times she could not eat at all and at yet others she
ate voraciously. She had dreams which she interpreted to her own
advantage. The most striking example came at the time when the
community were discussing an appeal against the procedures of
Péréfixe in August 1664. Seeing that Sr Thérèse Arnauld was reluctant to follow that line Flavie talked at her for hours and then the

next day she produced the 'conversation' she had had with the Bishop of Ypres (i.e. Jansen) in a dream persuading her to sign. She retailed it to Sr Thérèse 'word for word'! For this Mère Agnès and Angélique de Saint-Jean administered a cutting rebuke: 'It is not very strange that she dreamed at night about what she had been thinking all day'.[1]

So far so bad. What had happened to the monastic silence? But what is even more disturbing is that when Flavie joined the community in 1648 she was highly regarded and was soon made Mistress of the Children. One after another various nuns 'fell' for her, including the supercilious Eustoquie de Brégy who regarded her 'with much tenderness and kindness'. Neither did they or Angélique de Saint-Jean object strongly, if at all, to Flavie's strange devotions, her obsessive desire for relics and her prayers to the recent 'saints' of Port-Royal, such as Saint-Cyran, and to M. de Rebours who had been her confessor. To them and to others she attributed many of her cures. But many in the community, including Angélique de Saint-Jean, shared these 'devotions'.

There were also disputes about prayer, referred to briefly above. Flavie was directed by a M. de Rebours who seems to have been imprudent. He had a high esteem for her and went so far as to call her 'a second Catherine of Genoa for the charity she had for God and her neighbour'. The form of prayer that he and Flavie favoured was a prayer of the heart and the will while Angélique saw prayer as a methodical and mental exercise. She charged Flavie with neglecting the choir office – sometimes Flavie did not appear in choir for days!

After the betrayal, Angélique wrote an account which was, of course, very hostile to Flavie but in the course of it she revealed something of the life of Port-Royal in the years before there was any question of theological dispute. Angélique revealed only as much as she had to but, no doubt unwittingly, she shows that the marmo-

---

1. At p. 24.

real calm of the monastery suggested by the scenes and portraits of Philippe de Champaigne was far from the reality of the life. There were all those conversations, there was a certain amount of uncharitable gossip, and during the crisis of 1664 and afterwards nuns could be seen gathering in little cabals discussing their grievances and plotting resistance to the Visitandine nuns who had been put in charge of the house. Observance was far from perfect then and through Angélique's account we can discern that it had not always been what it should have been in the years before the troubles began. Perhaps we should not be surprised, tensions and disagreements can occur even in well-ordered communities. But Port-Royal liked to think that it was better than other religious communities and were not above saying so now and again. They were 'special' and the ordinary run-of-the-mill confessors could not understand their refined spirituality.

These revelations are important from another viewpoint. Generally speaking, the *whole* of the Port-Royal community has been regarded as Jansenistic; all of the religious were wholly given to the Jansenist doctrine, at least in the form in which Antoine Arnauld presented it. But it seems established that Angélique de Saint-Jean, with perhaps half a dozen of her disciples, was of this mind and it was she and they who led the rest. This becomes clear in an essay by Birgitte Sibertin-Blanc in the *Chroniques de Port-Royal, Biographie et Personnalité de la second Angélique* (1985), although she has a great admiration for her and calls her *cette grande figure.*[2]

---

2. The essay is based on her *Angélique de Saint-Jean Arnauld d'Andilly d'après sa correspondence* (Thèse d'École des Chartes, 1962). The fact that about a dozen of the religious 'fell' – signed and formed the community of Port Royal de Paris – shows that there was division in the community. Several others also signed but later recanted. Some of these suffered agonies of conscience and we may speculate that they would have been glad to have been left alone to make up their own minds.

Note B: The Physical Appearance of Angélique de Saint-Jean
Mlle Birgitte Sibertin-Blanc gives a description in her essay (p.75) based, it would seem, on a portrait of which there is a reproduction on the cover of the *Chroniques de Port-Royal,* mentioned above. Her general appearance is severe but marked by a keen intelligence and an intense inward-looking gaze. Under the veil the forehead seems high, the eyes are deeply set and widely spaced, the nose is long, the mouth large but the lips are thin and pursed; the chin is a little heavy, showing determination. There is a suggestion of masculinity. Her whole appearance breathes an air of distinction, intelligence and will.

7

JACQUES JOSEPH DUGUET

An Elusive Jansenist

Jacques Joseph Duguet is usually ranked with the 'moderate' Jansenists. He held on to the *droit* (Jansenist doctrine was right and orthodox) but surrendered the *fait*, the fact that the Five Propositions were in Jansen's *Augustinus*. But although he was a moderate, the second part of his life showed that he was extraordinarily tenacious of his views. In fact, he is much more interesting as a personality and as a writer than for his tenacity. He was highly intelligent, learned and, for many, an esteemed spiritual director. His conversation was enchanting and there were always ready listeners.

There was, however, another side to his character. He was elusive. Although he was a priest he never held any pastoral office and though enjoying certain kinds of company he evaded responsibility. He lived to be very old but by the age of thirty he was already fussing about his health. Early in life he had considerable success in instructing the young but ran away from it. Later, public lectures in Paris attracted large audiences but he pleaded ill health and asked to be relieved of the task. After pressure from the king on the teaching of Jansenist doctrine (or what was alleged to be such) he went into voluntary exile. It was his first great evasion and was characteristic of much of his life. One can hardly improve on Sainte-Beuve's description of him: *Talent qui se dérobe, style qui se dérobe, il a passé sa vie et mis son âme à se dérober.*[1] In fact, he went into hiding or self-exile some five or six times before the end of his life.

Like so many Jansenists Duguet was born into a legal family, in 1649. He received a good classical education at an Oratorian school and acquired an excellent knowledge of Latin and Greek to which he later added Hebrew. He entered the Oratory in Paris and during the first two years he spent there he came to know Antoine Arnauld and Pierre Nicole who informed him fully about the 'Peace of the Church'. Long conversations with them convinced him of the rightness of the Jansenist cause and he adhered to it for the rest of his life.

After two years he was sent to Troyes to teach philosophy (which he himself can only just have learned) and was charged with the humble task of instructing the poor in the Christian faith. Almost immediately he revealed his power of enchantment as a speaker and the fashionable world invaded his classes and crowded out the poor. He was horrified; he could not bear to see the poor he loved being excluded and he begged to be relieved of the task.

At Paris he studied theology and after his ordination in 1677 he was put to teaching positive theology, in which subject he developed his knowledge of the Fathers, especially the Greek Fathers.

When the royal embargo on the teaching of Jansenism came (1684) Duguet simply disappeared. Without a word to anyone, even his superior, and with the financial assistance of the wealthy Mme Fontpertuis, he made his way to Brussels to join Arnauld and his little community. It was his first evasion and seemed final. He stayed there for seven months.

Naturally the very secrecy of his departure caused public comment and his family complained bitterly that he had left them without any information. An apologia seemed called for and this appeared in two letters, the first addressed to his elder brother and the second to his father superior. To both he speaks of his need for solitude (but he is not going to become a Trappist), to both he makes sure that they will not suspect where he is, and to his superior, I regret to say, he is a little ingenuous. He begins by paying tribute to his kindness and to the way of life of the house. He has no complaints on that score but significantly and oddly he says nothing about the royal embargo, the very cause of his flight. But, he avers, although the Oratory may be tranquil, he however needs something more secluded: 'Day by day I am becoming more unsociable and so unaccommodating that I cannot live by the rules which the rest find so good. For a character so particular as mine I need a special place and I leave to seek one without knowing whether it will be suitable. I have however in view a place of solitude where I think they will put up with me. *But the one condition is that I preserve my freedom.*[2] If I do not find the quiet I am looking for, allow me, dear Father, to return and enjoy [the life of the house] once again with you.' This was pretty cool, perhaps an indication that Duguet had been a little spoilt or had come to depend on his charm.

In fact, the climate of Brussels, damp and cold in the winter, did not suit him, and though there are no signs of disagreement with Arnauld, it is possible that the lack of freedom was what Duguet found difficult to bear. He returned to France as secretly as he had left and found what he liked to think was a profound solitude (provided for him by Mme de Fontpertuis) in which he lived from 1685 to 1690. His first hiding-place was Troyes, a stronghold of Jansenism, and then Paris. He speaks of the roofscapes he could see from his windows, but the solitude was not all that profound. Almost certainly it was at Troyes that he found agreeable company and was able to walk about the town. And always, wherever he was, there was the stream of letters that came and went, letters from the ladies of the *beau monde,* often accompanied by presents – a *chapelle* (which seems to have been a *chape* or small cape), a great shawl, and the 'authentic powder of viper'! To all the fair ladies who sent presents he replied with letters that are subtle, diplomatic and touched with humour. It is no wonder that women liked him. It was also at this time that he took up knitting, which Sainte-Beuve found bizarre and hard to accept.

In 1690 Duguet regained his liberty though, as he was well known as a Jansenist or a Janseniser, conditions were imposed. At

the intercession of M. le Président de Ménars, a man well connected and approved of by the authorities, Père La Chaise, the king's
confessor, agreed to Duguet's release on condition that he did not
write on matters connected with the Jansenist dispute. Duguet
accepted the condition and for the next twenty-four years he lived
as a member of the Ménars household. As he said, he had at last
found the *tanière* (the lair) he had been looking for. He also kept
his promise not to engage in the Jansenist controversy except for an
intervention in 1696 when he wrote in support of Cardinal de
Noailles, Archbishop of Paris, who put out a statement hardly dis-
tinguishable from Jansen's teaching. Strangely, Duguet suffered no
ill consequences of his intervention.

It was in these years that Duguet's literary output became very
considerable. More will be said about this later. It was also at this
time that his correspondence became prolific. Writing so often to
women he had the ability to put himself in the position of the
recipients of his letters. He could identify himself with their condition as a rather mannered letter to a Mme Rieux shows. She is
unwell and he writes: 'After what you say, Madame, how can you
urge me to take care of myself? How can I take any interest in my
life if you wish to make it wretched for me? If you give yourself over
to suffering, how can I *not* feel it in the depths of my heart? Ask
yourself if that is right – it is for you to judge. I can only follow
your example and the less control you have over your will, the less
you let me have over mine. You can count on that, Madame. Suffer,
give yourself up to your suffering. I have not a word to say. But I
shall feel the reactions, and in the little troubles I have, I shall be
overwhelmed by yours'.[3] If there was a certain fashion of writing in
this way at the time, Duguet shows that he could conform to it
with the rest.

In the same letter he shows that he is *au fait* with another
fashion of the day and in so doing reveals his style of humour. He
writes of the little remedies he has to offer to a lady which differ
from those suggested by M. Hamon (the physician of Port-Royal)

and which do not suit her. Neither *caphé* (*sic*) nor chocolate are good for her stomach. He recommends tea and he cannot refrain from telling her how to drink it: 'I do not know whether you know how to take a liquid that is quite hot without burning your tongue. For tea, you must know, has a quite different effect if you can take it hot. You just need a little practice. You must take only one little sip at a time'. All this seems very un-Jansenistic, far away from the austerities of Port-Royal.

But if Duguet could be light-hearted, there were times when he was deadly serious. Mme de la Fayette, author of *La Princesse de Clèves,* was for many years the intimate friend of La Rochefoucauld of the *Maximes.* His death had left her disconsolate and, as her health began to give way, her friends became worried about the state of her soul. Not only had she been lax in her religious practice, she had also doubted and she verged on scepticism. Duguet was invited to give her what spiritual counsel might be appropriate to her case. She had written to him of her willingness to repent, of the thoughts that came to her in the moments in the morning between sleeping and waking. Duguet takes her up at this point: 'I believe you could not make better use of these quiet moments than by taking account of your life, already so long, a life of which you know better than anyone else its emptiness *(vanité).* Up to now the mist with which you have tried to smother religion has hidden you from yourself. We must examine ourselves and come to self-knowledge by referring all to Religion [God]. Now is the time to put everything in its place and you in yours. In vain do we resist, in vain do we dissimulate; the veil is torn apart as life and its desires disappear and the conviction grows that we must lead an entirely new life at the moment when [we know] we are no longer allowed to live. We must then begin with sincere desire to see ourselves as we are seen by our judge. That vision is overwhelming even for those who are most clear-minded about self-deception. Such a vision takes from us all our virtues and even all our good qualities as well as the esteem they have gained for us. We feel that up to that moment our life has been an illusion and that we have lived a lie. We realise that we have been nourished by the unreal form of food of a still-life picture and that we have taken on only the outward show of virtue. We have neglected what is fundamental because it demands that we should refer everything to God and to our salvation. In every sense of the word we have not despised ourselves. It is not a question of contempt of self out of a sophistical vanity or an enlightened pride or a fashion; we must despise ourselves on account of our unrighteousness and our wretchedness. [Here Duguet was attacking the contemporary form of Stoicism, propagated by, among others, La Rochefoucauld]. Then we are in the right way and we can see that we have misused everything because we have made care for self, our reflections, our friends and our virtues the purpose of our lives. As we see so prodigious a waste of a whole life we groan. Our affairs, even the most important, have degenerated into what were no more than pastimes because they have no final purpose. We are terrified by an almost infinite number of faults of which we have been hardly aware and we know that there is no excuse for the greatest of them though we conceal their horror from ourselves. Then we sink into an abyss of shame as, in bitterness of heart, we review all the years we cannot bear to think of. Even then we are not sincerely repentant because we are still so unrighteous that we excuse our weakness and love what was its cause'.[4]

Here Duguet is at his most severe. He understands Mme de la Fayette's condition very well. He cuts through the 'mist' and attempts to lay her soul bare. He is leading her from self-pity and mere remorse to true repentance. However, it seems that he was not successful. Mme de la Fayette's repentance took longer than perhaps he thought it would. Later she was reconciled by a priest of Saint Sulpice, the opposite pole of Jansenism, and perhaps the priest was less demanding or more perceptive.

When faced with Duguet's books, forty volumes on the Bible alone, one is reduced to near despair. It is not simply that he wrote so much but that he had the habit of spinning out his material to inordinate lengths. Thus his disquisition on the sacrifice and death of Abel covers four pages and by the time he has finished with him one feels there is not a great difference between him and the Redeemer of the New Testament. Unsurprisingly it took Duguet six books to complete his commentary on the Book of Genesis. However, he wrote well on the death and burial of Jesus Christ and he had a stronger and more personal relationship with him than was common among the Jansenists and, indeed, others at the time.[5]

There was another aspect of Duguet's commentaries on the scriptures which is less easy to justify or accept. It was an interpretation called the *sens figuré* from which Bremond coined the adjective *figurisant* (which is not in the dictionaries) and can be described as a debased kind of typology or, more accurately, a decadent form of allegory. Anything in the Old Testament could be made to 'stand for' whatever its practitioners chose to regard as parallels in the New Testament. What was even less healthy was the exploitation of the apocalyptic literature of both Testaments. Quite arbitrarily it was made to refer to contemporary events and to forecast a more or less imminent future. The 'Church', that is the Jansenist Church, was suffering persecution but there would come a time, perhaps soon, when popes and bishops would be either 'converted' or abolished to give way to a new hierarchy and a new Church which would endorse Jansenist doctrines and thus be restored to its primitive purity. These and other supposed events, such as the conversion of the Jews, were much in the minds of Duguet and some of his friends, and Bremond could say that Duguet's *passion figurisante* became almost a mania with him.[6]

Supporting and apparently encouraging these apocalyptic notions was a curious young woman whom Duguet came to know in the 1690s. She called herself Sr Rose of the Holy Cross, though she was not a nun, and her name was not Rose but Catherine. She was a young country woman without education but with apparently extraordinary gifts that seems to have impressed the unsusceptible Duke of S. Simon. He gives a lively description of her: '[she was] squarely built, of medium height, very thin', very ugly but 'with a very vivacious, eloquent... and impressive prophetic air... she uttered very extraordinary things, some about the past which were hidden and some about the future which in fact happened.'[7] Although two successive archbishops of Paris chased her out of the diocese Duguet fell for her and what attracted him to her was her alleged gift of prophecy which was very much in line with his apocalyptic views. In 1707 she prophesied that 'there will come a good pope who will bear witness to all the ancient [i.e. Jansenist] doctrines of the Church which will make it shine' for all to see. For Duguet her 'prophecy' came as a light from God and he regarded the coming of such a pope as imminent. When his friends expressed reservations he pointed to the papal nuncio in Paris, Mgr Cusani, who did in fact become a cardinal and so, technically, was *papabile*, but he showed no liking for Jansenism nor of course did he ever become pope. In any case Sr Rose's prophecy was shattered six years later with the publication of the Bull *Unigenitus*, the final and definitive condemnation of Jansenism.

As with most of his contemporaries Duguet's approach to the Bible was of his time but he was aware of the critical views that were emerging and in his *Traité sur les dispositions pour offrir les SS. Mystères* (1725), he writes of them with some irritation: 'They [the critics] grow old, bent over the scriptures, and learn nothing that would make themselves better. They know everything about the Gospel, matters one can ignore without danger, but they are children in all those matters on which their salvation depends. They are well versed in questions concerning times and places, ancient customs and the harmonisation of dates and circumstances that seem to conflict with each other. But apart from those thorns they know nothing of the fruit and never touch it; or if they do, they examine the rind and throw away the rest'[8]. This seems to be directed against Richard Simon (1638-1712) who, like Duguet, had belonged to the Oratory and, like him, had left it, but who is known today as a pioneer of biblical criticism. Duguet disliked his dry, critical temperament which contrasted so greatly with his own. It is however, an odd onslaught, coming as it does in a deeply spiritual book which is advising priests how to prepare to celebrate the 'sacred mysteries', i.e. the Mass.

As well as being a much sought-after spiritual director to the laity Duguet was from time to time invited to help the clergy in their spiritual duties. This was the origin of the *Traité* mentioned above and of his *Traité sur la Prière Publique* which appeared in book form in 1707 and retained a certain vogue even up to the twentieth century. The book is made up of two letters, the first addressed to a Canon Gillot and the second to a Canon Baudouin of Reims Cathedral. As appears from the *Avis du Libraire* many copies, apparently unauthorised, had been circulating in Paris and the provinces. The first letter had aroused criticisms of the Divine Office as it was and one of the canons used such criticisms to excuse himself from celebrating the office. Antoine Arnauld joined in the fray and, as was his wont, published severe criticisms of the *Traité* and made a strong plea for reform. Duguet kept out of this controversy, simply agreeing that the Office was very long and accepting that it posed a problem. The obvious remedy would be to reform it; some efforts in that direction were already being made in France[9] and Duguet was aware that some change was necessary. Part of the trouble was that, in addition to the Divine Office, on certain days the Office of the Blessed Virgin Mary and the Office for the Dead had to be said, as did prayers attached to certain 'pious foundations', usually for the dead. On these Duguet is scathing. He saw them as expressions of what might be called pious avarice on the part both of those who had asked for them in the past and of the clergy who had received them.

There were other undesirable practices. There were lay-clerks who, it must be supposed, did most of the singing and the psalms were recited at speed; they vanish like lightning, said Duguet, and what with this and the length of the offices 'the canons are bored at the beginning because they know they are going to be bored before long and the yoke of obligation remains when devotion has gone'. That gives Duguet the clue to his 'remedy'; the canons must be more concerned to reform themselves than reforming the Office!

That of course is where Duguet always wanted to bring those he directed and he has the basic remedy to hand. The sovereign remedy is to have charity in their hearts – *Caritas ex Deo est* (1 John 4:7, as Duguet notes) – since if a man's heart is full of charity he will be able to put up with the tedium of the office. But charity needs support and the first is obedience, on which Duguet discourses for thirteen pages.[10] The canon must be obedient to God and the Church; he is doing his duty when taking part in the celebration of the Office and he must not complain of the six hours a day he has to spend in Church. After all, the Desert Fathers spent their days and nights in unceasing prayer! What would they have thought of the 'few' hours the canon had to spend in Church? Not much comfort there for the canons, but the remark is all part of that idealised picture of the early Church which the Jansenists so much wanted to restore.

To give further support to the notion of obedience Duguet reminds his canons that they are delegated by the Church to pray for others, especially workers and the poor. It is in this context that a passage that became famous occurs. How much Duguet knew personally about the lives of the poor we do not know but, as Saint-Simon remarked, he noticed everything. Whether or not he was close to the poor he could empathise with them, as many of his contemporaries either could not or would not. Sympathy for the poor and practical help was the mark of the life of Mère Angélique of Port-Royal.

Duguet then gives a moving picture of working people and of the poor who would be only too glad to gather up the crumbs from the canons' tables: 'Harsh necessity keeps working people bent to the ground to get food for themselves and their families. From morning to evening they work without pause or respite. They turn their eyes to us with pious longing. They think us fortunate to have been freed from their crushing and oppressive burden and to have been dispensed from the hard and penitential life that is the heritage of Adam. They envy us who have been delivered not only from anxiety for the morrow but from the cares and troubles of today. We, they think, have already entered paradise from which the rest of humankind is excluded. In their view we are the delegates of the whole of the posterity of Adam, still in their suffering and wretchedness, appointed to plead to God in their name, to avert his anger from them, to offer him their tears and repentance and to bring them some drops of the heavenly dew that refreshes and consoles us. Thus we are called upon to lighten the burden they carry, to obtain for them what they lack and to thank God for what they have received. We must praise God on their behalf and groan for them; we must do what they cannot and offer whatever they can spare from their poverty. At all times we must speak to the Lord for them because we are always in his presence and always allowed to address him.'[11]

That the problem weighed on his mind can be gathered from another passage that seems to reflect his personal experience. He is writing of beggars who often stood outside church doors. What are they asking for? Not health, much less wealth. All they ask for are no more than externals, bread or clothes, or the smallest coin: 'Some refuse, but the beggar is patient. Many do not even deign to look at him and he suffers from their contempt. The smallest gift fills him with gratitude and if it is bigger than he expected he is filled with wonder at such liberality. He can hardly believe it and he throws himself at the feet of one who is no more than a man like himself. It is as if he owed to him his life. He waits for hours and often for whole days. He speaks little, his tears and sighs speak for him. And if one shows a little kindness and if one enters into the detail of his needs, this touches him so much that he cannot restrain his gratitude... His tears begin to flow faster and faster and one is drawn to wipe them away'.[12] Elsewhere in his *Traité des devoirs d'un évêque*,[13] he reveals his understanding of the poor. They represent Jesus Christ. Duguet's spirituality was radically Christocentric.

The rest of *La Prière Publique* is really a treatise on the spirtual life. There must be interior prayer before and after the Divine Office and the priest must have a sense of the majesty and holiness of God for whom he must have a 'holy fear'. This he finds in the Psalms and when speaking of them he has recourse to Augustine's *Enarrationes in Psalmos*, as we would expect. We should enter into the sentiments of the Psalms, he says, they are a picture of our wretchedness and an invitation to weep and lament but 'if it is a psalm of thanksgiving, recite it with gratitude; if it is full of hope, hope' (Psalm 30). The Psalms were not written for a particular time. They embrace all times and the needs of all. They are ours by right, they belong to us if we belong to Jesus Christ and if we are inspired by his spirit.

What can be regarded as a summing up of his thought on the Prayer of the Church shows his high regard for it: 'Public prayer is the source of almost all the graces that the Church receives when that prayer is pure, fervent, humble and supported by great faith and a lively hope. But when it is marked by the opposite qualities, the chastisements it calls down are almost incredible.'[14]

Duguet's *Traité sur les Dispositions pour offrir les SS. Mystères* follows the same lines as *La Prière Publique*.[15] It is a long, moralising disquisition in which favourite Jansenist terms like *misère* (wretchedness), *faiblesse* (weakness) and, above all, *corruption*, recur and the extraordinary number of virtues to fit a man to celebrate the Mass are listed. The impression given is that a celebrant would have to be a paragon of virtues before he could say a single Mass. He must watch his eyes and his ears, he must be in an almost continual state of alarm lest he should commit the smallest sin. Here Duguet was quite unrealistic and took no account of the life the parish clergy had to live in a city like Paris. Duguet's priest has to be tremblingly chaste yet in the rough and tumble of Paris that would not have been easy. One wonders whether Duguet had ever heard how Pascal, seeing an innocent country girl wandering round the streets of Paris and realising the danger she was in, took her to the clergy at Saint Sulpice (hardly his friends), gave them money and asked them to find a safe place for her, which they did. There were thousands of young women of the kind at the time and it is fairly certain that the clergy did not stop to think of the pious precautions of which Duguet wrote so eloquently when they had to deal with them and others a great deal less innocent.

Two other points may be mentioned. Understandably Duguet feels he must broach the question of how often a priest should say Mass. In the seventeenth century it was not yet the custom for every priest to say Mass every day. Duguet rather labours his answer, burdened no doubt by Antoine Arnauld's influence, stemming from the *De La Fréquente*, on the need for worthiness. At Port-Royal there had been a tradition of infrequent celebration. Some of the priests among the solitaries seem never to have celebrated at all, either because they had been, in their view, irregularly ordained (i.e. without an interior call) or because they had been pluralists, or out of sheer scrupulousness. Duguet debates the matter over thirty pages. All the Jansenist notions of the majesty of God, of his justice, and the need for anxious soul-searching about one's worthiness come into play. In the end, however, he allows a priest to celebrate three times a week and, if he is particularly fervent, four times. On certain great seasons of the Church's year he may celebrate even more often but then even greater care must be taken over his preparation.

The second point to be noted is the extraordinary absence of people. The impression Duguet gives is that the priest is not ministering to people but is conducting a spiritual exercise that concerns himself alone. It is to be presumed that he himself celebrated in his private chapel *chez Ménars*. He never held any public office and perhaps had little experience of celebrating in public, nor is there any evidence of his preaching in churches after his early days at Troyes and Paris. There is a similar lack of the sense of service of the people in his *Traité des Devoirs d'un Évêque.*[16]

Early in the *Traité* Duguet reveals the Jansenist view of vocation to the priesthood and, *a fortiori,* to the episcopate. As is well known, in seventeenth-century France (and elsewhere) the king nominated bishops, the pope appointed them and the metropolitan and his suffragans ordained them. Although there were good bishops at the time there were too many who were careerists without vocation. The Jansenist view, mentioned above, was that for a vocation to be authentic there must be an *interior call* that could not be denied. Making much of St John Chrysostom and others who had tried to avoid the episcopate, Duguet expounds on this and, as a *coup de grâce,* produces the saying (from the Code of the Emperor Justinian!) that no one is worthy unless he was ordained in spite of himself: *nisi fuerit invitus.*[17]

We may omit Duguet's long disquisitions on the qualities to be expected of a bishop, remarking simply that his spirituality is very individualistic, very demanding and near impossible: his bishop is to be *un prodige et un miracle de vertu!* Almost the whole of the second part of the *Traité* is taken up with the pious practices of the bishop. Thus it takes Duguet thirteen pages to get his bishop out of bed and into his clothes (he says nothing about washing) and another forty to get him out of his palace and into church. Meanwhile he has said the appropriate Offices, he has prayed mentally, he has studied the Fathers, the Church Councils and other approved authors. All this between 5.00 and 8.30 a.m. Then the bishop will either hear or say Mass, though Duguet does not approve of the former. *His* bishop is not to be like some of his colleagues who said Mass often enough as priests but who, once they become bishops, think it right to do so rarely. He should not only celebrate himself but do so in church where he will be able to give communion to his flock with his own hand. By so doing he will draw them into union with himself by associating them with the Eucharist which is the sacrament of unity.

After Mass, and still apparently without breakfast, the bishop goes to see the people who wish to speak to him, preference being given first to the poor. The public Mass and the interviews are the only occasions in the whole treatise when we find Duguet's bishop in contact with his people. After this the bishop has dinner. The food should be simple, a book should be read aloud and, if there is conversation, it should be seemly. After dinner there is no intermission, no siesta (and the poor man has been up since 5.00 a.m.) for the bishop is to continue his interviews or deal with other business about which Duguet will write later but never does. After all this the bishop will put aside business matters and give himself to prayer and recollection. He will retire at about 7.00 p.m.

The treatise peters out with some remarks on the subject of authority and service, supported by examples drawn from 'the prelates of Africa' – he means those of the third century! – and from the Fathers of the Church. Here the myth of the idealised early Church is at work – Jansenists regularly set it in sharp contrast to the Church as they saw it in their own time. Duguet here is using it as a backhanded criticism of the episcopate of his day and seems to have given a handle to the 'presbyterianism' of the fanatical Jansenists of the eighteenth century.

In 1700 Duguet was fifty-one years old and he had another thirty-two years to live, but this part of his life was very different from what it had been. From a life as a quiet counsellor of women he became something of a public figure and then a fugitive. The catalyst of this change in his way of life was the publication of the papal bull, the *Unigenitus,* in 1713, which condemned Jansenism once again in the shape of a hundred and one propositions drawn from the writings of the exiled Pasquier Quesnel who had taken on the leadership of the Jansenist cause. Duguet, who had long ago jettisoned the *fait* and all the dispute about it, but believed that the doctrine in Jansen's *Augustinus* was orthodox, regarded the *Unigenitus* as the most frightful calamity. When in 1714 the king, through an intermediary, asked him to write about the condemnation, Duguet became suspicious. Since the intermediary was the lieutenant of police his suspicions seem justified and, after his interview with that official, he disappeared. He exiled himself to Tamié in Savoy, just across the borders of France – rather like Voltaire who, in later life, lived just inside Switzerland! It is possible that Duguet chose Tamié as there he was able to have conversations with the dubious Sr Rose. He also spent his leisure time writing *L'Institution d'un Prince* which was highly regarded at one time.

On the death of Louis XIV in 1715 a new era seemed to be dawning. His heir was only a child and until he came of age the country was ruled by a Regency Council, headed by the sceptical Duke of Orleans. For a time there was a certain relaxation from which the Jansenists profited. In the hope of getting the *Unigenitus* and the oath attached to it withdrawn they decided to agitate. The result was that the old sanctions were re-imposed, not always with success, and even some bishops protested. One of these, Joachim Colbert, Jansenist Bishop of Montpellier, sent a strong remonstrance to the regent in 1724. For some unaccountable reason Duguet wrote an open letter to him, *Lettre à Monsieur l'Évêque de Montpellier*, congratulating him on his courage and at the same time arguing clearly and very strongly for the Jansenist position. It was the most public declaration he had ever made and, once again, he had to go into hiding, first at Troyes, from 1724 to 1728, and then, after a visit to Paris where the police got wind of his presence, to Holland. In 1730 he returned to Troyes and, after a year or so, to Paris, where he died suddenly at the age of eighty-four in October 1733.

In these last years Duguet had two afflictions to bear. One was domestic and concerned his niece, Mme Mols, who acted as his housekeeper and dominated his life. She was a busybody, impetuous and even violent, and she came between him and those who wished to consult him. One of these, the Marquise de Vieuxbourg, was severe in her criticisms. It was a pity, she said, that one had to excuse certain things in Duguet's behaviour on account of his old age. She conceded that he deserved some peace but that woman was not the right person to be in charge. Would that his nephew, André, also an Oratorian, were there. Along with others she had been refused the door and things were being kept from Duguet which he had a right to know. It sounds like the complaint of a disgruntled and offended great lady not used to being brushed off.

The second cause of Duguet's unhappiness was his rejection by the Jansenist party. This came as a result of the extraordinary happenings, the alleged miracles, that were said to occur at the tomb of the Jansenist deacon, François de Pâris, in the churchyard of St Médard. He had lived a life of great austerity and of charity to the poorest of the poor among whom he lived. He had rejected the *Unigenitus*. In spite of several embargos by the Archbishop of Paris and the civil authorities, crowds continued to flock there and then came the 'convulsions'. People threw themselves on the tomb, some inflicted on themselves various kinds of physical penances, even tortures, and one young woman, it was reported, had willingly undergone crucifixion. The purpose of all this and much more was to demonstrate by these 'charismatic' manifestations that the archbishop was wrong, that the government was repressive and that the *Unigenitus* was not of God. Duguet had been a consultant editor of the *Nouvelles Ecclesiastiques*, the organ of the Jansenist party, which was bitter, fanatical and well informed. Duguet condemned the 'convulsions', and thus fell out of favour with the Jansenists who had no further use for him.[18]

Bullied by his niece and rejected by those for whom he had worked and suffered Duguet thus came to a sad end. For a man of his distinction this was hard. He was intellectually gifted beyond the average, he was vastly learned and he combined learning with a sensibility that enabled him to enter into the thoughts, the feelings and the inner life of others. He was an able theologian with an extensive knowledge of the Bible, though his understanding of it was marred by his bizarre theories. He had a compassion for the poor but only a very limited experience of life. He sought solitude but was not temperamentally a hermit. His withdrawals were evasions of the harsh realities of life, rather than a desire for contemplation in the desert, a notion much talked about by the Jansenists but little practised. But he had an extraordinary tenacity, or stubbornness, and he stuck to his Jansenist convictions to the end of his life. It was this that brought his downfall and it is a pity that in old age he could not keep quiet. He was not made of the stuff of martyrs.

NOTES

Abbreviations

HLSR – *Histoire Litteraire du sentiment religieux en France.*

F&M – Fliche et Martin ed. *Histoire de L'église* (1946).

PR – *Port-Royal* of Sainte-Beuve.

Origines – refers to the volumes *Les Origines du Jansenisme*, I to IV.

Chapter 1: The Condition of the French Church

1. See Outram Evenett, *The Spirit of the Counter-Reformation* (Cambridge: Cambridge University Press, 1968), p.99.

2. *Origines,* II p.12.

3. See Joseph Bergin, *Cardinal de la Rochefoucauld: Leadership and Reform in the French Church* (New Haven and London: Yale University Press, 1987); and cf. review in *Historical Journal,* 52,3 (1989) pp. 707-708, by Dermot Fenlon.

4. See, inter alia, *The Lives of Anne de Joyeuse and Benet of Canfield,* ed T.A. Birrell (London and New York: Sheed & Ward, 1959), pp. xxvff.

5. Sainte-Beuve, PR, ed. de la Pléiade, Vol. 1, p.140.

6. See L. Chattelier, *The Europe of the Devout* (Cambridge University Press, ET, 1989).

7. See HLSR, *IV,* p.31. On Olier he wrote: 'Olier comme tous ceux de son école... se fait de la nature déchue l'idée la plus noire' (p.33). For the former quotation, see p.21.

8. See Louis Cognet, In *Le Coeur, Etudes Carmélitaines,* 1950, pp. 234-253. Cognet's article is an important example of the distinction that must be made between seventeenth-century Jansenism and that of the eighteenth century, if history is to be written correctly.

9. See Joseph Colomb PSS, 'The Catechetical Method of Saint Sulpice', in *Shaping the Christian Message,* ed. G. Sloyan (New York: The Macmillan Company, 1958).

10. Du Fossé, an old boy. See PR, II, p.419.

11. When he gave his whole time to his diocese of Meaux he continued to preach as he assiduously visited the parishes, often preparing his sermons in his coach. They are said to be winning in their simplicity.
12. Du Hamel was a follower of Antoine Arnauld but later 'weakened' in Jansenist terms, and Feydeau was an out-and-out Jansenist. See PR , I, pp. 1002-1009.
13. See F. & M. *Histoire de l'Eglise* (Leflon) (Paris: Bloud & Gray, 1949) t. 20, p.258.
14. See F. & M. *Histoire de l'Eglise* (Préclin and Jarry) (Paris: Bloud & Gray) t.19, p.158.

Chapter 2: Jansenism

1. French Jansenism was a very varied phenomenon. Historians identify three groups:
    i. The extremists who, however, were passive; they would have nothing to do with distinctions of *droit* and *fait* or any other controversial issues of the time. Truth would prevail. This is described as the attitude of Mère Angélique, the chaplain Singlin and Barcos, the nephew of the Abbé de Saint-Cyran.
    ii. The centrists who held to the distinction between the *droit* and the *fait*. This was the position of Antoine Arnauld and his followers, though they eventually agreed to the compromise of 1668, the Peace of the Church.
    iii. An extreme active group who campaigned against any kind of signature of the Formulary. This was the position of the Four Bishops (among whom was Henri Arnauld, Bishop of Angers and brother of Antoine) and of Guillaume Le Roy, Abbot of Haute-Fontaine, who is said to have influenced Mère Agnès and Jacqueline Pascal (Sr Euphémie).
    See Jean Delumeau, *Le Catholicisme entre Luther et Voltaire*, pp. 184-5.
2. The pope *lawfully and rightly condemned* the Five Propositions

as heretical. Arnauld and Nicole denied that they were *in fact* in the *Augustinus.*

3. As French scholars unanimously state, Jansen deliberately confused the will as 'faculty' with its action. It was the result of his contempt for the medieval scholastics.

4. The Fronde was a civil war in two phases, 1648-9 and 1651-2, when the nobility rebelled against the rule of Cardinal Mazarin, First Minister to the Queen Regent, Anne of Austria, during the minority of Louis XIV.

Chapter 3: Jean Duvergier de Hauranne

1. HLSR, t. IV, pp. 36, 46, 50.

2. Ibid. p.67.

3. See his *Port-Royal,* I, *passim.*

4. Orcibal, II, p.93.

5. *Correspondence de Jansénius,* ed. J. Orcibal (Paris/Louvain, 1947), pp. 4-5 (see Bibliography for details).

6. See J. Orcibal, *Saint-Cyran et le Jansénisme* (1961), pp. 7,8.

7. Later Vicar Apostolic in England.

8. The two men had first made a journey together of which the details are not known. Many years later it was built up as a secret meeting with a few others when they plotted to destroy the Church as it was, to undermine faith in the Eucharist and to establish deism! The place was supposed to have been Bourgfontaines and the alleged meeting there became part of the anti-Jansenist myth. It is exposed and refuted by Jean Orcibal, in *Jean Duvergier de Hauranne, Origines* III, p. 84, note 5.

9. *Saint-Cyran et le Jansénisme,* op. cit. p.46.

10. For the Jansenism of Saint-Cyran see J. Orcibal, *La Spiritualité de Saint-Cyran, Les Origines du Jansénisme,* V (Paris 1962), pp. 81-135.

11. *Origines* II, p. 419, n.4.

12. His position on this matter is in fact not clear.

13. Orcibal, in *Saint-Cyran et le Jansénisme,* op.cit. pp. 22, 23, gives the names of some forty-three distinguished people of the time.
14. PR, I, pp. 391-393.
15. *Origines,* II, p.450.
16. Orcibal, *Saint-Cyran et le Jansénisme,* op. cit. p.30.
17. In the Port-Royal library in the rue Saint-Jacques in Paris there is a framed fragment of a letter of Saint-Cyran. Evidently written in pencil (or something similar) the calligraphy is surprisingly elegant. One wonders whether it was not Robert Arnauld's handwriting, but M. André Gazier, the curator, was convinced that it was Saint-Cyran's.
18. The Bull was unsatisfactory in form and even modern historians have regarded it as legally dubious. Saint-Cyran also wrote: 'They have gone too far; we must show them their duty'. It is not clear who 'they' were. Lancelot in his Memoir applies it to the Roman Curia but, it seems, mistakenly. See J. Orcibal, *Saint-Cyran et le Jansénisme,* pp. 49-50. Saint-Cyran may well have meant the Jesuits.
19. I will spare the reader the grisly details of the dismembering of his corpse, the removal of his brain for inspection, the cutting off of his hands by Lancelot in the dead of night so that the nuns of Port-Royal could have them as sacred relics, and so on.
20. See HLSR, IV, pp. 161,164-166 and p.155.
21. See Y. Congar, *L'Eglise de Saint Augustin à l'époque moderne,* 1970, p.34, n5.
22. St Thomas speaks of *conversio,* the transformation of the elements into the body and blood of Christ.
23. The custom of reserving the Blessed Sacrament in a tabernacle on the altar began in Italy in the sixteenth century. Some ill-disposed people said that the suspension of the vessel over the altar was a sign that the nuns did not go to communion! In fact a sufficient number of altar-breads was given to the celebrant before Mass.

24. PR, I, p.535.
25. In his *Spiritualité de Saint-Cyran* (*Origines*, V, 1962) Orcibal traces the various influences on him. These were Francis de Sales, Bérulle etc., though not the Fathers. In the same volume he published a number of Saint-Cyran's MSS.
26. A disconcerting example of his apparent deviousness is his repeated affirmations that the pamphlets which went out under the name of Petrus Aurelius were not written by himself. He may have dictated them to his nephew Barcos who latinised some or all of them, so in that sense Saint-Cyran could be said not to have 'written' them. However, this seems to be a piece of the sort of casuistry that he condemned in others. The matter remains unclear.

Chapter 4: Angélique Arnauld

1. Louis Cognet, *La Réforme de Port-Royal*, 1950, p. 39.
2. Louis Cognet remarks that this was apparent in her facial morphology and in her handwriting and would be sublimated after her conversion, though it should be added, some years after her conversion (*La Réforme de Port-Royal*, op. cit. p.58).
3. Cognet, *La Réforme de Port-Royal*, op. cit. pp.73-74.
4. This seems to be the first instance of the plea of conscience which was to play so large a part in the Jansenist-Port-Royal affair later on.
5. *Relation de Mère Angélique de Port-Royal*, ed. L. Cognet, p. 49.
6. Cognet, *La Réforme de Port-Royal*, op. cit. p.102.
7. Cognet, *La Réforme de Port-Royal*, op. cit. pp. 115, 116.
8. Cognet, *La Réforme de Port-Royal*, op. cit. p. 118.
9. R.A. Knox, who was hostile to Angélique, writing of the *Journée du Guichet*, asks, 'Could not the same point have been gained with fewer tears?' He fails to take into account that he was writing of strong-minded French people of the seventeenth century who sometimes expressed their feelings with great vehemence. They did not have the inhibitions of a twen-

tieth-century Englishman. In the context he is attacking Angélique but who was it who gave way to unbridled fury? Knox's portrait of Angélique is a near travesty (See *Enthusiasm* [Oxford: OUP, 1950] p.189).

10. See Cognet, *La Réforme de Port-Royal,* op. cit. pp. 128-134.

11. See Cognet, *La Réforme de Port-Royal,* op. cit p. 156.

12. The account suggests that she laid *on* her or on her feet. If so, the poor sister would have been very uncomfortable, even unable to breathe. Another report tells how, when she visited the sick in the infirmary, which she did very frequently, everyone felt better and even thought they were cured. If that is a pious exaggeration, it shows what sort of woman Angélique was. Her vitality (and kindness) raised the sense of well-being of a company when she came into a room.

13. Moléon, *Voyages Liturgiques* (1718: Gregg reprint, 1969), pp. 238-41. To all this must be added the hours of adoration before the Blessed Sacrament.

14. Tavenaux, quoting A. Gazier, *Vie quotidienne,* p.34.

15. *Lettres de la Mère Agnès Arnauld, Abbesse de Port-Royal,* with an Introduction by M. P. Faugère; two vols (Paris, 1858).

16. Madame Acarie (1566-1618), cousin of Cardinal de Berulle, a mystic. Her house in Paris became a centre of spirituality. She supported her cousin in bringing the Carmelite nuns from Spain to make a foundation in France (1603). After the death of her husband she herself became a Carmelite.

17. Cognet, *La Réforme de Port-Royal,* op. cit.

18. Portions of these buildings still survive and are part of a hospital called La Maternité. Mass is still said in the chapel, now much reduced in size, on Sundays.

19. Sainte-Beuve, PR, I, pp. 242-46. He uses Angélique's own narrative which is far more vivid than any second-hand account. I have used the words 'police' and 'policeman' for the *archers,* as that seems the nearest equivalent though it can be presumed that they were soldiers.

20. 'Lord set a guard over my mouth and a door to my lips.'
21. PR, I, p. 250.
22. *Lettres de la Mère Agnès Arnauld,* Paris, 1858, ii, p.103.
23. For a brief summary of Angélique's friendship with Francis de Sales see Marc Escholier, *Port-Royal,* Paris, 1965, pp. 38-42.
24. Many years later Antoine Le Maître said that they discussed the state of the Church, which they both lamented, and Francis made guarded remarks about the corruption of Rome. He regretted that there was no prospect of a General Council which could undertake a 'reform in head and members'. Since this became a constant saying of the Jansenists, Le Maître's allegation must remain suspect. Angélique may have confused what she had subsequently heard from others with what Francis had said.
25. See Augustin Gazier, *Jeanne de Chantal et Mère Angélique d'après leur correspondence,* 1620-1641, Paris, 1915, pp. 54-57, text of the letters, pp. 138-140, 141-143. He thinks Angélique's letter showed feminine intuition.
26. His rehabilitation was undertaken by L.N. Prunel in his *S. Zamet, sa vie, et ses oeuvres. Les Origines du Jansénisme* (Paris, 1912). He portrays him in a better light than the Port-Royal writers do but independent critics say that his account is partial and hostile to Port-Royal.
27. *Lettres de Mère Angélique,* I, p.558.
28. *Lettres de la Mére Agnès,* I, op. cit. p.271.
29. *Lettres de Mère Angélique,* I, pp. 255, 263, 291.
30. *Lettres de Mère Angélique,* II, p.470.
31. The quotations in the previous paragraphs are taken from Cécile Gazier, *Histoire du monastère de Port-Royal,* Paris 1929, pp.133, 134, 135, 137.
32. Gazier, op. cit. p. 157.
33. For the foregoing on Angélique's last illness and death see Cécile Gazier, op. cit. pp. 159-162; PR, I, pp.643-549. Her body was laid to rest 'in the courtyard' and is still there, though its exact location is not known.

34. PR, III, pp. 644-5.
35. PR, III, pp. 643-4.
36. PR, III, pp. 645-6.
37. PR, III, pp. 646-7.
38. PR, III, pp. 647-8.

Chapter 5: Antoine Arnauld

1. This at least is what the experts conclude with some doubt. Several children died in infancy and Antoine was preceded by three other Antoines who died. See the table in PR, I.
2. PR, I, pp. 511-12.
3. PR, II, pp. 516-518.
4. PR, II, pp. 514-515.
5. It belonged to a priest in or near Banbury, Warwickshire, as appears from a statement on a fly-leaf, 'Mission of Banbury'. It is now in the Oscott College Library. See my article, *Worcestershire Recusant*, No. 41, June 1983, p. 2.
6. At p. 173.
7. At pp. 102-103.
8. L. Cognet, *Le Jansénisme*, p. 67.
9. See J. Steinmann, *Pascal* (ET, op. cit. 1965); Port-Royal-des-Champs was no longer a safe place.
10. PR, II, p. 652.
11. PR, II, p. 653.
12. PR, II, pp. 654-655, italics mine. M le Nain was not quite right about Barcos. He was learned but not very 'enlightened and judicious'. He had the unfortunate habit of causing minor rumpuses and he supported signature 'pure and simple', which Arnauld would never have done.
13. See Orcibal, *Port-Royal*, p.41 and pp. 38-42 for all this affair.
14. Orcibal, *Port-Royal*, pp.40-41.
15. 'It was not by dialectics that God willed to save man.'
16. The friend was a M. Brienne, not an entirely trustworthy witness, though Sainte-Beuve found no fault with his account.

17. See PR, II, 843-847, with the long footnotes. For the royal interview Saint-Beuve was quoting a contemporary account.

18. The book was called *La Perpétuité de la Foi de l'Église Catholique touchant*. It was a Massive argument from prescription (first used by Tertullian); what had always been in possession was the faith of the Church. Since Arnauld was now in favour, the government were willing to assist him and Nicole and diplomats in Constantinople were put to work finding Greek MSS and liturgies to help prove that the faith of Rome was in this matter the faith of the Orthodox Church too.

19. PR, III, p. 271.

20. PR, III, p. 273.

21. Extract from Emile Jacques, *Les Années d'exile d'Antoine Arnauld* (1976), p. 153.

22. His pitiful story can be found in PR, III, pp. 765ff. He seems to have been an excellent and most attractive man and his fate is one of the worst examples of the vengeful brutality of the Sun-King's government. He deserves a full biography.

23. For his liturgical activity see my *Lights in Darkness* (Dublin: Columba Press, 1996), pp. 52-62.

24. E. Jacques, op. cit. pp. 535-538.

25. See PR, III, p. 297, at the footnote, for these statements.

26. PR, III, pp. 296-297; E. Jacques, op. cit. pp. 464-465.

27. E. Jacques, op. cit. p. 688, n. 107.

28. See Jacques, op. cit. p. 669, and for further treatment of the whole subject see J. Steinmann, *Richard Simon et les Origines de l'Exegèse Biblique* (Paris, 1960). It is true that Simon was very provocative. He had more than one chip on his shoulder and he laid about him, sparing no-one.

29. *Enthusiasm* (1950), p. 197.

30. See my article 'Jansenism and the English Recusants', in *Worcestershire Recusant*, no. 41, June 1983, pp.6-7, 10-12.

Chapter 6 : Angélique de Saint-Jean Arnauld d'Andilly

1. C. Gazier, *Histoire du Monastère*, pp. 181, 199.
2. This is not just a matter of literary criticism. She was concerned to 'sanctify' the words, gestures and actions of her aunt and, indeed, other members of the community. R. A. Knox, for instance, speaks of the self-consciousness of Angélique; she was always watching as it were out of the corner of her eye to see what people would think. It is an unworthy suggestion, quite unlike Angélique, and Knox may have been misled through not realising who had written the history. (See *Enthusiasm*, p.189.)
3. *Histoire du Monastère*, pp. 192,193.
4. It is questionable whether the 'all' included the *Augustinus*.
5. Sainte-Beuve, PR, I. pp. 670ff.
6. PR, II, p. 679.
7. See J. D. Crichton, 'A Case of Conscience', *Heythrop Journal*, January 1981, pp. 19-31.
8. HSLR, IV, p. 231 fn.1, quoting Père Gazeau, *Études*, July 1875, March, 1876.
9. Cécile Gazier, op.cit. p. 205, says that Père Annat SJ 'inspired' the Ordinance. Other more objective writers agree with her.
10. 'Pretentious silly' – *pimbêche* – is very difficult to translate. It is the sort of word one fishwife would have used to another in Les Halles, and would have led to blows. Later the archbishop denied using it but in the temper he was in could hardly have remembered.
11. C. Gazier, op.cit. pp. 216-217.
12. The first two would have been her clothing and solemn profession.
13. See *Relation de Captivité* for all the foregoing, pp. 29-31. Saint-Beuve's comment is just: 'The pride with which she confessed her name comes from the pride of blood of d'Andilly, the weakness of the Arnaulds. They identified the cause of God with their own'. PR, II, p.707.
14. Ibid.

15. We have only Angélique's word that this is actually what Mme de Rantzau said.
16. *Relation de la Captivité*, pp. 46-59. Later in the day Angélique wrote a conciliary note of apology and the next morning before Mass Mme de Rantzau came to her and said she was sorry for the pain she had caused her and wished to be of service to her with sincere affection.
17. For a longer analysis of Angélique's 'affectivity' see J. Orcibal, *Port-Royal. Entre le Miracle et l'Obéisance*, 1957, pp.112-121: 'Her intellectual constructions were basically affective.'
16. *Relation*, pp. 64-66.
19. For the letter, see *Relation de la Captivité*, ed. L. Cognet, p.283, n.52. It ought to be said also that Angélique wrote her *Relation* when she was in prison and though she re-read it does not seem to have corrected it. The stringing together of long phrases in one sentence makes translation very difficult. I trust I have not distorted the sense. It was sent to Arnauld whom she asked to re-read it before sending it to Pavillon, the Bishop of Aleth. The letter quoted here is not much clearer.
20. In fact Liberius had condemned Athanasius for inaccurate reports.
21. For all the above see *Relation*, pp. 104-107. The sentence 'for there is no need...' is a very strong echo of what Saint-Cyran had once said.
22. *Relation*, pp. 118-123.
23. *Relation*, pp. 126-127.
24. 'Victorious grace on the lips of her enemies.' *Relation*, pp. 147-8.
25. *Relation*, pp. 163-171.
26. *Relation*, p. 259.
27. *Relation*, p. 260.
28. *Relation*, p. 261.
29. *Relation*, p. 261.
30. *Relation*, p. 263.
31. *Relation*, p. 264.

32. *Relation,* pp. 268-269.
33. This account is based on L. Cognet, *Le Jansénisme,* op. cit. pp. 82-83.
34. See Jean Orcibal, *Port-Royal, Entre le miracle et l'obéissance,* 1957, pp. 41-42. Although Flavie's testimony is suspect there is no doubt that this was Angélique's real mind.
35. Sainte-Beuve, PR, II, pp. 852-853.
36. *Choix de Lettres Inédites de Louis-Isaac de Sacy,* ed. G. Delassaut, 1959, trans. in F. Ellen Weaver, *The Evolution of the Reform of Port-Royal* (Paris, 1978), p. 144.
37. Orcibal, op. cit. p. 45.
38. F. Ellen Weaver, op. cit. p.145.
39. PR, III, pp. 735-6.
40. See F. Ellen Weaver, op. cit. p. 145.
41. For all the above see Jerôme Besoigne, *Histoire de l'Abbaye de Port-Royal,* t. I, p. 354 (1752), Slatkin reprint (Geneva), 1970.
42. Given in full in Besoigne, op. cit. p. 291.
43. Sainte-Beuve, PR, II, pp.732-733, note.
44. Sainte-Beuve, PR, III, p. 182.
45. *Discours de la R. M. Angélique de Saint-Jean, Abesse de P. R. des Champs, appellés Misericordes* (Utrecht, 1735). These were addresses on deceased relatives made at the request of nuns.
46. Sainte-Beuve, PR, II, pp. 733-734, III, 229.

Chapter 7: Jacques Joseph Duguet

1. PR, III, p. 48. 'Talented, yet he always wanted to evade publicity, his style was to conceal, he spent his whole life in escaping'.
2. This, I think, was the heart of the matter (italics mine). PR, III, p. 473.
3. PR, III, pp. 484-5.
4. PR, III, pp. 495-8.
5. See Bremond, HSLR, t. IX, p. 123, and *Dictionnaire de Spiritualité,* III, SV. 'Duguet', p. 1764.

6. HSLR, t.XI, p. 139.
7. PR, III, pp. 926-7.
8. Pp. 124-5. I have used the 1707 edition (which once belonged to Julien Green), described as the *troisième edition*. Another edition, brought out after Duguet's death was published by the 'Compagnie' (the Jansenists). I have noted no differences between them except for Duguet's refutation in a prefatorial letter of the accusation that he was teaching Jansenism in the book, a charge he easily refutes.
9. See my *Lights in Darkness* (Dublin: Columba Press, 1996), chapter 6.
10. Pp. 13-26.
11. *Prière Publique,* II, pp. 31-32.
12. Op. cit. III, pp. 129-130. One wonders whether Duguet had read La Bruyère. See La Bruyère, *Caractères,* XI, trans. Jean Stewart (London: Penguin Classics, 1970), p. 210.
13. III, pp. 91-2.
14. Op. cit. p. 206.
15. It is printed with that Treatise (1707) with separate pagination, 1-148. It too circulated in manuscript and was read by the Jansenising Bishop of Montpellier who greatly approved of it.
16. See *Recueil de quatres Opuscules fort importants de feu M. l'Abbé Duguet,* Utrecht, 1737, pp. 1-192. This was published by the eighteenth-century Jansenists and in the *Avertissement,* pp. 2-3, the editor reveals a touch of the 'presbyterianism' of the Jansenists of the time. He remarks that though Duguet is writing for a bishop his advice is also applicable to priests. He quotes St John Chrysostom's saying, *Inter est ferme nihil* (there is hardly any difference between priest and bishop).
17. *Traité,* pp. 18, 19.
18. For a full account of the deacon Pâris and all the affair of the *convulsionnaires* see B. Kreiser, *Miracles, Convulsions and Ecclesiastical Politics in Early Eighteenth Century Paris,* (New Jersey: Princeton University Press, 1978), chapters 2 and 6.

BIBLIOGRAPHY

The bibliography of Jansenism (and anti-Jansenism) is enormous, probably over 100,000 titles. The following list is chiefly of books referred to in the text.

Catholicism in Early Modern History, A Guide to Research (Ann Arbor, Michigan, 1988). Bibliographies up to 1988 in the principal modern languages with books reviewed by various authors: Pierre Blet, SJ, 'France'; Peter Burke: *Popular Piety* Jared Wicks SJ, *Doctrine and Theology* [Jansenists and anti-Jansenists], pp.241-245).

Bremond, Henri, *Histoire littéraire du sentiment religieux en France depuis la fin des guerres de la religion jusqu'a nos jours* (Paris 1916-1936 – reprint 1967) For Jansenism and Jansenists see tomes IV and XI.

Cognet, Louis, *Le Jansénisme* (Que sais-je?, 960; Paris 1961). Brief but comprehensive by an expert on the period.

Cognet, Louis, *La Spiritualité Moderne (Histoire de la Spiritualité chrétienne,* 3, Paris, 1966) See 2ieme partie, *La Préponderance française* and, in particular, *Le premier Port-Royal,* pp. 455-495. Unfinished.

Delumeau, Jean, *Le Catholicisme entre Luther et Voltaire* (Paris: Nouvelle Clio, 1971; (ET London: Darton Longman & Todd, 1977).

Gazier, Augustin, *Histoire génèrale du Mouvement Janséniste,* two vols (Paris 1922). Very partial to Jansenism but with much information difficult to find elsewhere.

Gazier, Cécile, *Histoire du Monastère de Port-Royal* (Paris, 1929).

Parker, Geoffrey, *Europe in Crisis,* 1598-1648 (London: Fontana, 1979).

Sainte-Beuve, C.A., *Port-Royal* (Bibliotheque de la Pléiade, I, 1953, II, 1954, III, 1955. Ed. by Maxime Leroy. All references are to this edition, by far the most convenient to use).

Racine, Jean. His *Abrégé de l'histoire de Port-Royal* (t.II Bibliothèque de la Pléiade, 1966) was a work of filial piety, beautifully written but never completed. It would probably have been much more useful if it had been as he had some first-hand information).

Taveneau, René, *Le Catholicisme dans la France classique* (I and II, Paris 1980).

Taveneau, René, *La Vie quotidienne des Jansénistes* (Paris, 1973).

Weaver, F, Ellen, *The Evolution of the Reform of Port-Royal.* From the Rule of Citeaux to Jansenism (Paris, 1978).

More Specialised Studies

Orcibal, Jean, *Les Origines du Jansénisme.*

Orcibal, Jean, I, *La Correspondence de Jansenius.*

Orcibal, Jean, II, *Jean Duvergier de Hauranne, abbé de Saint-Cyran.*

Orcibal, Jean, III, *Appendice, bibliographie et tables* (all Louvain – Paris, 1947-1948)

Orcibal, Jean, IV, *Lettres inédites de Jean Duvergier de Hauranne* (Ed. Annie Barnes, Paris, 1962).

Orcibal, Jean, V, *La Spiritualité de l'Abbé de Saint-Cyran* (Paris, 1962)

Orcibal, Jean, *Saint-Cyran et le Jansénisme* (collection, 'Maîtres Spirituels', Paris 1961).

Orcibal, Jean, Port-Royal. Entre le Miracle et L'Obéissance. Flavie Passart et Angélique de S Jean Arnauld d'Andilly (Paris, 1957).

The following comment on the importance of Jean Orcibal's work on Saint-Cyran and seventeenth century Jansenism is worth recording here:

'To Orcibal goes the credit for having recovered for us the dense spiritual physiognomy of Saint-Cyran and its relationship to the Bérullian tradition. (He thereby destroyed the idea that Jansenism was a uniform and undifferentiated monolith.) Nourished by an anti-humanistic bias, Saint-Cyran's spirituality is characterised by a tragic sense of human fragility and of acute need for salvation through grace. Saint-Cyran derives from Augustine not so much a doctrine of grace and predestination as a conception of Christian life. Like the Augustinianism of Bérulle, that of Saint-Cyran looks to lived Christian experience and does not attempt to form theories. An incomparable spiritual director, Saint-Cyran influenced individuals and communities: Antoine Arnauld, Angélique Arnauld, the nuns of Port-Royal and the 'recluses' of Port-Royal...'
To this may be added: 'The works of Orcibal, Cognet and Taveneaux have revealed that Jansenism was not only a theological dispute, not only a controversy with the Holy See... but also a life of prayer, of love of the Bible, of Eucharistic devotion, penitential discipline, and service of the poor – all elements rooted in a profound spirituality'. (Massimo Marocchi, in *Catholicism in Early Modern History*, p.181).

Documents of Port-Royalists (modern editions).

Arnauld, Antoine, *De la Fréquente Communion* (1643).

Arnauld, Angélique, *Relation écrite par la Mère Angélique Arnauld* (Ed. L. Cognet, 1949).

Arnauld, Angélique, *Lettres*, two volumes (1742). In this connection and for the life of Angélique until 1618 see L.Cognet, *La Réforme de Port-Royal* (Paris, 1950).

ould, Agnès, *Lettres de la Mère Agnès Arnauld, Abbesse de Port-Royal* (Introduction, M.P. Faugère, I,II, [Paris, 1858]).

Arnauld, Angélique de Saint-Jean, *Relation de Captivité d'Angélique de Saint-Jean Arnauld d'Andilly.* With an introduction by Louis Cognet (Paris, 1954).

On Mère Angélique de S. Jean see Brigitte Sibertin-Blanc, 'Biographie et Personnalité de la Seconde Angélique' in *Chroniques de Port-Royal* (La Mère Angélique de Saint-Jean [1624-1684], Paris, 1985).

For a theological exposition and critique of the teaching of Jansen see: Henri de Lubac SJ, *Augustinianism and modern Theology* (ET by Lancelot Sheppard, Geoffrey Chapman, London, 1969).

281

INDEX OF NAMES

separation of two houses, 229
'solitaries', 7, 38-39, 116, 118, 133, 134, 233, 235
spiritual directors, 60-61, 63, 118-21, 140, 142
Singlin, 132, 155
Zamet, 129-32
spiritual formation, 110-11
way of life, 39-40
work, 116
Port-Royalists, 16, 22, 23, 24-25
rejection of mysticism, 28
Precipiano (Archbishop of Malines), 181
Prières, Abbé de, 67, 68-69, 83

Q
Quersaillou, Claude de, 104, 106, 107, 109
Quesnel, Pasquier, 175, 176, 261
Réflexions morales, 174

R
Racine
Abrégé de l'histoire de Port-Royal, 146, 148-49
Rantzau, Madame de, 190
and Angélique de Saint-Jean, 200-204
Rapin, Père, SJ, 115, 185
Rebours, M. de, 244
Retz, Cardinal de, Archbishop of Paris, 139, 233
Richelieu (Cardinal), 11-12, 13, 15, 21, 90, 152, 153
and Abbé of Saint-Cyran, 52-53, 62-63, 65-69, 70, 71-72
L'Instruction Chrétienne, 53
Rieux, Mme, 250
Rose of the Holy Cross, Sr, 253-54
Ruth d'Ans, Edward, 175

S
Sablé, Madame de, 23, 133, 155
Saci, M. de, 22, 84, 171, 174, 233. *See also* Le Maître de Saci
death (1681), 242
Saint-Amour, Gorin de, 203
Saint-Cyran, Abbé de. *see* Duvergier de Hauranne, Jean Ambroise
Saint-Gertrude, Marguerite de, 190
Saint-Jean, Angélique de. *See* Arnauld D'Andilly, Angélique de Saint-Jean
St Maur (Benedictine Congregation), 13
Saint Paul Asseline, Dom Eustache de, 110, 111
Saint-Simon, Duke of, 254, 256
Sainte-Beuve, C.A., 73, 81, 84, 143, 152, 154, 163, 164, 166, 174, 226

and Angélique Arnauld, 117
and Angélique de Saint-Jean, 185, 190, 242
and Duguet, 247, 249
'miracle of the Holy Thorn', 146-47
Port-Royal, 7, 42
Sales, Francis de. *See* Francis de Sales
Séguier (Chancellor), 66, 160
Semi-Pelagians, 33, 34
Sénault, Père, 220
Sesmaisons, Père, 155, 156
Sévigné, M. de, 39, 142, 233
Sévigné, Madame de, 23, 211, 234-35
Sibertin-Blanc, Birgitte, 245, 246
Simon, Richard (1638-1712), 150, 254-55
Critical History of the Old Testament, 182
Singlin, Antoine, 132, 135, 140, 152, 155, 163, 165, 196
Sisters of Charity, 69
Smith, Dr Richard, 53, 60
Soissons, Mme de, 126
Suffren, Père, 121
Suireau, Marie Agnès de, Abbess of Port-Royal, 138, 148
Sulpicians, 14, 19, 23-24
Surin, Jean-Joseph, 18

T
Tardif, Mère Geneviève de, 132, 189, 235
Teresa of Avila, Saint, 110
Teresian Carmelites, 14
Tertullian, 29
Thomas Aquinas, Saint. *See* Aquinas
Thomists, 36, 37
Tillemont, Le Nain de, 164-65, 179, 233
Tremblay, Père Joseph de, 15, 61-62

U
Ursulines, 14, 18, 23

V
Vertus, Comtesse de, 39, 195
Vieuxbourg, Marquise de, 262-63
Vincent de Paul, Saint, 12, 13, 14, 17, 19, 28, 29, 68, 69, 155
Saint-Cyran's friendship with, 55, 62
Visitation Order, 13

W
Wadding, Luke, 35
Weaver, F. Ellen, 233-34, 235
William of Orange, 177

Z
Zamet, Sebastian, Bishop of Langres, 62-63, 64, 71, 129